MW00943589

LEAVES OF AUTUMN

Cheyenne Indians End Their
Domination Of The Kansas
Plains With An Attack On
Settlers In Lincoln County

by
James I. McArthur

Bloomington, IN Milton Keynes, UK

AuthorHouse™
1663 Liberty Drive, Suite 200
Bloomington, IN 47403
www.authorhouse.com
Phone: 1-800-839-8640

AuthorHouse™ UK Ltd.
500 Avebury Boulevard
Central Milton Keynes, MK9 2BE
www.authorhouse.co.uk
Phone: 08001974150

First published by AuthorHouse 9/13/2006

ISBN: 1-4259-5442-1 (sc)

Printed in the United States of America
Bloomington, Indiana

This book is printed on acid-free paper.

There is a monument in the small farming community of Lincoln, Kansas, dedicated to the memory of settlers killed or captured there by Indians on a sunny, spring day in 1869. Twelve were killed over a 10 mile stretch of the Spillman Creek and Saline River, and two women were taken captive. It is known as the Pioneer Monument.

Then a darker, drearier vision
Passed before me, vague and cloud-like;
I beheld our nation scattered,
All forgetful of my counsels,
Weakened, warring with each other;
Saw the remnants of our people
Sweeping westward, wild and woeful,
Like the cloud-rack of a tempest,
Like the withered leaves of autumn.

Song of Hiawatha, 1855
Henry Wadsworth Longfellow

INTRODUCTION

Over the past two miles the road had grown progressively narrower and more difficult to navigate. Deep ruts created by a heavy truck in some previous period of flooding jerked the wheels of the car this way and that, and large rocks half submerged in the clay-like soil shook the small passenger car viciously as it crossed over them.

The lane ended abruptly in the yard of a two story, dilapidated farm house, badly in need of paint and repair. One of the windows on the second level had been replaced by a large piece of cardboard. Several of the steps leading to the house were broken, and one of the pillars supporting the roof over the front porch was missing. The overhang sagged dangerously. The home was surrounded by fields of corn almost eight feet tall. A small creek meandered through the northeast corner.

I turned off the ignition and got out of the car. For the first time I became aware of the man sitting in a rocking chair on the shady side of the veranda. He had a tattered straw hat pulled low over his forehead, and was wearing an old, faded pair of overalls. Under this was a grimy set of long-johns with sleeves coming half-way down his arms. It wasn't his attire that caught my attention, though, but the double-barreled shotgun lying across his lap.

"State your purpose, Sonny, or turn around and skittle out of here," he shouted. The muzzle of the shotgun shifted slightly as he spoke so that it was pointing more or less in my direction.

I was quick to answer. "Hello. My name's Stanley Houston. I'm looking for a gentleman named Joe – I don't know his last name. I was interested in the Indian massacre of settlers that occurred here in 1869. You know, the one they have that monument for in town. I wanted to learn a little more about the Alderdice family, and that couple that came over from Germany – what was their name – Weichel? Fellow working at the gas station told me that someone he called 'Old Joe' who lived out this way was the one I ought to talk with. Said Old Joe knew all about it."

"Indian massacre, you say." I thought his voice softened just a little. "What are you, a writer?"

"No. Well, maybe. I guess I've given some thought to writing a book about the attack. Haven't decided for sure. That's why I was looking for someone who might know a little about it."

The old man studied me carefully before replying.

"I guess I know as much as anyone about those days. Always kinda enjoy talking about them with someone who's really interested. Matter of fact, I've been kinda waiting around just to tell the whole thing to someone who might put it to print." He definitely had a friendlier tone to his voice. "Come on up here so's I can see you better."

At close range I noted that his face was badly wrinkled. Furrows that reminded me of a plowed field covered his forehead and cheeks. He had a day old white stubble beard and heavy white eyebrows. It was impossible to determine his age, but I could see why they referred to him as 'Old' Joe in town.

"Sit down," he said, pointing to a rickety straight chair with a cloth pad on the seat. "Tell me about yourself."

For the next fifteen minutes we talked about the weather, the corn crop and my interest in the Indian attack. I was getting impatient to turn the conversation to the raid itself, but the old man seemed to be in no hurry. During the course of our talk he bent forward in his chair and laid the shotgun gently on the deck of the porch.

Finally he said, "So you want to know the story of the massacre, do you? Well, I guess I'm the best one you could have come to. I remember it as if it had happened only yesterday."

I wondered briefly what he meant by "I remembered" since these events would have occurred long before his time, but assumed *he meant that he remembered the stories of the attack and not the attack itself.*

"It all began when the Cheyenne first came to this land. They used to live in Asia, you know. It was many years ago that they crossed over. Game was getting pretty scarce, and the winters were bad. There wasn't many of them on that first journey. Their medicine man ..."

"I really wanted to know about the raid itself," I interrupted, afraid he was going to spend all afternoon talking about the origins of the Indian tribe, in which I had no interest. I wanted to get down to the particulars of the events in 1869.

Old Joe gave me a long, accusing look. *"Sonny, supposin' you saw a bright crimson leaf caught in an eddy in the creek and you decided you wanted to write about that leaf. Where would you start? When you first saw it circling in the whirlpool? Or maybe when it came around the bend when it was floating down the river? Or maybe, if you really wanted to tell the story of that leaf and how it ended up in the backwaters of the creek, you would start when it budded out in the spring of the year, when winter had passed and everything was green and fresh."*

I could think of no reasonable response.

Old Joe glowered at me for several seconds more, before settling back in his rocking chair and continuing. *"As I was sayin', the Cheyenne were looking for a new home. Our medicine man told everyone he had ..."*

"Excuse me," I interrupted him again. *"You said 'our' medicine man. Are you an Indian, or part Indian?"*

"Did I say that?" The old man chuckled softly to himself. *"Well don't that beat all? I guess sometimes I don't know what I am. When you get real close to a story you start identifyin' with everyone in it. Like you was kin, almost."* A far away look came in his eyes as he stared into the distance. I could tell he was seeing something in his mind other than the corn fields that glistened in the afternoon sun.

"I can picture old Black Kettle even now, standin' alongside Roman Nose wearing that magical war bonnet of his," he mused. "And Tom Alderdice and big old Eli. And Maria. Sweet Maria."

I waited impatiently until Old Joe suddenly jerked his head to one side, cleared his throat, seemed to return to the present, and once again began his story.

CHAPTER 1

The Cheyenne were looking for a new home. They came silently, one by one, through the freezing, swirling fog, clutching their hide robes tightly about them. They were tired, they were cold, and they were hungry.

Their holy man had promised them a new land, full of wild game and running streams. But now they came to an icy, rocky shore, and only the freezing salt water lay ahead. They had no way of going any further. They huddled together in small groups, full of despair.

The holy man rose shakily to his feet. He was so weak that for the past few miles he had been unable to walk, and had been carried by his people. "We have been led to this place for a purpose," he stated. "I will go off to a hill we passed a little way back. I will strip to my breechcloth, and lie down there, and wait for a vision."

"But you will surely die," some of the people cried. Others muttered that they were all going to die soon anyway, so did it matter if the holy man made his peace now.

Four braves carried the holy man to the crest of the hill, and left him there as he directed. When they returned to the group, they discussed what they should do. There was little choice. They were weak and without food, and were at the end of their stamina. Their only sustenance was a little moss and the hides they wore over their bodies, which they chewed to assuage the pangs in their stomachs. The babies cried in hunger, but the older children huddled silently, staring out of gaunt, sunken eyes. Here and there some of the braves began to sing their death songs as they prepared to die. Finally a great silence descended on the camp.

But at the dawn the silence was broken by the loud booming of thunder. "What was that?" the people cried. "It is the sound of our death approaching," some replied. "Perhaps the holy man has met with his ancestors," others responded.

Those who still had a little strength left went to the holy man to see if his spirit had departed. But when they found him he was sitting up and waving with great excitement.

"I have had a vision," he exclaimed, though his voice was so weak that even those near him had to bend their heads low to hear. "In my vision a small herd of buffalo wandered into our camp, and our braves killed them all. Their meat renewed our strength. And in the vision I saw how to make boats out of their hides. I saw how to dry the hides, how to shape them like the buffalo, how to use the willow rods to give the skins strength. I saw our people embark on these boats towards the rising sun, through the icy mist and freezing rain, and saw them land in a new world."

The braves carried the holy man back to their camp, and everyone heard the story of his vision. And just as he had dreamed, so it happened. The people left the rocky shore, proceeded through the fog and mist, and landed in a new place. Over a period of many, many moons, the people prospered, and the tribe grew. They gradually moved southward and eastward to the land of the Great Lakes and finally to the wide prairie. And that was how the Cheyenne came to this place.

Before the Europeans arrived in this country, the Cheyenne, like most other Indians, were in the process of shifting from what the anthropologists call a hunter-gatherer society to one based on agriculture. They began to rely more on crops they could grow themselves than on game they could kill or wild berries they could gather. They lived in what is now Minnesota in permanent villages along the streams, and grew squash, corn and beans. Occasionally they hunted the buffalo, but it was difficult for men on foot to kill enough buffalo to sustain the tribe.

By the 1700's they had been driven further West by the Sioux and were living in what is now South Dakota, still dwelling in permanent homes and raising crops. Then came the horse, introduced by the Spaniards.

The horse. Seldom has a single event changed the life of a society as greatly as did the arrival of the horse for the Cheyenne. Now a handful of Indians could kill enough buffalo in one hunt to feed the tribe for many moons. And on the plains were thousands upon thousands of such animals.

According to Cheyenne legend, they had been told about the coming of horses by their medicine man, the mythical Sweet Medicine, long before they were introduced into this country. The horses would be brought by white-skinned strangers, he said, and would change the Cheyenne way of life forever.

And indeed the horse did change the Cheyenne way of life. With the horse a warrior could wander many, many miles in a single day to run down buffalo. Soon they forsook their permanent villages, and became a society of nomads, roaming the vast reaches of the plains, following the buffalo, and once more became a hunter-gatherer society.

They were great warriors, raiding neighboring tribes for more horses and to earn honor in the tribe. Young braves were raised to be fearless fighters. One of the greatest awards a combatant could earn was to touch his enemy with his hands or with some object while his foe was still alive. This

3

was called 'counting coup.' Until an Indian boy had counted coup on an enemy, he couldn't consider earning the affection of a young maiden.

"That's the way it was in the early 1800's." Old Joe said. "Pretty idyllic existence you might say. Then the white men from all over the world began movin' westward into the 'new world,' smack dab into the sacred hunting grounds of the Cheyenne Nation. Created a real problem for the chiefs. Old Black Kettle in particular."

"Black Kettle. He's one of the Indians that was really stirring up trouble for the settlers, wasn't he? I've heard of him. Did he lead the attack on the settlers in 1869?"

Old Joe gave me one of those looks that said plain as day that I must have been the dumbest kid in the class. "No, Black Kettle didn't lead any attack on the settlers in 1869. Matter of fact he was dead by then."

I was confused. "If he was dead how could he have been involved?"

"Well, Sonny, let me tell you about old Black Kettle."

CHAPTER 2

A soft breeze stirred in the high reaches of the mountains and then began its journey down the slopes and through the canyons of the snow capped peaks. It eventually found its way to the high plains of Colorado, and continued in an easterly direction. In the Smoky Hill region of central Kansas it massaged the tall prairie grass and stirred the drying leaves of the cottonwood trees.

It also cooled the weathered face of the man sitting at the crest of a hill, facing to the west and the setting sun. It was a strong face, and stern, with a wide mouth and prominent jaw that told of fierce determination. The man was called Black Kettle, or Moka-ta-va-tah in the Cheyenne tongue. Black Kettle, in the 44th year of his life, had just been elected to be one of the four chiefs of the Wotap band of the People. This was a great honor, but also carried great responsibility. Black Kettle appealed to the spirits of the wind, the mountains and the prairie to provide him with the wisdom to justify the faith that his people had shown in him.

There were ten bands in the Cheyenne nation. Each elected four chiefs to lead them. In addition there were four other, older chiefs that provided continuity and stability to the group. Together they were known as the Council of

Forty-four. These men governed the day-to-day affairs of the tribe, resolving problems, making treaties, and declaring war when necessary. Although the Cheyenne were a single nation, they lived in villages scattered across the plains where they could find grass for their horses and game for their families. Periodically they would come together for special occasions, such as the renewal ceremony for the sacred medicine arrows, or a sun dance called by one of the clans.

Black Kettle was thinking about his life, how he might draw on his experiences to help make him a better leader. Although he sat quietly, he was aware of all about him. He noted the coolness of the breeze that swept over his brow and that played with the single feather that he wore in his head band. Our summer is about over, he thought, and another season will soon be upon us. He let his mind think about this, about the seasons of the year, and the seasons of his life.

As a boy he had been taught by his father and uncles about honor and responsibility. Every Cheyenne boy was trained to be a great warrior, to be considerate of others in his tribe, and to obey the dictates of his elders. Most of all every young man yearned for the day that he could count his first "coup" on an enemy.

Black Kettle remembered the day when that had happened for him. It was with his good friend, Lean Bear, and three other young braves. While on a hunting trip the five spotted the camp of three Utes who had just killed a buffalo and were busy skinning it. Black Kettle and his friends decided they would steal the horses, which were wandering loose about 30 feet away. The Cheyenne youths followed a dry creek bed to within 50 feet of their enemy.

They came out of the gulch and charged into the camp, shouting and yelling. While the other four circled the horses and began driving them to the north, Black Kettle rode directly up to the three braves, who were scrambling for their weapons. Leaning from his horse, he slapped one of them on the back, sending him sprawling.

The Cheyenne boys escaped unharmed with the horses, and returned to their village. Black Kettle remembered the pride he felt when he told the others of his exploit. His father had given him a warm smile, clasped his shoulder and said, "You have done well, my son. This day you have earned much honor."

Black Kettle's thoughts drifted to another season of his life. When he was eighteen, he was accepted into the Crooked Lances society, also known as the Elkhorn Scrappers. A young Cheyenne warrior could choose from one of five different social-military groups: the Bowstring, the Dog Men, the Crooked Lances, the Kit Foxes or the Red Shields. Each had an important role to play within the tribe, and had its own costumes, ceremonies and dances.

As he thought about those days, Black Kettle pulled an elk horn rattle from his tunic. It was colored blue and yellow, and had a snake's head painted on one end and a tail on the other. Every member of the Crooked Lances society carried one of these magic rattlers to remind themselves that they would always help each other in time of war or difficulty. Black Kettle gently shook the rattle as he continued his contemplation.

He remembered the great battle with the Kiowa and Comanche in the year of 1838. The Cheyenne together with their friends, the Arapahoe, killed almost 60 of the enemy that day. Black Kettle had been a 'wolf' in that campaign - a runner sent ahead of the rest of the tribe to seek out the enemy's position. He had located it, and he and the Crooked Lances led the charge into the stronghold.

The thing Black Kettle remembered most about the Kiowa, however, was that a few years later the Cheyenne and Kiowa made peace with each other. They exchanged many presents, joined together in a big feast, and had become staunch allies. The Council of Forty-four had been wise, Black Kettle thought. How much better to be friends with the Greasy Wood People, as the Kiowa were known, than to be at war.

But the Cheyenne had never made peace with the Pawnee, even to this day. Black Kettle thought about a battle the Cheyenne had fought with the Wolf People only two years ago. Black Kettle had been selected to carry the Sacred Medicine Arrows into that fight. It was a great honor. The Arrows had been given to the tribe by their legendary holy man, Sweet Medicine. There were four of them, and they protected the tribe from sickness and ill fortune, and gave them strength and victory in battle.

The setting sun now almost touched the earth, and was a bright, crimson ball of fire in the west. The warm glow reminded Black Kettle of Little Sage Woman, his first wife. He wondered where she might be, and if he would ever see her again. His heart ached at the memory. She had always been at his side, even during the time of the white man's sickness - the evil spirit they called cholera. Almost half of Black Kettle's tribe had been killed by that disease in the winter of 1849.

Little Sage Woman had been lost during the war party against the Mexicans. The dark skinned white men had killed two Cheyenne warriors and stolen many horses. Black Kettle was enraged, and determined to lead a war party of around 40 warriors into Mexico to seek revenge. Little Sage Woman and Red Eye Woman offered to accompany the avengers to tend to camp chores.

The raids were successful, and many rancheros were burned and scalps taken, but on the return the fighters ran into an overwhelming number of Utes, another enemy of the Cheyenne. Black Kettle and his group were quickly surrounded by their foes. Little Sage Woman was thrown

8

from her horse and captured by the Black People. Black Kettle tried to fight his way to her side, but was beaten back on every occasion. Finally he gave up his rescue attempts, and with his companions fought their way out of the encirclement. They escaped, but both of the women had been taken captive by their enemies.

Black Kettle often thought about Little Sage Woman. Was she a slave of the hated Utes, or perhaps even married to one? Or maybe she had been traded to the Mexicans, which often happened, and was a prisoner on some ranchero. He wondered if he would ever know.

In time another maiden had captured his eye, and Black Kettle took a new wife, Medicine Woman Later. She is a fine woman, Black Kettle thought. She was from the Wotap band of the tribe, and as was the custom, Black Kettle came to live with his new wife's clan. He was greatly admired and respected by his new family, and now found himself elected to be a chief of the Wotap.

As the last rays of the sun faded away, Black Kettle arose and said a final prayer to the gods of the wind. He knew there would be much to consider in the months ahead for his tribe. Not only would there continue to be conflicts with their ancient enemies, but now a new question had to be considered. The question of what to do about the white man.

Old Joe leaned back in his chair, pulled out a corn cob pipe, filled it with Prince Albert tobacco, and struck a match to it.

"Black Kettle had every reason to worry about the whites. At first it was only the traders and hunters. They got along pretty well with the Indians, often taking an Indian wife and living with the tribes. But then came the pioneers headed for California and Oregon. They didn't try to understand the people whose lands they were traveling through. They cut down scarce trees along

creek banks, and killed the buffalo and deer. But at least they weren't hangin' around permanent like."

"Then gold was discovered in Colorado, in the Pikes Peak region. Now the whites were comin' into Indian Territory to stay. Towns grew up overnight, and the traffic along Cheyenne roads got pretty heavy. But the real problem was when the settlers started movin' in and turning favorite Cheyenne camp sites into farms."

"Old Sweet Medicine warned about the whites. He said someday they would come and try to lure the People with presents while they took the land. He predicted they would bring a great sickness, and in the end the tribe would lose respect for their elders and start quarrlin' among themselves. They would drive the People crazy, he said."

Old Joe paused for a moment, then asked, "Did you ever hear of Chickamauga?"

"Well, sure," I replied. "But that was something in the Civil War. Nothing to do with the Indian raid that I know of."

Old Joe gave me another of his dour looks. "Chickamauga was the reason that Tom Alderdice came out west. And you said you wanted to know about the Alderdice's didn't you?" He puffed on his pipe for a few seconds, trying to keep the embers going. When he finally had a red glow in the bowl, he relaxed, and said, "Yep, I guess you could say that destiny came to old Tom at Chickamauga, in a round about way."

CHAPTER 3

Company E of the 44th Mississippi Infantry came to the river early in the morning. The Sergeant surveyed the situation, and then turned back to his men. "OK boys. We gotta cross this here little ole puddle of water before we're gonna find any Yankees to kill. Let's get movin'."

Private Thomas Alderdice, Company E, groaned. "Nothing I hate more," he said to the soldier next to him, "than fighting with wet feet." He sat down on the bank and untied the laces on his boots, pulled them off, and tied them together. He put his tobacco and gun powder and a few other valuables in the boots, threw them around his neck, and holding his rifle high, waded across the river.

On the other side, he sat down again, pulled off his stockings, and wrung as much water out of them as he could. As he was putting his boots back on he turned to one of his new-found friends - Buck Jackson - and said, "I wonder if this magnificent body of water we just crossed has a name."

Buck replied, "They tell me this here's the Chickamauga. Indian name meaning 'river of death.'"

Thomas thought about it for a minute, before saying, "Guess I could have gone all morning without knowing that piece of information." Thomas was a slim man of medium height, with a thin face sporting a closely clipped mustache. He had brown hair, and his dark eyes glowed with a subdued sense of humor mixed with an ample supply of intelligence. He had been born and lived part of his life in Pennsylvania, but when war came he was residing in the South and had sided with them in their rebellion against the Union.

Thomas and his company pushed on for several more hours before stopping again to rest. It was approaching 10:00 in the morning on September 19th, 1863, and the Confederates, under the command of General Bragg, were moving towards the northwest to attack the Union Army under General Rosecrans. Bragg had been in retreat several days before, but received major reinforcements at Lafayette, and now turned back to launch an attack against the pursuing Union Army. It was estimated that the Federals numbered almost 55,000 men, while the Rebs now had close to 70,000.

While Thomas and Buck were reclining under a large tree, the Sergeant came by and said, "I need a few volunteers. Alderdice and Jackson - pick three more of your friends to accompany you on a scouting trip."

"I thought I heard the word 'volunteers'," Thomas replied. "I sure didn't see my hand up in the air."

The Sergeant ignored the remark. "Some of the boys say they heard some voices off there in the woods a little while ago. I need someone to investigate. See what's in them there trees and brush."

Thomas scanned the forest to which the Sergeant pointed. It was thick with foliage, and he wasn't able to see more than twenty-five or thirty yards into the maze. The canopy of leaves overhead, now starting to show the brilliant reds and oranges of fall, blocked the sun's rays from reaching the ground. The bushes growing throughout the woods were almost five feet tall.

"Yes, sir," Thomas replied. "Whatever you say."

Thomas and Buck picked three more of their comrades, and started off into the dense growth. They spread out until they could barely see the man on their left and on their right. After twenty minutes of pushing through the underbrush they came to a break in the trees, and before them in a green meadow, they could make out hundreds of Union soldiers assembling for battle. The patrol drew back, and sent a messenger to their commanding officer, Lt. General Longstreet.

Thomas waited in the trees, trying to stay out of sight. But the Bluecoats were too busy readying their gear for battle to be paying much attention to the fringes of the woods. Finally Thomas heard his Confederate comrades moving up behind him. The soldiers took their positions, still undetected by the Union camp.

Thomas clutched his rifle tightly waiting for the command to attack. As soon as it came, he gave a loud yell, and joined his fellow Rebs in a running attack on the boys in blue. The charge caught the enemy completely by surprise, and they began to fall back in confusion, before being rallied by their officers. Soon bullets and cannon shells were screaming from both sides, and casualties began to fall. The sound in the glen was deafening, and the scene was one of utter confusion, as men in Gray surged forward, only to be met with fierce resistance from those in Blue. For a while it looked like the Southerners might have the Union soldiers in a complete rout, but then the Northern officers would gather their men and lead a counter-attack. For several hours the battle lines surged forward, then back, then forward again.

In one of the major Southern charges Thomas and Buck found themselves in the leading edge of the attack. Men were falling all around them, but still they charged on. Then Buck stumbled and slipped to the ground, gasping for air, and Thomas could see a patch of red blood beginning to form on his chest.

As he ducked behind a fallen tree, he paused to look around, and realized that he was alone. His comrades had either fallen, or had retreated, and now the Union soldiers were advancing rapidly. A bullet slammed into the trunk of the tree he was crouching behind, sending splinters into his face and momentarily blinding him. Rubbing his eyes, he started to leave the shelter of the fallen tree to race back to his lines when he found himself surrounded by a half dozen soldiers with their rifles leveled at him.

"Give it up, Reb!" one of the soldiers barked. "Drop the gun and fall on your belly. Now!" Tomas took only a moment to size up the situation before letting his rifle slip to the ground and unbuckling his pistol. He lay down on the ground.

"Shucks," one of the other soldiers muttered. "Why don't we just shoot him? Bet he shot a few of our own today."

"No, we can't do that," the leader of the group said. "We got to honor the code. A prisoner gotta be treated with respect. Besides, if we take a prisoner back we get out of this here dog fight for a while anyway."

They ordered Thomas to his feet, and two of them motioned for him to start marching with them back towards the Union lines. For Thomas Alderdice, aged 22, the war between the States, which pitted brother against brother, was over.

Nearly a year later, on a hot and humid October afternoon, Thomas was lounging on a cot in the prisoner of war camp at Rock Island, Illinois, reading a week-old newspaper.

A large fly circled his head, creating a loud buzzing in his ears. It finally lit on the back of his hand. Tom twitched his arm a little, and the fly left. But in a minute it had returned, this time alighting on Tom's pants leg. Again Tom rather absent-mindedly brushed the fly away. But the fly was persistent, and after a few seconds was back, landing almost at the same spot on his pants. This time Tom concentrated a little more on the fly, and tried to swat it with his hand. He missed, and the fly, thoroughly aroused, buzzed angrily in his face, before perching on his left sleeve. Now the fly had Tom's full attention. He rolled up the newspaper, ready to smash the insect into oblivion, when a Union soldier came into the building and ordered everyone outside.

The prisoners moved out in the sun, wondering what the commotion was all about. A colonel that Thomas had never seen before stood on a box crate in front of the men and began talking in a loud voice. "Now listen up everyone," he shouted. "Any of you boys tired of these here quarters? Like to get out of here and be free men again?"

A derisive chuckle passed through the ragged bunch. "How's that, Colonel?" one of them shouted back. "The Union ready to surrender are they? Want to give up your arms to us?"

"No, the Union is not going to surrender," the Colonel replied. "In fact it ought to be pretty obvious to everyone that the war is all but over. The Confederacy can't last much longer. But you boys could be set free right now, if you were of a mind. All you got to do is pledge your allegiance to the United States of America – the Union – and sign up for a year's active duty in the Army, and away you go."

"Sign up in the Union Army?" another of the prisoners scoffed. "And go fight our own boys? No way are we going to do that!"

"Sign up in the Union Army – yes," the Colonel replied. "But not to fight against your own. To fight Indians out west. Probably out to Kansas. We wouldn't expect you to pick up arms against your own Southern brothers."

"Yeah, go fight Indians out west to free up your boys to fight Rebs. No thank you," a prisoner on the front row shouted.

"Well now that's not exactly the case," the Colonel replied. "We've pretty much pulled our troops out of the west already – much as we could. The problem is, that leaves women and children out there without much protection against the Indians. You would be doing a brave and honorable thing. Think it over, men. Any of you decide you would like to trade your present circumstances with helping to protect innocent settlers in the west against marauding Indians, you let me know."

With that the Colonel stepped down from his platform, and the prisoners were dismissed.

Thomas mulled over the Colonel's proposition that night, and thought about the South's - as he now perceived it - losing fight. Thomas had been fighting because he lived in Dixie, not because he had a plantation or family or job to defend. There was really nothing pulling him back to Mississippi. By morning he had made up his mind. He would take that oath, join the U.S. Army, and seek his fortune in the west.

CHAPTER 4

Even as Southern prisoners in Illinois were being urged to join the Army to chase Indians in Kansas, people in Kansas earlier in the summer were being solicited to fight Southerners. There were persistent rumors that General Price of the Confederacy planned to make an incursion into Missouri and perhaps Kansas. In early July, 1864, while Thomas Alderdice was still sweltering in a prisoner of war camp in Illinois, Governor Thomas Carney of Kansas received a request from General Curtis, Commanding Officer of the Department of the Missouri, for a voluntary regiment of infantry to serve 100 days in the defense, if needed, of eastern Kansas.

The sun beat down with great intensity on the family sitting around tables in the yard of the Michael Ziegler homestead, just to the north of Salina, Kansas. The Ziegler clan was a large one, consisting of Michael and his wife, Mary, and nine children. Two of the children were married, Susanna, the oldest, to James Daily, and the next, Mary, to John Alverson.

"Well, I guess I just feel like it's my duty to sign up," James Daily was saying. "The Governor has called for volunteers to fight the Rebs. The regular army is spread pretty thin, trying to take care of the Indians, and here come

17

the darned Southerners to take advantage of the situation. It isn't going to hurt my homestead claim any if I sign up for 100 days."

Susanna mustered a brave smile, but it wavered just a little at the corners of her mouth. She was worried about being left alone with her son, now just a little over a year old, and a new one coming on.

"But James," she said, a little defensively. "I don't see why you have to be the one to go. You've got a family to think of, you know."

James gave her a loving smile. "I wouldn't go if I thought it would in any way jeopardize you and the boy, Susanna. You know that. Your family is right here, and they'll make sure you are alright. And it's only for 100 days. I'll be back by time the new one there is ready to stick his or her nose into the world." Then, turning to John Alverson, he asked, "How about you, John? Think you might join up with me? The Army sure could use someone with your frontier savvy."

John Alverson took several minutes before replying. It was true that he was an experienced frontiersman. He and his father had made their living killing wolves in the Kansas winters, and living in the wilderness, often camping with Indians. But now he was married to Mary, and much more of a family man. Besides, he was pretty much of a free spirit, and not too sure about having to take orders from some Army Lieutenant. Still, he couldn't deny the threat posed by the Southerners, who might try to make a grab for Kansas.

"Guess I'll have to give it some thought," he finally replied. "I'm not too sure I want to be leaving when all this Indian trouble is starting to flare up."

Eli Ziegler, the eldest boy of the Ziegler children at 12 years of age, interrupted, "Boy, I wish I was old enough to go. I bet I'd be as good as any of the others."

James and John both smiled at the boy's exuberance. Eli was big for his age, and there was no doubt but what he could take care of himself, even at this young age.

"Likely you would be at that," John replied. "You sure do know your way around in the woods. And a pretty good shot with the rifle, from what I hear." Eli was beginning to get quite a reputation as one of the best shots in the county. "But I reckon someone has to stay home and keep the Indians away."

The mention again of Indians caused a worried frown to appear on Susanna's face. "What do you think, John?" Susanna asked. "You've been out there with Indians when you were hunting wolves. What do you think about them?"

John thought about this last question several minutes before replying. "I guess in one way Indians are a lot like white folks. There's good, peaceful Indians, and there are some that are just down right mean. And there's a difference between tribes, too. Some tribes are farmers and don't go looking for trouble, but there are others that are raiders and pretty belligerent. Out here, our Indians are mostly Cheyenne, and they are warriors."

"For a Cheyenne brave the most important thing in the world is to prove just how manly and courageous he is. Why it's even more important than living to a ripe old age. A Cheyenne believes that it is far better to die in his prime, fighting for his honor and his tribe, than to live to be an old man who has lost his teeth and is useless to everyone. For him to go steal horses from an enemy, or go kill a Pawnee, is as normal as going to hunt rabbits is for you and me."

"Yeah," Eli replied. "But one main difference, rabbits don't shoot back."

"Well, if you really wanted to match the Cheyenne in bravery, Eli," James chimed in with a slight smile, "you'd have to let your hair grow real long – all the way down to your toes. I've heard tell that some of the Cheyenne Dog Soldiers wear their hair so long it reaches the ground, and the reason is so's that if a battle seems to be going the wrong way they'll have someone tie their hair to a stake in the ground so that they can't run away, and then they'll stand there and fight the enemy until they're killed, or until the rest of the tribe fights back to save him."

"You two make the Indians sound very noble," Susanna stated. "That's not exactly how I hear it, of how they rape women and brutally kill children."

"There's certainly that side of it too, Susanna," John remarked. "Within the context of their own tribe the Cheyenne are a pretty civilized bunch, maybe even more so than us, but they are totally brutal to their enemies. They can indulge in torture and inhuman acts with their perceived enemies without a bit of conscience or second thought. Take women for instance. Their women are highly respected and virginity in a bride is very important. When a brave marries, he leaves his own tribe and goes to live with his wife's family and joins some society in her tribe. But a woman captive, especially a white woman, is held in no such respect. They will rape her – the whole tribe maybe – and the squaws will beat her and work her to death. Better for a woman to take her own life than be taken captive by a war party."

Susanna shuddered at the thought.

"Well, they all sound like a bunch of savages to me," Mary said. "I don't see any redeeming feature in any of them."

"I guess it depends how you look at it," John continued. "If you just consider an Indian in the confines of his tribe, he is probably the 'Noble Red Man' you read about in the papers back East. There's a lot of admirable traits in a Cheyenne warrior. He places high value on honor and loyalty to his people. But when it comes to his enemies or captives, he can be a savage beast."

Susanna thought for a moment before observing, "Doesn't seem to me like there's much chance of ever living peacefully with them."

"I think you're probably right," John replied. "Comes the fall and winter months they decide they want peace 'cause their ponies are weak and it's cold out. But soon as spring comes the juices start running and the young braves are out looking for honor and excitement again. And the tribal elders don't have much control over them. One or two braves, or maybe a half dozen, will strike out to raid ranches or steal horses, while the rest of the tribe maintains that they are peaceful. Then, when the warring braves get tired, they return and are welcomed back like the proverbial wayward son that returns to the fold."

"So there is no chance of living with them in peace?" Mary asked again.

John thought a moment before replying. "I guess I can't see much chance of it. Like I said earlier, there's no such thing as either a good or bad Indian – there's just Indians. And they're unpredictable. We can't seem to keep them on their reservation, and as long as they're wandering around the countryside you can't be sure that your women or children will ever be safe. If we want to sleep well at night," he finally said, "best to just get rid of them, one way or the other." The other men nodded their heads in agreement.

"Do you think we are in any danger here, John?" Susanna asked.

"Well, likely not, I guess. The Cheyenne keep pretty well to the west of the Elkhorn. But I sure would keep my eyes open and my gun handy if I was you."

The talk turned away from the Indians and the Civil War to other things. The progress that was being made with the Union Pacific Railroad which would soon be coming west, the prospects of a good corn crop, and the mosquitoes that were beginning to swarm around the picnic table.

John Alverson and James Daily both signed up to serve with the 17th Kansas Volunteer Infantry. General Price did push up into Missouri, and was nearly successful in taking St. Louis. Meeting stiff resistance there, he turned westward towards the Kansas border. He was defeated in a battle at Independence, and veered off to the south. There were several skirmishes along the Kansas border before Price finally returned to Arkansas.

James Daily served most of his 100 days at Fort Leavenworth, and then, just a few days before his enlistment expired, contracted typhoid fever. He died at the hospital in Leavenworth on November 25, 1864, never seeing his second son, Willis, born in early October.

Old Joe tapped his pipe against the arm of the chair to loosen the burnt tobacco, then dumped the contents onto the porch. He pulled a toothpick from the front of his overalls, and cleaned the rest of the ashes from the bowl. It was getting late in the afternoon, and I was afraid we were never going to get around to the Indian massacre of 1869.

"1864 was a key year leadin' up to that raid of yours," he said, almost as if he had been reading my mind. "Tom Alderdice comin' out west, James Daily dying and leaving Susanna and her two children all alone. And that's the year that all Hell broke loose with the Indians. The Lean Bear trouble, and Sand Creek. Most of all, Sand Creek."

Old Joe paused, and got that far-away look in his eyes again. I wanted to prod him, but figured I'd better let him take his time. Trying to hurry him along didn't seem to work.

"The year actually started out pretty good for the Indians," he finally said. "Sam Colley, the Cheyenne Indian agent, invited some of the chiefs to visit Washington the year before and meet with the Great White Father, old Abe Lincoln. I think the idea was to impress them with the strength and numbers of the whites, and convince them that it would be futile for the Indians to make

war on the pale faces. Lean Bear and Black Kettle were among them. Worked pretty good, too. These two old chiefs recognized that it would be disastrous for the Cheyenne and white men to fight each other. They became great peace advocates."

"But early in 1864 the trouble started. A Cheyenne war party, Dog Soldiers, headed out to make a raid on their old enemies, the Crow, when they found four stray mules and took them into their camp. The rancher who owned the mules demanded them back, and the Indians agreed to give them up. At least kinda' agreed. They insisted, however, that they should get a reward for their efforts in roundin' them up. The rancher refused, and reported to the Army that the Indians had stolen the mules and were on a rampage, terrorizing ranchers in the area. The Army set out to recover the animals and teach the Indians a lesson."

"The troopers found the Cheyenne party, and demanded the mules be returned. The Dog Soldiers complied, but then the Army tried to take the rifles away from them. That was a big mistake. There was no way the Indians were going to give up their arms, and fighting broke out. There were casualties on both sides. But the main outcome was that the Indians were enraged that the Army was embarking on a campaign to disarm them."

"That was the beginnin'. After that groups of Cheyenne, mostly Dog Soldiers, began raiding ranches here and there, stealing cattle and horses and sometimes killin' someone. The soldier boys were in hot pursuit, hunting down Indian villages. When they found one it didn't matter who the Indians were, or whether they had been peaceful or not, they were attacked and the lodges were burned to the ground."

"Old Black Kettle was trying his best to keep the young men in his camp in line, but it was getting more and more difficult. Then came the Lean Bear affair. That was the last straw for the Dog Soldiers."

The old man leaned back in his rocking chair, and puffed on his unlit pipe.

CHAPTER 5

Black Kettle lifted the flap of the tent, bent slightly, and walked inside. Lean Bear, one of the most respected of the chiefs of the People, was expecting him. Black Kettle sat beside his good friend and they spent several minutes in quiet contemplation.

Lean Bear finally spoke. "Do you still cling to the vision we have shared, my brother?"

"It is so. The vision is not one to my liking, but it must be. You and I have been to the white men's cities in the east. We have seen their strength and numbers and prosperity. We cannot defeat them in war. We must learn from them and adopt their ways. But it will be hard. It may not happen in the seasons that you and I have left to travel this earth."

Lean Bear nodded. "Your words are true. But we must grasp this vision of peace and hold it close to our heart. We must not let it go, even when it seems to slip from our grasp. The land has been generous to the Indian. It has provided him with sweet grass and wild berries and game to feed our people. But now the game grows scarce. The wild berries are picked by the settlers who travel through our country. Their wagons crush the sweet grass. Now we must ride many miles and spend many suns trying to find enough food to keep our bellies from growling in hunger."

"The land may have been generous to the People," Black Kettle replied, "but it has opened its heart and shared its innermost secrets with the pale faces. While we hunt with great difficulty for food, these men from across the sea raise enough grain and vegetables on a small plot to feed entire villages. If our tribe is to survive, we must learn the ways of the white man. Our young men must be made to see this."

"This is so, my cousin, but tell me this. If you were a young man again, which life would you choose? One that ties you to a small patch of land which must be tilled every day, or one where you can ride the wide prairie on a sleek pony, with the wind at your back and the stars over your head? The change will be slow to come. And the white men are looked on by many of our tribe as our sworn enemies."

"We were once great enemies with the Greasy Wood People, the Kiowa," Black Kettle remembered. "Then the Council of Forty-four made peace with them, and it has been good. We must follow the same path with the pale faces. Our young men, especially the Dog Soldiers, do not understand. They think the whites can be driven off, and that we can continue in our old customs. We must try to show them the way."

The two chiefs lapsed into silence again. After a while Lean Bear leaned forward and with his finger stirred the dust on the ground on which they sat, and said, "There will be much trouble this summer. The soldiers kill our people with no cause, and our warriors retaliate with attacks against the ranchers and new settlers. The Dog Soldiers especially are angry. You and the other chiefs spoke with our agent Colley at Fort Larned?"

"We spoke. We warned him that our Sioux brothers were filled with anger, and that they were planning raids this summer along the Platte and Arkansas. We told him the Sioux sent the war pipe to us, that they wanted us to join them. We informed him, however, that we did not smoke this pipe, that we want to live in peace with our white brothers."

Black Kettle paused, then added," Now the Army attacks villages not too distant from our camp. It is time to take our lodges to the Smoky Hill as the Council has discussed, and join our brothers who are already there."

Lean Bear grunted, signifying his agreement. Later that day a tribal crier was sent through the village of 250 lodges informing the people that they would move.

Black Kettle and Lean Bear rode at the head of the column as it threaded its way to the east. The afternoon had been hot and dusty, but now large, dark clouds were building in the west. Lean Bear stopped his pony and turned to survey the procession behind him. The mood was festive, as it always was when the tribe was moving to a new camping ground. Children were running along the line, laughing and playing games as they moved forward. The women were engaged in animated conversation as they walked along the travois being pulled by the horses. The men were riding in small groups, making jokes and bragging about their exploits. It was good to see the people happy.

"We will have rain soon," Lean Bear observed, noting the darkening skies on the horizon. "It is best that we stop early and let the women prepare the meal before it comes."

Black Kettle agreed. "We have traveled many miles this day."

The two chiefs held up their arms to signal to the rest of the people that it was time to halt and prepare for the evening. They rode back to where their women were already unpacking cooking utensils and bedding for the night. The children gathered wood, and soon many fires sprung up throughout the camp. This life is good, Black Kettle mused, but it is coming to an end.

His thoughts were interrupted when a warrior that had been scouting in advance of the tribe raced into the center of the camp. He pulled his horse up in a cloud of dust in front of Lean Bear and Black Kettle.

"There are many soldiers coming. They have cannon, and they ride in this direction." The alarming news spread rapidly throughout the camp. Nervous warriors readied their weapons, and women gathered their children near them.

"We have nothing to fear from the white soldiers," Lean Bear said in a loud voice. "Do not be afraid. I will ride out and talk with these men and assure them that we are at peace."

"I will ride with you," Black Kettle said. A chorus of yells and shouts from the surrounding braves assured Lean Bear many others would come also.

"No," Lean Bear replied. "We do not want to alarm the blue coats. Only a few will ride with me. Black Kettle, you stay here and watch over the camp." Lean Bear fumbled for a moment with a satchel tied to his waist, and extracted a large medal tied to a bright ribbon. He placed it around his neck.

"I will wear the medal given to me by the Great White Father, and they will know that we are their brothers." Lean Bear rode off with 30 warriors to meet the advancing troops. Soon they spotted the cavalry headed in their direction. There were over 80 men in the contingent. When they saw the Indians riding towards them, they halted and formed a defensive position.

"The rest of you remain on this hill," Lean Bear told the warriors gathered around him. "I will ride down and parley with this officer, and see what it is they want."

The soldiers watched as Lean Bear detached himself from the rest of the warriors and slowly advanced towards their position, making signs of peace. When he was close, the commanding officer, Lieutenant Eayre, ordered his troops to open fire, and Lean Bear was cut down in a hail of gunfire. The soldiers then opened fire on the rest of the Indians.

These warriors, seeing their beloved chief so brutally killed, rushed down the hill in a head long charge, yelling and screaming and firing their rifles as they came. The soldiers held their position, not overly worried since they outnumbered the Indians almost 3 to 1. But back in the main camp, the Cheyenne warriors heard the shots, and rushed to the aid of their comrades. Soon there were over 500 enraged warriors surrounding the outnumbered Army troops. Black Kettle was among them.

When he learned that Lean Bear had been killed, he was filled with great anger and resentment. He clutched his rifle tightly, and prepared to join his people in the fight. The death of a Cheyenne chief would be avenged. But then he remembered Lean Bear's words, spoken only the previous day. "We must grasp this vision of peace and hold it close to our heart. We must not let it go, even when it seems to slip from our grasp."

Black Kettle sat quietly on his horse in the midst of the chaos surrounding him. If we kill all of these soldiers, he thought, the Army will never rest until it has killed every Cheyenne man, woman and child. Suddenly he sprang into action, riding into the front lines of his people and yelling, "Stop! Do not fire! Go back! We must not kill these men." He rushed into the thick of the fighting, and grabbed the reins of the horse of one warrior, then another. "Turn back. Return to our camp," he yelled. One by one, the braves began to heed his commands, and pulled away from the fight, until finally they were all gone. A silence settled onto the prairie, punctuated by thunder in the distance as the rain clouds moved in from the west.

Lt. Eayre watched in amazement as the last of the warriors disappeared over the hill. He couldn't believe that he and his men were being allowed to escape. He had never dreamed there were so many Cheyenne in the vicinity, but as he made a hasty retreat to Fort Larned, he was already thinking about the great victory he would claim when he met with Colonel Chivington, who had ordered Eayre to kill all Indians that he might come across. Chivington would be pleased that they had killed a major chief of the Cheyenne.

Four soldiers died in this battle, and several others were wounded. The Cheyenne lost three warriors and many others were injured. But the murder of Lean Bear put in motion a confrontation between the Indians and the whites that would set the plains on fire during the summer of 1864.

About this same time the citizens of Denver were shocked by the brutal murder of a Mrs. Hungate and her two children – one a little girl of four and the other an infant –at their ranch southeast of Denver by a band of Arapaho. The woman was scalped and raped, and the children's heads had been nearly cut off. Their bodies were brought into Denver, where the citizens were in an outrage.

The highly ambitious Governor of the Colorado Territory, John Evans, began a campaign to convince authorities in the East that Denver was in imminent danger of Indian attack. In August he received authority to raise a 100-day volunteer militia to defend the territory. This was the Third Regiment of the Colorado Volunteer Cavalry, responsible to Colonel Chivington, who was the commanding colonel of the military district of Colorado. Many, if not most, of the volunteers were renegades and drifters.

Chivington had been, and still was on occasion, a Methodist minister who had earlier distinguished himself in a battle with Southern forces in New Mexico. He was, however, an outspoken foe of all Indians, and a hellfire and brimstone preacher. His solution to the Indian problem was genocide. He also believed that the Cheyenne were at the heart of the Indian unrest, and as far as he and the Colorado

Volunteers were concerned, all Cheyenne were considered hostile.

The Third Regiment saw very little action as the 100-day enlistment period was coming to an end. In Denver they were often referred to as the "Bloodless Third." Both Chivington and Evans agreed that they needed some kind of dramatic victory before the militia was disbanded.

Although Black Kettle had been able to hold his warriors in check in the fight with Lieutenant Eayre's troops, he was not able to keep his young men from exacting vengeance on stage lines and ranches in the months that followed. Raids were made all the way from Fort Larned in central Kansas to Fort Riley in the east.

Later in the summer the Council of Forty-four decided that it was time to renew the power of the sacred Medicine Arrows. This was a four day ritual, and at the end the people elected new chiefs to serve on the governing body. Black Kettle and most of the current chiefs were re-elected. The new Council discussed the problem of the white men, and whether they should make peace or war. Most of the leaders still sought peace, although one chief in particular, Tall Bull of the Dog Soldiers, held out for war. When he was outvoted, he told the council that he and the Dog Soldiers and any others who thought as he did would go to the north, and smoke the war pipe with the Lakota Sioux. The Dog Soldier society had declared war on all whites. The summer was a deadly one for any caught unprotected along the Platte River and open prairie of western Kansas and eastern Colorado. Travel on the Overland Trail was virtually shut down, and supplies were cut off to the citizens of Denver.

Black Kettle and the peaceful chiefs moved their people to the Hackberry Creek branch of the Smoky Hill River. The camp numbered almost 2,000 Cheyenne and Arapahoe and over a hundred Lakota Sioux.

One day in the latter part of August, William Bent rode into camp, where he was greeted with great enthusiasm. Bent had been the first white man to settle in Colorado Territory when he established Bent's Trading Fort in 1834 along the Arkansas River. He was a friend to all the tribes, and married a Cheyenne maiden, Owl Woman. They had four children, including George Bent. When Owl Woman died, William married her sister, Yellow Woman. They had one son, Charles. When they were old enough, William sent four of his children, including George and Charles, to Westport, Missouri to attend school. George and Charles had recently rejoined the tribe, preferring to ride with the Indians over the wide prairie than live in a city with the white men. The Cheyenne, and most of the other tribes, respected William Bent and trusted him, and were happy to have the Bent brothers by their side.

Now Bent sat in Black Kettle's lodge and smoked the peace pipe with all of the leaders of the tribe. "The white chief, Governor Evans, has issued a proclamation," he said. "All friendly Cheyenne are to stay away from those that are at war, and are to go to Fort Lyon where they will be safe. This order was issued many moons ago, but I have been unable to find you and give you this message until now."

"This word that you bring is good," Black Kettle replied. "We have wanted to live in peace with the pale faces, but they attack our villages for no reason, and shoot at our young men. Some who are here have been on the warpath this summer, but now join us in wanting peace. However, the Dog Soldiers and those that ride with them in the north are still angry over the death of Lean Bear, and do not want to shake the hand of the white men. We cannot speak for these people, only for those who are here with us. How can we let this chief Evans know that we do not want war?"

"I reckon the best way to start would be to write your agent, Sam Colley, and try to set up a meeting with the

Army. I see that my son, George, is here with you. He knows the white men's words and can put them to paper as you direct."

The chiefs murmured their approval, and Black Kettle dictated two letters, one to their agent Sam Colley and the other to the commandant of Fort Lyon, Major Edward Wynkoop. In the letters, he emphasized that the Indians with him, which included groups of Kiowa, Comanche, Arapahoe, Apache, Sioux and Cheyenne, wanted peace. He said that they had seven captives in their various camps, which they would like to exchange for Indian prisoners the Army held in Denver. He would await their reply.

CHAPTER 6

Major Edward Wynkoop surveyed his desk once more. It still didn't look quite right. He moved the jar holding the pencils further to the right and repositioned the name plate bearing his name and rank to the middle. He studied the "in" and "out" boxes, and wondered if it was better to have the "in" on the left and the "out" on the right, or the other way around. He finally decided that he should go from left to right.

There was a knock at the door, and an orderly stuck his head into the office. "Major, there's a couple of Indians just arrived. Said they had a message for you. They're Cheyenne."

"Cheyenne? Do they know we are at war with all Cheyenne? What do they want?"

"Said they want to talk peace, Sir."

Wynkoop thought for a moment. He had spent almost three months now in his new command at Fort Lyon, and was inclined to be wary of any Indian peace offer. Wynkoop was a tall, slim man around 35 years of age. His dark hair was receding slightly on the left side of his temple, but to compensate for this he sported a long, droopy mustache that extended well below his jaw. His face was narrow and his lips thin, giving him a rather sober look, but his dark brown eyes seemed to dance from some inner amusement. . He had participated in several campaigns against the Indians, but knew very little about their habits or culture.

"Well, show these peace ambassadors in, by all means," he told the corporal. "We sure don't want to keep them waiting."

The orderly turned back, and in a few minutes ushered in two Indian men and one woman. "Sir, this is Chief Lone Bear and Chief Eagle Head of the Cheyenne tribe. The woman is Lone Bear's wife. They have a letter for you from Black Kettle and some of their other chiefs."

Wynkoop studied the three visitors, who returned his scrutiny with equal candor. He had to admit they presented themselves with a quiet dignity and calmness. It was obvious they were trying to judge his character just as he was trying to determine theirs.

Lone Bear pulled Black Kettle's letter from his tunic, carefully unfolded it, and handed it to Wynkoop. "Our people have received the proclamation from your big chief Evans," he said. "We wish to accept his offer, and desire to meet with him to see what we can do to move this thing ahead. We want to live in peace with our white brothers."

Wynkoop rose from his chair, walked to the front of the desk, and took the proffered letter. He read it several times before responding. "You say in this letter that you have some white prisoners?"

"Seven captives, which we would exchange for our brothers held by your troops. We wish you to ride to our camp and meet with all of our chiefs so that we can arrange this thing and talk peace." Wynkoop studied Lone Bear's face as he made these comments, but he could see no sign of uneasiness or duplicity in the chief's demeanor.

Wynkoop read the letter one more time, then sat on the edge of his desk. "If I were to ride out to your village, how do I know that I could trust you? How do I know this letter isn't just a way to get our troops exposed and in a vulnerable position so your tribe could attack us?"

Lone Bear replied. "My people have given their word that you would not be harmed. If they broke their promise, I would prefer that you kill me rather than live with this shame. My life, and that of Eagle Head, are your assurance that we do not speak with a crooked tongue."

Wynkoop was impressed with Lone Bear's apparent sincerity, but nevertheless had the Indian chiefs locked up while he considered their request. The letter very well could be an attempt to get soldiers out of the fort and into an ambush, but the prospect of liberating white prisoners, presumably women, was something he could not ignore.

Several days later he rode out of Fort Lyon with 127 soldiers, two cannon, and his three hostages to show the way to the Indian villages. By the fifth day Wynkoop was growing uneasy and skeptical of their mission. They were well beyond any hope of assistance from any other commands if they should be riding into a trap.

It was late in the afternoon when movement on a hill far to their right caught Wynkoop's eye. He brought the troops to a halt and turned to his First Lieutenant, Robert McPherson. "Bob, give me your binoculars." He scanned the ridge, then the next hill further to the front of their position, and handed the glasses back to McPherson.

"Bring the chiefs up here," he yelled back to the Sergeant. Lone Bear and Eagle Head, along with Lone Bear's wife, were brought to the front of the line beside Wynkoop.

"I reckon you know we are being watched," he said. "There's Indians off to the right on that hillside, and more up ahead. Tell me once more that this is not a trap you are leading us into."

"If it were a trap, you would not be seeing them," Eagle Head replied. "We are nearing our village, and these are our people. They watch to see your intentions. You bring many soldiers and cannon - they are suspicious."

A voice from deep within told Wynkoop to turn around and high-tail it out of there while they still had a chance. But the chiefs had seemed to come in good faith. He had decided at Fort Lyon to trust them, and now he guessed he was pretty much committed. He formed the soldiers into a battle line, and gave the command to proceed at a slow pace.

"Bob, tell the men that if anyone shoots without me giving an order, I'll personally see him tarred and feathered and drummed out of the service." For the next 20 minutes they rode with rifles at the ready, nervously watching the Indians who were becoming more numerous to the right of their column. Then they came over the crest of a hill and found themselves facing around eight hundred mounted Indians, yelling and brandishing weapons. Wynkoop brought his troops to a halt.

"Lone Bear! Eagle Head!" he said to the Indian chiefs riding by his side. "I guess now we find out if your words are true. Ride out there and tell them we received their letter and that we come in peace. I will keep your wife here by my side, and if there is even a single shot fired I will personally put a bullet through her head. Do you understand?"

The two chiefs grunted, and rode ahead to meet with the Indians. Wynkoop followed slowly with his troops, ready for an attack. "Steady, men," he said. "If any of you know any prayers, now might be a pretty good time to offer them up."

One of the chiefs rode out in front of the wild and belligerent mob, raised his hand, and gave what sounded like an order. The Indians lowered their weapons and gradually stopped their shouting. They rode forward to meet the advancing troops. The Indian who had quieted the horde approached Wynkoop, and said, "I am Black Kettle. My brothers Lone Bear and Eagle Head, whom we sent to you, tell me that you have come in peace and to talk. It is good. You are safe here with our people. Make camp for the night, and in the morning, when the sun has chased away the shadows, we will talk."

Wynkoop nodded his agreement. He hoped his overwhelming sense of relief wasn't evident to the old chief. "Is George Bent with you?" he asked. He had met the Bent brothers several times at the Fort. "It would be good if he could join us and interpret all of our words to make sure we do not misunderstand each other."

"He will be here," Black Kettle replied. He moved forward and shook Wynkoop's hand, saying, "My heart is happy that you have come. This gives me much assurance that there will be peace." He turned his horse and rode back over the hill.

"Wynkoop met with Black Kettle and the other chiefs the next morning," Old Joe said, "and it didn't start out too well. Some of the chiefs, especially the Dog Soldiers who were with Black Kettle's camp, were openly hostile to Wynkoop, and demanded to know why he had come to them with troops and cannon. Wynkoop told them he was aware that some would not welcome him, and he was prepared to fight if he had to. He also told them he was not a big enough chief to talk peace with them. They would have to come in and talk with the Governor of the Colorado Territory, John Evans."

"After awhile they got around to talking about the prisoners the Cheyenne claimed to have. The chiefs didn't want to give up any captives till the soldiers released some Indians being held in Denver, but Wynkoop insisted that it would be a great show of sincerity on the part of the tribes if they would do so. The chiefs finally told Wynkoop they would need to talk about all of this, and asked him to make camp about 12 miles away. They'd let him know their decision in a few days."

"I can tell you, Sonny, those troopers were pretty nervous. Many thought the Indians would end up attacking them, and they begged Wynkoop to get out of there real fast. But Wynkoop had looked deep into Black Kettle's heart, and figured he could trust the old chief. And sure enough, in a few days they brought in four hostages, two women and two children, and turned them over to Wynkoop. They said they would need to bargain for the other three who were being held by the Sioux. You see, Indians didn't just give up their prisoners, they had to be bought. Black Kettle was trading some of his best stock for these here captives."

"The chiefs also told Wynkoop they would send a delegation back with him to meet with this Governor Evans." Old Joe thought for a moment, then added, "That was sure the dog-gonest worse thing they could have done."

I looked off to the west, and saw that the sun had turned into a dull, red ball and was slipping behind clouds on the horizon.

"It's getting pretty late," I told Old Joe, "and we haven't even talked about the settlers I was interested in. Just the Indians. And I don't think any of these Indians you've been telling me about were even involved in that raid. Are you sure you know all about the massacre?" I gave him an accusing look.

"Well, Sonny, I can understand your interest in the people who were killed in that attack. And we're getting there. But you know, those people were really just innocent victims that were in the wrong place at the wrong time. Oh yes, they had ambitions and feelings and it was a great tragedy and we need to know about them, but the real story in that massacre is with the Indians. What made them come down Spillman Creek that Sunday morning, full of hate and anger? That's where the real emotion and drama lies, with the Indians. They're the ones that did the killin'. That's why I'm telling you about these things that led up to the attack."

"I guess you're right," I admitted grudgingly, "but it's almost dark, and I need to be getting back to town. I'll have to come back another time, maybe tomorrow?"

Old Joe looked around, apparently noticing the lengthening shadows for the first time. "Well what do ya know?" he said. "It is getting to be that time of day, isn't it? Time sure do fly. But before you go, I need to finish the story of Sand Creek. That was the most devastatin' thing to happen in the whole litany of events leading up to your massacre."

I resigned myself to hearing him out, and got as comfortable as I could on my straight-backed chair.

CHAPTER 7

Wynkoop escorted the chiefs, including Black Kettle, White Antelope, Lone Bear, Bull Bear who was a Dog Soldier, and several Arapahoe chiefs, Left Hand, Neva, Heap of Buffalo and Knock Knee, to Denver to meet with Governor Evans. Evans didn't really want to see them. He had taken a hard stand against the Indians and had convinced Congress that Colorado needed the 100 day volunteers for protection, and now he didn't want it to seem that he had exaggerated the dangers. But eventually he agreed to join Wynkoop and the chiefs, along with Colonel Chivington, at Camp Weld, just outside of Denver

At this meeting a belligerent Evans berated the chiefs for every atrocity that had occurred in Colorado over the past year. He accused the Cheyenne of joining with the Sioux in smoking the war pipe, and said the chiefs were unable to control their young men. He wouldn't commit to peace, saying the Indians would have to deal with the Army on that issue, and turned to Colonel Chivington.

Chivington told them that the Indians had declared war, and peace could not be made until all the Indians gave up their arms and surrendered. Black Kettle wasn't quite sure what Chivington meant some of the time, but at the end of the day the chiefs were told to move their lodges close to Fort Lyon and to place themselves under the jurisdiction of Major Wynkoop.

Black Kettle, White Antelope and Left Hand took their people to the semi-dry Sand Creek, as directed by Wynkoop, about 40 miles northeast of Fort Lyon. There they erected over 100 lodges, and felt that they were safe under the protection of the Army. The Dog Soldiers, however, refused to accept the terms Chivington laid down, and moved to the north where they continued their raids along the Platte.

Wynkoop issued annuities to Black Kettle's group, and felt confident that he could keep these Indians peaceful. A bond developed between Black Kettle and Wynkoop, and each grew to trust the other's words.

In the early part of November Major Wynkoop was abruptly relieved as commander of Fort Lyon, and reassigned to Fort Riley. Chivington was furious that Wynkoop had issued rations to Indians he considered as hostile, and with whom they were still at war. Major Anthony, the new fort commandant, was an avowed Indian hater, and Colonel Chivington's choice to head up the camp. Black Kettle and the other chiefs were concerned about this change of command, and went in to meet with Anthony. He told the chiefs that he personally couldn't make peace with them, but that they should remain in their camp along Sand Creek until they received further notice.

This was the situation early in the morning of November 29, 1864, when Black Kettle's people were sleeping peacefully in their tepees.

Black Kettle raised his head from the blanket with a start. What had awakened him? He listened carefully, but could hear nothing. Medicine Woman Later was still sleeping peacefully next to him. Then he realized what it was that had disturbed him. It was not what he had heard, but what he felt. It was the faint trembling in the earth from the pounding of many hoofs. Could it be buffalo? Was there a buffalo stampede headed for the village?

Black Kettle leaped from his blankets and threw open the flap of his teepee. The morning was still dark, with only a faint glow in the east. And it was cold. Black Kettle could see his breath in the still of the dawn. Then in the dim morning light he saw what had awakened him. It was many white men – cavalry – riding into camp. Black Kettle was sure they meant no harm. The soldiers knew his camp was peaceful, and under the protection of the Great White Father. Black Kettle ran back into the teepee and retrieved a package from the back of the tent. He removed the buffalo skin from around it and unfurled an American flag. This was a flag that had been given to him by Colonel Greenwood, who had escorted the chiefs on their trip to the East, and who told him as long as he flew this flag his people would never be harmed.

He tied the flag to a pole and a white cloth just above it. He ran back outside, waving the flags back and forth, his wife at his side. He tried to calm his people, and told them not to fire at the soldiers. But then the soldiers started shooting. Within minutes the scene changed to a horrible, bloody massacre. His people were running in all directions trying to get away from the cavalry, while the soldiers were riding through the camp, firing indiscriminately at anyone they could find – which was mostly women and children. Most of the men had ridden out several days before to hunt buffalo.

Black Kettle watched in horror as one soldier cut the head nearly off of a 12 year-old girl running from her teepee. His people offered only sporadic, uncoordinated resistance. Black Kettle looked to the west where White Antelope's and War Bonnet's camps were located, and saw people running in panic with soldiers firing at old men, women and children without distinction. The same was true for Left Hand's Arapaho camp to the east.

White Antelope, who had traveled to Washington with Black Kettle, was one of the first to die. He could not bring himself to fire on his white brothers. Now Black Kettle watched in dismay as White Antelope stood in front of his teepee with his arms folded, singing his death song: "Nothing lives forever, only the rocks and the mountains." In the next moment White Antelope was cut down by a rain of bullets slamming into his body.

By now the camp was in total chaos; soldiers, Indians and horses milling in a confused mass of blood and movement. Around 100 of his people had gathered around Black Kettle and the flag, but suddenly they broke and began running in all directions. Black Kettle stood a moment longer, still clutching the lodge pole with the U. S. flag in his hands, before coming to life.

Dropping the flag he grabbed Medicine Woman Later and together they ran for the creek bed. As they drew near the edge of the camp he heard a cry at his side, and his wife stumbled and fell. She had been shot, and blood poured from her shoulder. Black Kettle stood for a moment in indecision. He realized that to help her now would be futile. The soldiers would easily cut them down. With a cry he once more started for the river bank. Glancing back, his heart sank as he saw a soldier fire several more shots into his wife's body as she struggled to get up. Images of Little Sage Woman, his first wife, flashed through his mind as he stumbled on.

He passed the body of White Antelope, who had been scalped. Mutilated bodies were everywhere. Many of the soldiers had dismounted and with their knives were cutting souvenirs from the bodies of the fallen Indians. They weren't content with taking scalps but were removing organs and private parts from both men and women. Black

Kettle felt that he was drowning in the screams and blood of his people.

A deep gulley angled off of the main creek bed to the North. Black Kettle, running as fast as he could, headed up this ravine. Rounding a sharp bend in the dry creek bed he came upon a soldier leaning over the dead body of a teen-aged girl. With knife in hand the soldier was preparing to desecrate the girl's body. Black Kettle recognized the lifeless form of Little Dove, his niece.

The man turned, and seeing Black Kettle, fumbled for his revolver. He fired two quick shots before the gun clicked on an empty chamber. Both shots missed, and in the next instant Black Kettle leaped on him, clamping his strong hands around his neck. They rolled in the dust as the blue coat gasped for air. The soldier's struggles weakened and finally stopped altogether.

Black Kettle came to his feet and saw a group of the attackers riding on the edge of the creek bed, firing on Indians fleeing below. Far to the south, a band of approximately 50 Cheyenne and Arapaho were gathered in a tight defensive line against the creek bed, surrounded by the white men on horseback, firing into the group from a safe distance. Just to the north another cluster of men, women and children was gathered against the back of a tall ravine, digging pits in the sand, and firing at the raiders riding by.

Black Kettle picked up the dead soldier's rifle and grabbed the reins of the renegade's horse. With an agility that belied his years, he leaped into the saddle and rode to the north, towards the band of Indians that had formed a defense perimeter against the creek bed. He began to sing his death song softly to himself as he rode through the line of men firing at the Indians. They didn't seem to notice him in their frenzy, and suddenly he was in the open and then into the ring of his people. He was off the horse before it had come to a stop, and took up a firing position with the defenders.

He found himself next to George Bent. "We don't have much in the way of guns or ammunition," George said. "We won't be able to hold them off for long."

But the soldiers, who Black Kettle now saw were not regular army, but a rag tag bunch of volunteers, had little appetite for real danger. Instead, they stayed just out of range of the Indian's gunfire, riding back and forth, looking for stray Indians hiding in the bushes or behind rocky ledges.

For the first time Black Kettle had time to think about what was happening, and the thoughts were a heavy weight on his heart. Many of his people were killed in the first rush of the treacherous raid, and the rest would surely follow before the day was through. Black Kettle was a brave and stoic warrior, but tears welled in his eyes. It had been at his urging that they had come to Sand Creek – it was his counsel that spoke of peace and brotherhood with the whites. Other chiefs and war leaders had called him a fool, especially Tall Bull and the Dog Soldiers. But he had believed the white men – had trusted their words.

And now it was ending in this senseless massacre. Black Kettle thought it would be better if he did not live to see another sun. When the soldiers charged, he would not fire his rifle, but do as White Antelope had done. He would stand tall and sing his death song to Heammawihio, the Wise One, who watched from above. Then he could travel the white road in the night sky to meet this great warrior and be with his ancestors where white men would never come.

The hours passed slowly on the bleak and cold winter's day, but the final attack never came. It was as if the white men had no stomach for real fighting. Periodically a group would ride past, firing into the barricaded Indians, but these forages became less frequent, and the sounds of shooting more distant. To the south Black Kettle could see smoke rising in the afternoon sky, and he knew their lodges were being burned.

Just before dusk the band of Indians that had been downstream left the safety of their shelter and joined Black Kettle's group. Now and then others in small numbers or individually hastened into their confines.

As the sun slipped below the hills to the west Black Kettle held a conference with the other braves. The soldiers had left, but many felt they would return in the morning to finish what they had started. The group decided that the band had to move out now in the cold and darkness and try to reach another Cheyenne camp far to the north. Black Kettle looked at the rag-tag cluster of survivors, and his heart was sore. Most had run from their teepees without coats or blankets, and were already shivering with cold as the dreary gray of the afternoon sky gave way to the still, cold night. Silently the band picked up what few belongings they had with them, and started on their journey.

Black Kettle waited until they were on their way, then turned back to look for Medicine Woman Later. It was pitch black now, with no sign of stars or moon in the overcast sky. Yet Black Kettle's eyes pierced the darkness, and not once did he stumble or fall as he sped along the creek bed. He passed the body of Little Dove, his niece, and with increasing bitterness raced on to where his wife had fallen.

When he reached the spot, he could not find her body. Confused, Black Kettle knelt on the ground and tried to think on what might have happened. As he crouched in the darkness he heard a moan coming from a rocky ledge some distance to the east. Black Kettle was instantly alert. In a few minutes the low cry of anguish was repeated. Black Kettle arose and without making a sound glided towards the ledge. Again the sound was repeated, and Black Kettle pinpointed the spot from which it came.

In another few seconds he was holding his wife in his arms. He could not believe she still lived. He examined her wounds, then pulled her to her feet, and with his arms about her started after the rest of the tribe. It did not take long to catch up with them, as their progress was slow.

The hours that followed were a nightmare that none of them would ever forget. The ragged bunch of Indians, staggering through the freezing night with almost no clothing, with many of them wounded and in great pain, was a pathetic sight. The march continued until the early hours of the new day. At last Black Kettle realized they could go no further, and called a halt to the torturous procession. The entire group fell to the ground, totally exhausted and frozen.

Very few heard the sound of the horses riding down on them from the north. Black Kettle was one who did, and rose to his feet. If the white men were coming to finish them off he would die proud and tall, unafraid. The horsemen could now be seen dimly in the early dawn as they rode over the crest of a hill. After a few minutes, a single rider detached himself from the rest, and rode into the camp. He halted his horse directly in front of Black Kettle.

The last thing Black Kettle remembered as he slowly crumbled into an exhausted unconsciousness was looking into the stern, strong face of Tall Bull, one of the chiefs of Hotamitanio, the Cheyenne Dog Soldiers.

Old Joe filled his pipe again, and now paused to put a match to it. "You wanted to talk about a massacre, Sonny. Well, this here massacre at Sand Creek was one of the worst depredations ever committed by white men against friendly Indians, and was one of the factors that led to Cheyenne attacks on whites throughout the west over the next four years. The man behind it all was Chivington and his Colorado Volunteers, not the regular Army. Chivington planned the attack from the very moment he met with Black Kettle and the other chiefs at Camp Weld. He claimed that he had killed between 400 and 500 Indians, although a more accurate estimate is probably around 140, and most of these were women and children. The butchery these so-called soldiers did to their victims' bodies was unthinkable."

I could tell that Old Joe was disgusted as he thought about the atrocity committed by the whites. "Did Chivington ever get in any trouble over the raid?" I asked.

"Well, Chivington and his rag-tag bunch of volunteers were treated as conquering heroes when they returned to Denver, where they proudly displayed their grisly souvenirs. He claimed a great victory over hostile Indians, maintaining that he had broken the uprising that the people of Denver feared."

"But gradually the truth of the attack came out. Regular Army soldiers were pretty mad at the senseless slaughter of women and children. Religious groups started protestin' the actions of the Third Volunteers. In Fort Riley, Wynkoop was furious at what had happened, and was reassigned to Fort Lyon to conduct an inquiry into the matter. Several Congressional and Army investigations were initiated, and all of them found the slaughter of the Indian camp to be unconscionable, but no charges were ever brought against old Chivington."

"He retired from the Army shortly afterwards, and led a rather unremarkable life for the rest of his years. In fact, he spent much of his time and efforts in trying to defend the righteousness of the attack at Sand Creek."

"What happened to Black Kettle and his people?" I asked.

"They joined with the rest of the Cheyenne and moved to the north, and together with the Sioux and Arapaho started a bloody war of revenge. The uprising that Governor Evans feared became a reality. Stage stations were attacked, ranches were burned, and settlers were forced to abandon their homes to seek safety in the towns. The west never saw such killing and plunder as followed the aftermath of Sand Creek. Weren't nobody safe – white man or Indian alike."

"Old Black Kettle was ridiculed by the Dog Soldiers, and most of the young men of the tribe, for his faith in the white men. But even as they engaged in an all-out war against the advancing tide of miners, ranchers and settlers, Black Kettle still held out hope that there might be peace."

"You mentioned that Major Wynkoop had come back to conduct an investigation of the attack. Did anything come of that?"

"Not much, but the good thing for the Cheyenne is that Wynkoop, disgusted with the army, resigned his commission and became the Indian Agent for the tribe."

By now the sun had disappeared below the tall stocks of corn on the west side of the yard, and the cool breeze that had sprung up was filled with night sounds – the chirping of crickets under the porch, a dog barking somewhere in the distance, and the far-off wail of a passing locomotive. The yard was filled with hundreds of lightning bugs, glowing as they meandered this way and that. I hadn't seen this many of the insects since I was a child. It was good to know that the pesticides hadn't killed them all off.

"Joe, I can't stay any longer. Will you be here tomorrow? Could we continue our little talk then? You still haven't told me about the settlers involved in the attack."

"Why sure, Sonny. I'll be here. You just come on out whenever you've a mind, and we'll pick right up where we left off."

As I pulled out of the drive and down the bumpy road, I looked back at the house. There was no light in it. I wondered about the old man – who he was, why he lived out here in this isolated place, and how he knew so much about the happenings of 140 years ago. I decided I would have to find out more about him.

CHAPTER 8

The next morning I was at the farm house shortly after the sun had risen. Old Joe was sitting on the porch just where I'd left him, rocking back and forth and smoking his pipe. I didn't see any sign of the shotgun that he'd had the day before. After we'd exchanged a few pleasantries, I pulled a piece of paper from my shirt pocket.

"I've got a list here of the settlers involved in that attack in 1869," I said. "You talked about Thomas Alderdice yesterday, the Southerner that joined up with the army to get out of the prisoner of war camp. You mentioned Susanna Daily, whose husband died at Fort Leavenworth of typhoid fever. Now I don't have a Susanna Daily on my list but I do have ......"

Old Joe held up his hand to stop me. "OK, Sonny. You win. Let's talk about some of those settlers who were movin' into Cheyenne hunting grounds. There's one thing they all had in common. They shared a dream of a new land and a new opportunity, where a man could forget his past and be whatever he wanted to be. One of the biggest dreamers of all was Tom Alderdice. He finished his year of service with the Union Army in Salina, Kansas, and decided this was as good a place as any to make his fortune. That was the same year as the signin' of the Treaty of the Little Arkansas."

"Treaty of the Little Arkansas? What was that?" I could have bitten my tongue off as soon as I asked, knowing this would lead Old Joe into talking about the Indians again.

"Well, that was another attempt by the government to make peace with the Indians, and to open up the west to all the settlers moving into the territory. Things were pretty bad off by 1865."

Old Joe's thoughts were back with the Cheyenne, thinking about their turmoil.

In the months following Sand Creek, the Indians in the northern plains spread fear and devastation across western Kansas and Nebraska, and eastern Colorado. Many of the raids were by small groups, maybe four or five, out to prove their manhood and to earn coup. Sometimes the numbers were larger, up to 25 or 30 in a war party. And sometimes the attacks came as well-coordinated and well-planned assaults involving hundreds of warriors.

Julesburg was a stage stop and Army camp in northwestern Colorado, about 200 miles from Denver and about the same distance from the Saline Valley in Kansas. In addition to the fort, there was a station house with a place to feed travelers, a stable, blacksmith and repair shop, granary and storehouses, and a big corral. There was also a general store selling goods to travelers and wagon trains, and an Overland Telegraph Company office. Just beyond these buildings was the fort, housing one company of the 7th Iowa Cavalry.

On January 6, 1865, nearly 1,000 Cheyenne and Sioux warriors descended on this settlement. They were careful to conceal their presence behind sand dunes several miles from the fort. Then a few Indians on horseback rode close to the camp, hidden by a dry ravine. When they saw some of the soldiers walking outside of the barricade, they attacked with much noise and fan-fare. In short order 60 soldiers rode out of the fort in pursuit of the Indians, who led the soldiers towards the rest of the warriors hidden in the hills. The decoy was only partially effective, because the young men among the warriors couldn't wait for the trap to be sprung, and burst out prematurely towards the charging cavalry while they were still a little distance away. The soldiers whirled back to the fort. Most made it safely, but between 14 and 18 were killed.

The Indians didn't see much use in trying to attack the blue coats sheltered behind the walls of the barricade, so they turned back to the stage station and loaded up with the supplies and store goods found there. They spent all day looting the place, hauling their spoils to the hills.

On February 2, they returned to Julesburg, once again taunting the soldiers within the fort to come out and fight. But the cavalry had no such intention, and stayed within the confines of the garrison where they were well protected. As before, the Indians looted the stage station and store, taking the rest of the goods they missed in the first raid. Never had the Cheyenne taken so much loot. They burned the buildings to the ground, and slowly rode off, laden with their plunder.

Shortly after this the Cheyenne headed north to the Powder River country to join their cousins, the Northern Cheyenne, and the Sioux under the leadership of Red Cloud.

Black Kettle and his followers, however, broke off from the rest of the tribe and journeyed south to the Arkansas River in the southern part of the state. He continued to hold to his vision of peace with the whites, a vision that would lead him down a long, dark path. He and his band of 75 lodges moved on to the Cimarron River in what is now Oklahoma, where he joined with camps of the Kiowas, Comanches and Prairie Apaches. The newcomers had little in the way of possessions, having lost everything at Sand

Creek. But the other tribes welcomed them, and presented the Cheyenne with many presents and horses.

Black Kettle was thankful for their acceptance, but found himself once again in the midst of warriors that were angry with the white soldiers. These three tribes had been attacked the previous November by the Army, led by Kit Carson, and had been forced to move from the South Canadian to their present camps along the Cimarron. They were planning a major offensive in the spring, when the ponies would be fattened and strong for battle. Many of Black Kettle's tribe were stirred by the war talk, and planned to join them.

In early spring the tribes were visited by their new Indian agent, Edward Wynkoop, and William Bent, who as noted earlier was the founder of Bent's Fort. Bent was married to a Cheyenne woman and was considered a trusted friend of the Cheyenne.

These two men pleaded with the Indian chiefs not to go to war, and to meet with a Presidential Commission who wanted to make a new peace agreement with the tribes of the Upper Arkansas, which included the Cheyenne, Arapahoe, Kiowa, Comanche and Prairie Apache. Initially the chiefs were not inclined to talk with them, but later in the summer relented and agreed to the parley.

It was a brisk October morning as Wynkoop and Leavenworth, agents for the five tribes, watched the procession of Cheyenne move into camp along the Little Arkansas River, near the present city of Wichita. Black Kettle had brought 80 lodges of his people to be near the council meetings. Wynkoop was glad to see his old friend, and greeted him warmly. He was grateful that Black Kettle did not hold him responsible for the betrayal at Sand Creek.

The sessions began on the morning of October 12.

Black Kettle, looking majestic in his robes and single feather in his head band, filled the ceremonial pipe with tobacco and lit it with a burning twig from the council fire. When the tobacco in the bowl was glowing with fire and the smoke was traveling freely through the stem, he passed it to the man on his right, Major General William S. Harney, president of the peace commission. Harney took a deep puff, exhaled the smoke and passed it on to the next man sitting in the circle, Judge James Steele, representing the Bureau of Indian Affairs. It slowly made its way around the negotiators - Thomas Murphy, William Bent, Kit Carson, Major General John B. Sanborn, and Colonel Jesse H. Leavenworth. The chiefs included Black Kettle, Little Robe, Black White Man, and Seven Bulls from the Cheyenne, and Little Raven, Spotted Wolf and Big Mouth from the Arapahoe.

Harney opened the talks after the pipe had made its rounds.

"The Great White Father in the East recognizes what a great wrong was committed at Sand Creek. The attack did not reflect his desires, but was the work of a few bad soldiers. He realizes that these actions forced the tribes of the Upper Arkansas to make war on the whites. But now the time has come to put all of this behind us, and to take each other by the hand so that we may have peace once again."

"The great war between my countrymen has come to an end," he continued, "and soon there will be many people coming to the west, to the lands of eastern Kansas and Nebraska, and western Colorado. Our President is afraid there will be much trouble between them and the Indians unless the Indians agree to move to a new place set aside for them, where they can live forever."

"And where is it the white father wishes us to move?" Little Robe asked.

"Lands have been set aside north of the Platte River where your northern brothers would go, and south of the Little Arkansas River for the five tribes represented here."

Black Kettle spoke for the first time. "The people that are with me are happy that there is peace talk once more. But we are only a few lodges, 80 or less. There are over 400 lodges of my brothers to the north, and I cannot speak for them. The same is true for my friend Little Raven and the Arapahoe. It would not be possible for us to put our marks to any new agreement without consulting them."

Black Kettle paused a moment, then spoke directly to General Harney. "It seems that whenever the white soldiers come to us to make a treaty, the lands that are to be ours shrink in size. Fifteen seasons ago we signed the Treaty of Fort Laramie in which the hills you now want to take away from us were guaranteed to be ours forever. Only a few years ago we signed another treaty at Fort Wise, and our lands were greatly reduced, but were still in the plains of Colorado. This new treaty you put before us asks us to give up all of our old hunting grounds and move to a territory that has already been promised to the Comanche and Kiowa."

"We will make arrangements with these tribes," Harney replied. "You will be welcomed there. Each chief that signs the treaty will be given 320 acres for his own use, and each of the children and squaws who lost husbands or parents at Sand Creek will be given 160 acres, to keep forever."

Little Raven said, "It would be a hard thing to leave the lands that God has given us. It is where our chiefs are buried, where our blood has been shed, where the buffalo are plentiful. We need the buffalo to survive."

"In this treaty," Sanford replied, "you can continue to hunt the buffalo on the plains as long as they are there. But your permanent lodges must be kept below the Little Arkansas."

The sessions went on for two days. Wynkoop and Bent argued with the chiefs that it was in their best interest to sign the new treaty, that they probably would never get another offer as generous. In the end, Black Kettle and the other chiefs gave in and on October 14, 1865, put their mark to the Treaty of the Little Arkansas, in which they ceded all rights to the Great Plains.

"So if the Indians signed the treaty, that pretty much opened up the west to the settlers, didn't it?" I asked.

"A lot of folks thought so," Old Joe responded. "But you've got to remember two things. Number one is that Black Kettle and the chiefs believed they still had the right to hunt buffalo there, and number two, the great majority of Cheyenne were to the north, as Black Kettle told them, and they would refuse to recognize the treaty as valid."

"I thought you said Wynkoop and Bent were friends to the Indians. Sounds to me like they didn't do them any favors, talking them into giving up all their land."

"Well, Sonny, you got to consider the alternative. Those two were trying to get the best deal they could for the tribes, but most of all they was trying to bring an end to the fighting. There was a lot of folks thinking extermination was the best answer to the Indian problem, and Wynkoop and Bent just wanted to get them out of the way where they would be safe."

"What did the Dog Soldiers and their chief – what was his name? – Tall Bull – think about Black Kettle signing the treaty?"

"Tall Bull was just one of the chiefs of the Dog Soldiers, but he was an important one. What did he think? He was hoppin' mad, I can tell you."

CHAPTER 9

Early in 1866, when the grass began to turn green, the Southern Cheyenne who had gone to live with their northern brothers and the Sioux, became home-sick for their hunting grounds in western Kansas and eastern Colorado. They decided they would return to their old haunts and visit their friends and relatives who had gone with Black Kettle below the Arkansas River. On a warm, spring day, they started their journey south.

Tall Bull could sense the excitement that was spreading through the tribe. It had been there the previous night around the camp fires, after a long day's journey. He felt it in the animated storytelling of the old men, in the joking among the women, and in the boisterous play of the children. This morning, as they broke camp to continue their homecoming, it had been more subdued, but still a solid, tangible thing. Now, as they traveled past familiar rivers and old camp sites, the feeling of anticipation was building to a new high.

The time with their cousins in the north had been good, but still they longed for the gentle, rolling slopes of the Smoky Hill, where the winters were not so harsh, and for their favorite camp sites along the many streams and tributaries that threaded the country. This was their hunting ground, which the Great Father above had given to them. There were still many buffalo to support the tribe, and the song of the meadowlark and crooning of the prairie chicken were present to soften the warm, summer evenings. The warriors would drive the white men out of the country if they bothered them anymore. And if they had to die, better to fight and die in their own land than off to the north in the land of the Sioux.

Tall Bull watched a half dozen of his group, including the Bent brothers, the half- breed sons of William Bent, race off to some remembered hunting ground of previous years. Both had been at Sand Creek when the tribe was attacked by Chivington's volunteers. George had escaped with Black Kettle's group of survivors while Charlie had been captured and narrowly escaped being executed when one of the regular Army officers had intervened on his behalf. Both brothers were embittered by the attack, and had joined Tall Bull and the Dog Soldiers.

As Tall Bull thought about Sand Creek and the Army, he wished that Roman Nose had come south with them. Roman Nose had many followers among the young braves of the Dog Soldiers for his daring feats in battle, but had delayed coming with them at this time. He had promised to join them shortly, however. "Roman Nose is a good leader for war," Tall Bull mused to himself, "but he is too hot tempered and headstrong to be a permanent chief among his people. Good traits in battle, but not for being a wise and thoughtful leader for his people. Still - it would be nice to have him along."

Tall Bull's thoughts were interrupted by the sound of gun fire. The shooting was coming from just beyond the hill over which the Bent brothers and the other young warriors had ridden. The echo of the shots had hardly died away before Tall Bull pulled his rifle from its sheath and urged his horse forward to a full gallop. Crossing the ridge, Tall

Bull found the young men reining in their horses just out of range of a new stage station.

Tall Bull had never seen a station built like this. It was dug into the soil with the sod-covered roof rising only a few feet above the ground. Loopholes were cut into the wall at ground level through which men inside were firing sporadically. A few dozen yards to the west was a corral with 15 fine horses. One large black and white mare stood out from all the others.

Little Wolf, Okohm'ha'ku, leader of one of the Cheyenne bands, was engaged in animated conversation with the Bent brothers.

"Charlie," he drawled out the "e" at the end of Charlie's name, "you and George make big attack with morning sun to your back. Make big noise - big skirmish. I sneak in from other way and get horses - give one to each of you."

"Well, Little Wolf, I sure would like to get me one of those horses alright - especially that black and white mare. But it doesn't look like we could storm that dug-out very well without us all getting killed."

"No - black and white horse for me," Little Wolf grunted, "other horses for you."

Tall Bull laughed. He knew Little Wolf's love for fine horses. "I have a better idea," he said. "Charlie and George attack from east. You attack from north, Little Wolf, and I will sneak in and steal the horses. I will give one to each of you."

Everybody joined in the laughter. It was obvious that there was no way to get to the animals, but they were in a jovial mood.

"Or even better," Tall Bull continued, "I think George should ride down there and get those horses all by himself. If you think Black Kettle's niece, Magpie, still has eyes for an ugly half-breed like you, you'd better be getting as many horses for barter as you can. You will have need for them."

George squirmed on his horse, as once again the band fell into loud laughter. He looked out of the corner of his eye at his brother. He knew Charlie didn't approve of his wanting to take a wife, especially if it meant that George might abandon the Dog Soldiers and decide to live with Black Kettle's group. Charlie's hatred of his white heritage had grown stronger over the past two winters, and in his view Black Kettle was nothing more than the white man's puppet.

But George didn't know whether Magpie would be waiting for him or not. It had been many moons since last they had seen each other. For all he knew she might have married another brave by now - one that had followed the wisdom of Black Kettle. He put such thoughts from his mind. Probably she had grown fat and ugly over the past 18 months anyway.

Tall Bull and the Bent brothers rode back to the main party together. All were feeling the exhilaration of the day - of returning to their home. Nothing could dampen their spirits.

When they rejoined the main body of the tribe, Tall Bull guided his bay to where his wives were hauling their lodge. White Buffalo Woman, his first wife, was harking at the two younger wives to stop their silly jabbering and to pay attention to one of the bags of belongings that was coming loose from the travois. Tall Bull felt a real sense of affection for White Buffalo Woman, and remembered their first time together. But it was his new wife, Moon Flower, who made his blood race now. He stirred his horse to her side, and slapped her soundly on her bottom.

"Do not wear yourself out, my little one," he advised. "Tonight in my lodge we will look further into the matter of your qualifications to be the wife of a great chief."

Moon Flower smiled. It was not a coy smile, but open and brazen, which seemed to convey a great deal of knowledge and competence in understanding the duties of a Cheyenne wife. "So," she replied, "and perhaps also we look into your qualifications to be the great chief you would have everyone believe you are."

Tall Bull's other two wives, White Buffalo Woman and Lost Feather, listened to the exchange without emotion. They both accepted the Cheyenne custom of a brave having as many wives as he could support, and one could certainly not expect a Chief of the Dog Soldiers to have only one wife. It would not reflect well on his strength and prowess. But still, it was impossible not to feel a little jealous at this new wife who received the bulk of Tall Bull's attentions.

The Cheyenne continued on their journey for several more days before making camp. It was then that George Bent made up his mind to join a group that was going further south to visit Black Kettle. He wanted to see all of his old friends who had gone to live below the Little Arkansas, and of course to see Magpie. Also he wanted to visit with his father, William Bent.

Charlie became angry when George told him he was going. "I thought you were Cheyenne - a Cheyenne warrior," he said. "Now you want to go to Black Kettle, who has betrayed his people and is a disgrace to his tribe. And you want to visit with that man you call your father. Bah! He is no father to me, and he is no father to you! He is a white man that has desecrated our mother."

"Charlie" George said, "it is bad for you to be filled with such hate. Our father loves us, and has done much for us. And Black Kettle is a good chief. It was not his fault that the renegade soldiers betrayed him. We have avenged what happened at Sand Creek. The pony soldiers and the settlers have paid dearly for that attack. And it wasn't even the regular soldiers who killed our people."

"Go then," Charlie shouted. "Go and grovel with our enemies. But return immediately with or without your precious bride, or you will be lost forever as a warrior of our tribe – and as a brother to myself."

Charlie whirled around and stalked away, not waiting for an answer.

Several weeks after George and the others left for the Little Arkansas, two riders appeared over the hill and rode into camp. Shouts of joy and friendship erupted from the returning Dog Soldiers. The visitors were two of the young men who had gone south with Black Kettle, and who had many friends and family with Tall Bull's group.

After many handshakes, and a dozen eager inquiries about loved ones, Tall Bull asked whether the soldiers were still hunting the Cheyenne here in the Smoky Hill region.

"You have not heard?" the young men replied in unison. "Black Kettle has signed a peace treaty with the white men. We are not at war with them."

"Black Kettle!" Tall Bull exploded. "Black Kettle signed a peace treaty? By what right did he sign a treaty? He is too old and his heart is too weak to speak for the Cheyenne. And what has this old man promised in return for the white man's peace?"

"Black Kettle signed what he had to sign," the younger man replied. His loyalty to Black Kettle was evident. "Many chiefs signed – Little Robe, Seven Bulls, Little Raven of the Arapaho. Many others. We counseled with Little White Man, William Bent, whom you all know to be a friend of the Cheyenne. He told us that he tried to persuade the Great Father to grant us permanent rights to this land between the Smoky Hill and the Republican, but the request could not be granted because already a stage and railway are being brought through the land."

"But the white man is sorry for Sand Creek," the other young man interjected. "They know the Cheyenne at Sand Creek had done no harm, and were attacked without cause.

The new treaty allows us to hunt in this land, although we must live south of the Arkansas."

"My father has betrayed us," Charlie Bent muttered. "I will kill him when next we meet."

Tall Bull was beside himself. "Who is to say where the Cheyenne can live but the Cheyenne? I tell you now that the Cheyenne can hunt in this land and the Cheyenne can live in this land!" Tall Bull stalked from the assembly of braves, leaped on his horse, and rode off across the hill.

"There will be trouble," the young brave prophesied. "Much trouble."

Several more weeks went by, and the Cheyenne continued to revel in being back in their old hunting grounds. Occasionally several of Tall Bull's band would embark on a horse stealing adventure, and once five of his young braves shot up a stage wagon. But they were not bothered by the Army, and the buffalo seemed plentiful. It was good to be back in their land again.

Several weeks later, when the sun was high in the sky, there were loud shouts at the southern edge of the camp, as one of the tribe's scouts rode into the village. He raced his pony through the tepees and came to a sliding halt at Tall Bull's lodge.

"George Bent is coming over the hill," he exclaimed. "He has a white man with him. Also three of our brothers from Black Kettle's camp. The white man is the Major Wynkoop from Sand Creek."

Wynkoop! Tall Chief, as he was known to the Cheyenne. Tall Bull knew from the two braves who had visited the camp several weeks earlier that Wynkoop had left the Army shortly after Sand Creek, and was now the Indian Agent for the Cheyenne. Although he held much anger against Wynkoop, he decided to hear what the white man had to say.

"Let them come to our camp," Tall Bull told his warriors.

When the visitors arrived, Tall Bull, George Bent and Wynkoop went into Tall Bull's lodge to talk. Tall Bull's quick eyes noted that George seemed to reflect a happiness and contentment that had not been there when he left. His courtship of Magpie must have been successful, Tall Bull thought.

The main focus of his attention, however, was on the white man seated before him. His face seemed open and honest. His eyes looked directly into Tall Bull's when he spoke. They were steady, and seemed to speak true. No deceit or attempt to hide the thoughts of his mind.

Wynkoop opened the parley by recounting the events prior to Sand Creek, and the dishonor that Chivington had brought on the Army. "The Cheyenne and the white man were friends before Sand Creek," Wynkoop related. "Those times had been good, and the Cheyenne and white man respected each other. Both lived alongside each other in peace."

"The big mistake at Sand Creek has changed all that," Wynkoop admitted. "But the fight at Sand Creek was not at the wishes of our Great White Father who lives in the East. He wants to make a new peace with the Cheyenne, and return to the days when there will be no more shooting and killing."

"Black Kettle and chiefs of the Arapaho have signed a new treaty," Wynkoop continued, "and peace has been restored with them. It is a good treaty. I am happy to see Tall Bull and the Dog Soldiers return to their old hunting grounds. The Cheyenne are free to hunt the buffalo and not be bothered by the white men. But in return the Cheyenne must agree to make their lodges south of the Little Arkansas on land that has been designated for them. I ask that you,

Tall Bull, and your chiefs ride into the fort with me and sign this new treaty. Then all will be well."

Tall Bull remained silent and impassive during this speech by Wynkoop. Now he gathered his robe about him, and spoke for the first time.

"I believe that Tall Chief speaks as a friend of the Cheyenne. I believe that his words come from his heart. But it is not the heart of a Cheyenne. It is not the heart of one who has seen over a hundred of his brothers and sisters killed without warning at Sand Creek. How can such a heart ever again put faith in the words of your Great White Father, or his officers?"

"You say that the red-eye Chivington is disgraced and no longer wears the uniform of the Army. What does this mean to the Cheyenne? Has he been punished, as you would punish a Cheyenne who did such a thing? Why was the red-eyed one not hung from a rope in the style of the white man's justice? Or imprisoned in a stockade? Or driven from the land in exile, as the Indian would do? Why were none of these things done? Your justice does not work to protect the Indian, only to protect the white men."

"The words of your chiefs have no meaning. They speak of peace and they hope to be reassured that the Indian will leave them alone, while at the same time they build railroads across our land, destroy our buffalo, seek to move us from the place that God has given us, and kill our women and children."

"If the white man wants peace, he can have peace. But he must stop shooting at our young men, stay off our hunting grounds, and stop building railroads across our hills. If he does this, the Cheyenne will not bother him. But the Cheyenne will not agree to move from this place that is ours, and will sign no peace treaty. We have signed peace treaties before, and they are without meaning."

"I tell you now that we will not harm the white man as long as he leaves us alone. But when the white man comes onto our land to build homes, or railroads, he will be driven off. These are my words and you can tell them to the Great White Father."

Wynkoop was silent for a long time following this speech. He could not disagree with the logic and reasonableness of Tall Bull's words. Yet he knew that if Tall Bull did not sign the treaty the cavalry would be out to hunt him down. Times were changing, whether Wynkoop liked it or not. The number of settlers, many of them Civil War veterans, and their families, was increasing every day. In Washington they dreamed of the "Manifest Destiny"; one nation stretching from the Atlantic to the Pacific. There was no mood anywhere in the country to tolerate obstruction from a bunch of "savages."

Wynkoop felt the only hope for the Cheyenne was to strike as good a bargain as they could, and the present treaty seemed to be the best they would ever get.

The talks lasted for several hours, but Tall Bull was adamant in his position, and at last Wynkoop had to acknowledge the failure of his mission. Wynkoop warned Tall Bull that if he insisted on putting up his lodges in this country, he would probably be attacked by the soldiers.

Tall Bull stated in return that this was Cheyenne territory, and the whites could not dictate to the Cheyenne where to put their lodges. They would fight the soldiers if they came. It would be better to die here defending their land than to move off to some other place to be the white man's camp dog.

When the conference was over, George Bent looked around for his brother, Charlie. He saw him with a group of braves gathered in front of Tall Bull's lodge. Their eyes met for a moment before Charlie turned and walked away without speaking. George made no attempt to go after him.

He knew Charlie wouldn't like it that he had ridden in with a white man, and tried to talk peace with Tall Bull.

As they rode out of the camp, Wynkoop turned back in his saddle and saw Tall Bull still standing by his tepee, and his heart ached for what he knew would come.

Although Tall Bull had promised Wynkoop that he would hold his braves in check unless provoked by the whites, this did not happen. Roman Nose joined the group on the Smoky Hill, and in August, he and war parties of Cheyenne visited Fort Wallace and other stage stations, threatening to kill all who were still there in two weeks time if they didn't leave.

Tall Bull also grew increasingly belligerent as he thought about the white man's offer, and swore that he would embark on a campaign to drive all of the soldiers and settlers out of Cheyenne territory. But an early winter slowed his plans. A major offensive would be taken early in the spring, he vowed. As soon as the grass was green and the ponies strong.

"You mentioned an Indian named Roman Nose," I said. "I think I've heard of him. Wasn't he one of the Dog Soldiers?"

"Nope. He was a member of the Crooked Lances Society, the same clan as Black Kettle. But at heart he was a Dog Soldier, and led them in many a battle." Old Joe chuckled at the thought. "Him and that magical war bonnet of his."

"That's what I remember about him. He had a head dress that was supposed to protect him from bullets."

"Yep. That's him. Ice Bear, one of the Cheyenne medicine men, made it for him. The Cheyenne were a spiritual people, you see, and believed that magical beings dwelt in almost everything: animals, birds, rocks."

"Even in inanimate things like rocks?" I asked.

"Sure. Spirits can be found anywhere. Why I wouldn't be surprised if even this old house wasn't infested with spirits."

*He looked down the length of the porch, and then back at the
dilapidated walls of the structure.*

"Yes sir, probably a strong spirit lives right here."

*I thought Old Joe was getting a little carried away, but
said nothing.*

*"The Indians thought the energy of these forces could be
harnessed by special medicine and put to use for the good of a
particular recipient," he continued. "They might keep the person
from growin' old, or protect him from disease, or lead him to a
happy marriage. And in some cases, they could maybe ward off
white men's bullets. That was one of the jobs of the medicine
man, to capture these influences and make them available to the
leaders of the tribe."*

Ice Bear (also known as White Bull), whose Indian
name was Ho-tu-a-hino-lao-mas, sat quietly on a magic bed
of pine needles and reeds. He had made the resting place
in the middle of a mystical spot on the side of a spirit hill
known only to himself.

He had previously covered his body with magic lotions.
Then he performed a ritual dance and repeated the secret
chant taught to him years ago by Dark, one of the most
powerful of all the Cheyenne medicine men. With great
deliberation he chewed on some herbs that he had gathered
earlier in the day, and concentrated on the problem of the
white men. He awaited a vision. He sought special medicine
to use against the pale faces, to delay the day which he knew
would inevitably come, when the intruders would push the
Indians out of their land.

After a while, he noticed that the trees on the other side
of the clearing seemed to be swaying in motion. "Ha!" he
thought. "They are trying to mimic my dance." He laughed
quietly at the thought. Then one tree in particular began to
stand out. It was a strong tree, and was taller than the others

around it. It reminded him of Roman Nose, who was over six feet tall, and much bigger than other Indians.

Without warning a fire erupted at the base of the tree. Although the flames surrounded the tree and burned brightly, the tree did not seem to be harmed. Except for a few pieces of charred wood at the base, the tree itself withstood the fiery blast.

Unexpectedly a kingfisher flew into the clearing, circled the burning tree three times, and flew straight into the flames. Then a bat darted into the clearing, and followed the kingfisher into the inferno. With a loud "swoosh" four eagles appeared over the tops of the trees, and they also flew directly into the fire. The eagles were a bright red in color.

Then a very strange thing happened. A woman appeared out of nowhere, and with a stick tried to retrieve the bodies of the bat and kingfisher. She was about to succeed, when she saw a metal fork lying on the ground. She dropped the stick she was using, grabbed the metal fork, and once again tried to get the birds out of the fire. Suddenly she gave a shrill cry, and was enveloped in flames. She fell into the burning tree, and could not be seen again.

As Ice Bear watched these strange proceedings, the kingfisher and bat that had flown into the fire came to life, flew out of the flames unharmed, and disappeared over the hill. Just as suddenly the four eagles appeared out of the inferno and soared into the distant sky. But instead of being bright red, they were now blackened by the fire. As White Bull turned to watch the birds fly away, he saw a snake at the perimeter of the circle, watching the whole thing. But it was very odd, because the serpent had one horn right in the middle of its head. As he watched, the snake slowly turned away, and followed the kingfisher, bat and the eagles over the hill.

The fire now died out and only the smoldering ashes remained.

Ice Bear sat a while, thinking about these things, then lay back on the bed, and went to sleep. When he awoke, he pondered once more the meaning of his vision. He looked around, and saw a tree which he had not noticed before. It had been burned on one side, but had healed itself and was now strong and healthy. Ice Bear went to the tree and knocked some of the charred wood from the trunk, and placed the pieces in his sack.

He destroyed his bed, picked up all of his things, and removed all traces of his visit to this place. The meaning of the things he had seen in his vision was becoming clear. In his mind, he now envisioned a magic war bonnet, a head piece that would be more powerful than any that had ever been made before. A war bonnet for Roman Nose, one of the most powerful of the Cheyenne warriors.

When it was finished, the bonnet had a single horn in the center of the head band instead of the customary two, and the tail was so long that it almost touched the ground when Roman Nose was on horseback. The length of the bonnet was made from a piece of buffalo hide, and was covered with eagle feathers. The feathers alternated with four red ones, four black ones, then four more red ones, and so on for a total of 40 feathers in the bonnet. Ice Bear only used native materials – nothing that came from the white man, such as metal or cloth or thread. The buffalo hide was painted with charcoal from the burnt tree.

On top of the head dress was the skin of a kingfisher. When a kingfisher dives into a pool, the water fills in around it almost instantly. In the same way the magical skin of the bird would cause the skin of the warrior to close in around bullet wounds, as if they weren't even there. Next to this was a dead bat, which would allow the wearer to see and be safe at night.

But powerful as the war bonnet might be, there were rituals and taboos that had to be followed to ensure its magic. Each time that Roman Nose wore the head piece, he had to follow a sacred ceremony. He would hold the bonnet over the embers of a fire to catch the smoke from the embers, and would shake a powder from a medicinal herb on the top. Then he would lift the bonnet to each of the four directions – north, east, south and west – before placing it on his head.

And there were certain taboos, things that Roman Nose could not eat and places that he must avoid, like not entering the tepee of a newborn baby until four days after it's birth. But most of all, Ice Bear warned, Roman Nose must never eat any food that had been touched by metal. If he were to break this taboo, he most certainly would die in his next battle.

This mystical bonnet was effective, and in many fights with the white men Roman Nose rode back and forth in front of a skirmish line, with soldiers firing at him, and escaped unharmed. Roman Nose, and his war bonnet, became a part of western lore. But its magic would be put to the test in the months ahead at Beecher's Island.

CHAPTER 10

It was a brisk October day, and Thomas Alderdice was hurrying down the main street of Salina to keep an appointment at the Saline Bank. His head was down, and he was deep in thought. As he rounded a sharp corner he ran headlong into a young lady, knocking her flat on the ground.

He knelt by her side. "Golly, I'm sorry, mam. Are you OK?"

The woman sat up and gave him a withering scowl. "I seem to be, no thanks to you. Have you ever considered looking where you are going? Lots of people do, you know."

For the first time Thomas got a good look at her face. She was not exactly pretty, he thought, but still it was a face that was pleasing to look at. The eyes were a deep blue, and at the moment showed a fire burning from within. The nose and chin were perfectly proportioned with full lips. She had straw colored hair which showed from beneath a slightly dislodged bonnet.

Thomas helped her to her feet. He started to brush some of the dust from her back, but caught himself just in time. Don't want to seem too familiar, he thought.

"It was my fault, mam," Thomas said. "I guess I was just preoccupied and not paying attention to what I was doing. Are you sure you're not hurt?"

"I'm just fine, Mr. .....?"

"Alderdice," Thomas stammered. "Thomas Alderdice."

"Well, Mr. Alderdice, I trust you will be a little more careful with the other ladies in our town." She walked away as Thomas tried to assure her that he certainly would. After she had gone, Thomas realized he had not even asked for her name.

Twenty minutes later he finished his business with the bank, came back outside, and was preparing to light a cigarette he had rolled from his package of Bull Durham, when he spotted the young lady down the street. She was talking with another couple, a man standing with his arm around a younger woman. Thomas thought the man looked familiar, then realized it was an old Union Army buddy, Houstan Anglin.

Houstan, like Thomas, had been in the Confederate Army, was captured, took the oath of allegiance to the Union, and signed up in the 2nd U. S. Volunteer Army. Thomas had heard that Houstan was recently married. A very young girl named Ziegler, he thought. Sabra Ziegler – that was it. Without hesitation he threw down his cigarette and strode over to them. He greeted Houstan warmly. "Hey, Houstan," he said, "how you been? Haven't seen you for a long time."

Houstan broke into a wide smile. "Hello, Thomas. Been just great. Don't believe you ever met my wife have you? Sabra, this here's an old Army buddy of mine, Thomas Alderdice."

"I'm pleased to meet you, Sabra." Thomas replied

"And this here's her sister," Houstan continued. "Mrs. Daily. Susanna Daily."

Thomas suppressed a twinge of disappointment. She was already married. But he took her hand, and said "Pleased to meet you, too, Susanna." He looked a little longer into her eyes than he needed and decided that she was indeed a striking woman.

"I believe Mr. Alderdice and myself have already met," Susanna said. "A rather brief but interesting encounter. Have you managed to steer clear of the other ladies of Salina, Mr. Alderdice?" There was a twinkle in her eye as she gazed at him.

"I have, indeed, Mrs. Daily. One such meeting was quite enough. I have felt no need to try to impress myself on anyone else after running into you, so to speak."

Susanna rewarded Thomas with a broad smile, indicating that she bore him no ill will. Sabra and Houstan looked on with a puzzled expression. Neither Thomas nor Susanna tried to enlighten them.

"Where are you staying these days, Thomas?" Houstan asked. "We need to get together and get caught up on things."

"Oh, I've got a room in the hotel just down the street. Thinking of laying a claim on some farm land as soon as I can scout around some. Just got discharged."

Neither Thomas nor Houstan mentioned the fact that they had fought for the Confederacy before signing up with the Union Army. Kansas was not particularly friendly to the cause of the South.

The four of them chatted for a while before Thomas took his leave. Once again he gave Susanna an appraising look, regretting that she was a married woman.

Later that afternoon as Thomas was resting in his hotel room, Houstan banged on his door.

"Hey, Thomas," he said as soon as the door was opened, "why don't you come join us for supper tonight at Sabra's folks. They live just north of here. Big family gathering, and Sabra wanted me to invite you."

"Oh, I don't know, Houstan. I wouldn't want to be imposing." Thomas was thinking a single man surrounded by a bunch of married couples and noisy children probably wouldn't be his idea of a lot of fun. Still, a home-cooked meal wouldn't be hard to take.

"Shucks, don't you worry about that. Sabra's already headed over there. Splash some water on your face and come on with me. Sabra's folks been here for some time. They could probably give you some tips on homesteading."

Thomas and Houstan arrived at the Michael Ziegler home just before dusk, and Thomas was introduced to the family. Besides the Zieglers, and Houstan and his wife, there was one other married couple – John Alverson and his wife, Mary. She was the second oldest of the Ziegler children.

Thomas tried hard to remember the names of all the Ziegler young ones as he shook their hands. One, however, was easy. Eli, thirteen years old, was a big strapping youth – taller than Thomas – but then Thomas wasn't exactly a giant. Eli looked like the kind of a kid that would be good to travel the river with, as the old saying went.

Susanna was there also, and Thomas met her two children, John and Willis. No sign of her husband, however.

The food tasted wonderful to Thomas, with plenty for everyone. Afterwards, as the women cleaned up, the men sat around the table and discussed the prospects of a good crop next year (always the first and often the only subject men discussed). But also the Indian situation.

"I 'spect I'd be pretty careful about moving onto Spillman Creek," the elder Ziegler said. "That's getting into their old hunting grounds." This started a round of observations about treaties, and the ever present danger of being molested by Indians.

Thomas participated in all of these discussions, but kept wondering where Susanna's husband might be, and why nobody ever mentioned him. Finally he got up enough courage to ask, "Does your husband homestead around here, Susanna?"

There was an awkward silence, before Susanna replied, "My husband is no longer with us, Mr. Alderdice. He died of typhoid fever a year ago while serving in the Army. I and my children have been living here with my parents."

Thomas was ashamed of the excitement he felt as he heard her words. "I'm sorry to hear that, Susanna," he managed to say. He turned back to John Alverson and Michael Ziegler and asked about the land to the west, soil conditions, availability of water and other concerns of a man about to become a homesteader, while trying to keep his mind off of Susanna. Everything he heard sounded good, and he was anxious to get started with his new venture.

"Have you heard they've moved the Butterfield Stage line down here from Nebraska?" John Alverson asked. "Set up a relay station down at Ellsworth. They say you can ride from Atchison to Denver now in only 12 days."

"Yeah," Houstan replied, "that is if the Indians don't give you any bother."

Thomas only half listened to this conversation. He couldn't help stealing a glance in Susanna's direction every few minutes. Several times she caught him staring at her, and turned away with a deep blush. Once, Mary also saw Thomas's interest, and gave her older sister a playful dig in the ribs with her elbow. Both girls turned their backs to the men with soft giggles.

When Thomas left the Ziegler home that night, he knew the direction in which his new life was headed.

The next year, the year that Tall Bull and the Dog Soldiers returned to the Kansas plains, Thomas and Susanna were married, and together with Susanna's two children, settled on a homestead further to the west of the other settlements, near the present town of Lincoln, Kansas. Well into the hunting grounds of the Cheyenne Indians.

"So that's how Thomas and Susanna met," I said – more of a statement than a question. "But what about the German couple – Maria and George Weichel? What can you tell me about them?"

"Well, I can tell you by all accounts that she was a very pretty girl."

"But what brought them out here to the wilds of Kansas?"

"Ever hear of the Seven Weeks War?" Old Joe said. "That was one of the things that headed them in this direction, along with an awful lot of advertisin' about the glories of owning land in the west."

CHAPTER 11

There were a number of things happening in the year 1866 that would contribute to the growing number of settlers coming to central and western Kansas.

Among these was the Homestead Act, signed into law in 1863, which encouraged settlement of "public lands." With the signing of the Treaty of the Little Arkansas, all of western Kansas and Colorado were considered to be in that category. Under this law settlers could lay claim of up to 160 acres if they lived on it and made improvements over a five year period. The law was in answer to those who demanded "land for the landless," and who sang a popular song of those days, "Uncle Sam is rich enough to give us all a farm." At the close of the Civil War the law was amended so that a homesteader could deduct the time served in military service from the five year residency requirement. This brought thousands of families uprooted by the war into the west in search of new beginnings. Within ten years 26 million acres of public lands would be claimed by new settlers.

The Union Pacific Railroad reached Fort Riley in 1866, and plans were well underway to proceed through the heart of the Cheyenne hunting grounds. The railroads, eager to drum up business for their new lines, circulated hundreds of leaflets in America and abroad describing the wonderful opportunities of land ownership in the west. Transatlantic steamship companies joined in the promotions, hoping to draw large numbers of foreigners to cross the ocean on their ships.

And in Europe the advertisements found a receptive audience among those going through the unrest of the Prussia-Austria War. In 1866 a number of German states were unified under the German Confederation, which was dominated by the two "super states" of Austria and Prussia. Prussia, led by Otto von Bismark, embarked on a campaign to eliminate Austria's influence in the confederation. Bismark maneuvered Austria into declaring war on Prussia in 1866, and in the Seven Weeks War, as it was later called, quickly defeated them.

George and Maria Weichel, along with their good friend Fred Meigerhoff, were only a few of the thousands that would have their lives changed by these events. On the night that war broke out, George had asked Maria, a girl much younger than himself, to attend the annual Hanover musical festival with him.

The 19th century German singers marched vigorously on the stage in Hanover's new, open air theater as they performed songs from the love story of Tristan und Isolde, Richard Wagner's tragic opera which had premiered the year before. Overhead the spring-time celestial stars provided a bright canopy which seemed in complete harmony with the tender lyrics of the opera.

The year was 1866, some 18 months after the Sand Creek massacre in that far away region of western United States. That episode of frontier life had been little noted in the cities of Europe, who had problems enough of their own. In particular the incident was totally unknown to the pretty, dark-haired girl who was listening intently to the words of the musical.

During one of the more tender love songs the girl, Maria, stole a sidelong glance at the man sitting by her side. Once again she noted, with satisfaction, his strong features and the pleasing profile of his face. Well, perhaps his nose could have been a little less pronounced, and maybe his jaw could have been set in a slightly less determined look, but these were minor imperfections in his overall appearance. With a sigh, she decided, as she had already done on several occasions over the past few months, that he was really quite good looking, though just a little on the somber side. But after all, he was ten years older than she, and maybe had a right to look serious and worldly.

"Isn't this a wonderful opera?" she asked. "Herr Wagner is quite talented." As she said these words, the music stopped abruptly. The players on the stage were milling around in apparent confusion. At the front of the theater people were beginning to shout and get up from their chairs

"What is it, George? What is happening?" Maria asked, and grabbed him by the arm.

"I don't know, but something is wrong, that much is certain. Wait – someone is coming onto the stage."

A small, wiry man, whom Maria recognized as the Burgomaster of Hanover, was standing with his arms raised for silence. Slowly at first, the crowd began to quiet down, and then total silence descended as the audience waited to hear what the Burgomaster had to say.

"Ladies and Gentlemen," the Burgomaster began in a loud, but tremulous voice. "I have momentous news to bring to you. We have just received word that Hanover, along with our good friend and neighbor, Austria, has this date declared war on Prussia. A time of terrible conflict and great uncertainty lies before us. I suggest that we conclude these festivities and each of us depart now, quietly, from this theater, and go to our homes to prepare for the days that lie ahead. Pray for our success against the Prussians and the dictator, Bismark. Thank you, and God bless us all."

For a moment there was a strained silence as the crowd digested the significance of what they had just heard. Then the theater erupted with loud cheers, yells and screams. Throughout the audience young men stood on chairs and waved their hats, amid growing chants of "Death to Bismark. Death to the tyrant."

George Weichel, age 27, and one of Hanover's most accomplished businessmen, was as excited as any at that open-air theater. He too hurled insults at the Chancellor of Prussia, Prince Otto von Bismark. But in the height of his excitement, he was caught once again by the beautiful, if somewhat fearful, eyes of the girl by his side. Grasping her arms he lifted her in the air in a half pirouette before putting her back on the ground.

"Oh, Maria, do not look so troubled. The Bismark will be overcome swiftly, and once and for all we shall put an end to his shameful ambitions to rule the continent. With Austria at our side, we cannot lose."

"But George! Surely you will not be involved in this war. You are a successful businessman, the owner of Hanover's best brewery. Surely this will not affect you."

"My dear, you do not understand. Men like the Bismark must not be allowed to rule the destiny of others. He is a cruel despot who lusts for power. Immediately on the morrow I shall volunteer to serve with the army to help defeat the Prussian warmongers. Herr Meigerhoff can manage the business while I am gone."

"Herr Meigerhoff? Fred? I know he has been your trusted assistant since you were but a boy, but surely he cannot manage the business without you?"

"Fred has been with me as long as I can remember, and served my father before me. Fred can run everything with great efficiency – and anyway, it won't be for long."

As he spoke, George felt a twinge of anxiety in spite of his words. The fear was not at the prospect of war, however, but at the thought of having to leave the girl he now held in his arms. At that moment George knew with a certainty that this was the woman he wanted for his wife.

He held her at arm's length in order to make a cool appraisal of her charms, much as he would assess the merits of a prize steer, or waving field of grain. Recognizing that his emotions were not quite under control, he still concluded that by any standard this was quite a beautiful and adorable woman. Her dark hair flowed to her shoulders and framed a face that was at the same time intelligent and seductive. Her lips were a bright red, and were never more inviting than when she pouted slightly, as she was now doing. But it was her eyes, her deep blue eyes that really set her apart.

"Maria, listen to me. There is so much I want to say. Tomorrow I will offer my services to fight the Prussians, and tonight I must find Fred and make preparations. But Maria, you must promise me that you will – that is – if you want –," George stammered to a halt, as he groped for just the right words.

Maria, her own face flushed with excitement and anticipation, wanted to help, but dared not speak a word lest it spoil everything.

"What I mean to say, Maria, is that I love you and want you to be my wife! I realize that this is very sudden, and that I am older than you, and that I am not very good with words, and certainly not the most dashing man you have ever met, but I am steady and have a good business and can take care of you, and..."

"George- George," Maria interrupted, laughing with happiness. "Are you going to let a poor girl have her say or are you going to keep talking all night?"

"Yes – yes – please what do you say?"

"Oh yes, George! Yes! I love you and I will be honored to be your wife."

And for that moment time stood still for these two young people, as they stood locked in an embrace in the middle of the theater, with the bright spring-time stars twinkling overhead.

It was exactly one month to the day before Maria heard from George again. It had been a dreary day with intermittent rain ranging from a light mist to heavy downpour. Thankfully there had been a slight let-up at the graveside where they had buried her father.

Now Maria was back in the house that she and her father had shared since her mother passed away several years ago. She wanted to be alone and sent her friends away. Her father's death was so unexpected that she could hardly grasp that he was gone. There had never been any indication that his heart was giving him trouble, right up to the moment that he died.

It was the war that did it, she told herself. All he could think of was the war – and the war had gone badly. Bismark secured the aid of Italy against Austria, and was able to keep France neutral. The Prussian soldiers quickly overran Hanover, and were now everywhere visible, standing on street corners, or in the cafes. The crowning blow had been the crushing defeat of the Austrians at the Battle of Koniggiatz on July 3, ten days before her father's death. He was never quite the same after the news of that stinging defeat reached them there at Hanover. And worst of all, she had no idea where George might be, or even if he were still alive.

The rain was coming down in earnest now, as Maria sat by the window, oblivious to the darkening shadows of the premature dusk. Her somber thoughts were interrupted by a knocking at the door. She moved to the front of the house and peered out the window. A dark figure, drenched by the rain, stood on the front step with a coat pulled over his head. She went to the entry and called out, "Yes? Who is it please?"

"Maria - it is me. George. Let me in. Quickly."

"George!" She flung the door open and pulled the soaked figure into the house. "Oh, George. Is it really you? Are you all right?"

"Yes, yes. At least I will be if I can ever get into dry clothes again."

"Look at you. Soaked to the bone. Oh, George, I have been so worried about you. The Prussians are searching the city for soldiers who fought against them. They haul them off in box cars. We may never see them again. You must be so careful."

"I know, darling. The war is over, and now we must suffer the consequences. I cannot stay but a minute. I have been to see Fred and made arrangements for him to sell the brewery. I am on my way to Switzerland - to Bern. He will join me there when everything has been settled here. Maria, Fred told me about your father. I am so sorry. He was a great man, and a wonderful father to you."

"It was so sudden, George. But he had such pride in you, fighting the hated Prussians."

"Maria, I couldn't leave without seeing you. And asking you - would you come to Bern when Fred comes? We can get married there. I know that I can make a good living in Switzerland. We could be so happy."

"Oh yes, George. Yes! I will come to you wherever you may be."

The conversation was interrupted by the sound of horses on the street outside of the house. George rushed to the window, pulled back the drape and peered out. A wagon carrying a dozen soldiers had stopped in the middle of the block. The Prussians jumped out of the vehicle and divided into two groups. An officer said something to them, and one group went up the hill to the beginning of the block, and the second group scurried the other direction. The officer stood by the carriage.

"They're doing a house-to-house search," George said. "I've got to leave. Promise me you will come to Bern, Maria."

"I promise, my darling. I will be there."

George pulled Maria close, gave her a hurried kiss, and rushed to the back door. He opened it and edged outside, careful to examine every inch of the yard. He could see no one. The rain had changed to a slow, cold drizzle. George went around the corner of the house and moved slowly to the front. The officer was still there. He would not be able to go in that direction without being seen. He returned to the back yard. Beyond the fence was an open park. George started to climb over the enclosure, but then paused. If the soldiers were doing a door-to-door search, and the officer was keeping watch in the front to make sure no one came out, wouldn't it be logical that they would also have someone posted in the park to make sure nobody escaped in that direction?

George hesitated, unsure of what to do. The soldiers were at the house next to Maria's now. One came out on the back porch with a lantern which contained a funnel around the base, focusing the light into a beam. Holding it high he examined every inch of the yard.

George dropped to the ground and crawled to a large lilac bush. He made himself as inconspicuous as possible, hugging the ground and waiting for the men to come to Maria's house. He shivered from the cold and dampness.

It seemed an eternity before the back door opened and two soldiers appeared on the porch. George kept his face down as the light from the lantern played across the yard. It swept past the lilac bush he was hiding behind and moved on to the right. Just as George started to relax, the beam came back and focused on the bush. George tensed, ready to jump up and make a run for it over the back fence, when the light moved on once again. A few minutes later the men went back in the house.

George stayed where he was until he heard the soldiers gather in the street where they loaded back into the truck. When they drove off, George got up, shivering and shaking, and went to the back door. Maria answered his knock almost immediately, and pulled him inside.

"Take off those wet clothes right now," she demanded. "Tonight you will sleep in my father's bed while they dry. You will find a pair of his pajamas in the drawer. Go now, while I warm a bowl of soup."

George was too cold and tired to protest.

I was busy making notes of all of the things that happened in 1865 and 1866. Black Kettle and the other peace chiefs signing the Treaty of the Little Arkansas, Tall Bull and the Dog Soldiers returning to Kansas, the railroad poised to move into Cheyenne country, Tom Alderdice and Susanna Daily getting married, and now George and Maria Weichel trying to get out of Hanover.

"Tell me, Joe," I asked, "how is it you know so much about all of these events? Did you read a book about them somewhere?"

"Me? Read a book? Shucks, Sonny, I can't even spell my name." He gave a sly look from the corners of his eyes, chuckled softly, and said "Don't suppose you'd believe me if I said it was 'cause I was there?"

I laughed along with him. "Don't believe I would," I replied. "That would make you well over 140 years old. Nope, I don't believe I'd buy into that story."

"I was a' guessing that'd be your response. Well, let's just say that sometimes I see things, things that happened in the past. Things that seem so real I think I'm livin' them right now."

"You mean, like premonitions?"

"Not exactly premonitions. Those are things you sense that are going to happen in the future. More like mental telepathy I'd say. Pictures that just come to your mind like someone sent them to you. Kinda like Uncle Mart used to get."

"Uncle Mart? Who's he?"

"Why, old Martin Hendrickson. He's another of those settlers you want to know so much about."

I pulled out my list of names of those involved in the raid of 1869.

"You won't find him in that there list of yours, Sonny, 'cause he didn't get himself killed. But he was there alright. Him and those feelings he'd get out of nowhere."

"You don't really believe in all that stuff, do you?"

"Believe? You bet your sweet potatoes I believe. Just look at that there telephone you got stuffed in your pocket. Why it can send pictures thousands of miles to another telephone, clear as a bell. And that's just one little ole computer talkin' to another. Now the human mind is much more complex and powerful than a computer could ever be, so why is it you don't think your mind could be a sendin' pictures to another mind programmed to receive them? Sure does sound logical to me."

I decided not to get into that argument. Besides, if someone was sending pictures to Old Joe, they'd have to be 140 years old. Or sending them from the grave.

"But I'm gettin' sidetracked," Old Joe said. "Uncle Mart comes later. Right now I want to tell you about the Old Man of the Thunder, as he was called by the Indians. What a jackass."

Old Joe was right about one thing. I was getting as interested in the story of the Indians as I was in what happened to the settlers.

CHAPTER 12

"With the end of the war between the states," Old Joe continued, *"the nation turned its attention to the Indian problem out west. Religious groups were pretty upset over the slaughter of Black Kettle's camp at Sand Creek, and the sorry treatment given to the tribes. But a lot of others saw the Indians as nothing more than a stumblin' block towards uniting the East coast with the West. Something they called our Manifest Destiny. A tricky sounding phrase invented by some politician, I guess. But it dominated the thinking of many Americans. The problem was becoming more critical, because Congress realized that they couldn't just keep moving the natives further west. Some more permanent solution had to be found."*

"Then in December of 1866 Crazy Horse and a band of Sioux dealt a devastating blow to the U. S. Army. Eighty-one troopers under the command of Captain Fetterman were ambushed and slaughtered on the Bozeman Trail in Wyoming. The Fetterman massacre, as it came to be known, had a considerable affect on the military brass. They were convinced that the Indians needed to be dealt a decisive blow to subdue them into accepting peace."

"Wynkoop and Leavenworth, the Indian agents for the five tribes of the Little Arkansas - the Cheyenne, Arapaho, Kiowa, Prairie Apache and Comanche - insisted that these tribes were peaceful and not causing any trouble, in spite of Roman Noses's

threats. But the Army and Indian agents were increasingly at odds with each other, and the accusations between the two sides became bitter and acrimonious."

"General Winfield Scott Hancock, Commander of the Military Department of the Missouri, stationed at Fort Riley in eastern Kansas, got all hepped up over reports of Indian atrocities in western Kansas, although most were unsubstantiated. But the Cheyenne Dog Soldiers refused to sign the Treaty of the Little Arkansas which would have cleared the way for settlers to move into the plains. Moreover the Kansas Pacific Railroad was laying tracks well inside of the territory, Indians or no Indians. For all of these reasons Hancock felt it was time to get Tall Bull and the Dog Soldiers to sign the treaty and move south with the other Cheyenne."

"He figured he knew exactly how to do it. No more coddling, no more negotiating. The time was here when the military needed to get tough. Either the Indians would agree to the terms of the treaty, or else. And the "or else," General Hancock thought, needed to be visible and decisive. It was time to send a "peace-keeping" expedition into western Kansas and get the Indians to agree to peace, or destroy them. His personal views ranged more to the latter solution. But he needed to have the support of his boss, General William Tecumseh Sherman, Commanding Officer of the Military Division of the Missouri."

Old Joe had a rather harsh look in his eyes as he continued.

Corporal Higgens wished there was some way he could hear the conversation going on in the next office between the two men in charge of the Army of the Missouri. He knew that Hancock was thoroughly aroused over the increasing reports of Indian hostility in western Kansas, particularly over the murder of two station hands at Chalk Bluff, and was hoping for permission to lead a major expedition against them. General Sherman, who had just completed a fact finding tour of the west, was reportedly a little less convinced that the Indians represented a major threat at this time.

His thoughts were interrupted when the door to Hancock's office opened and the General called for him to come in. As he entered, he could tell at a glance from the satisfied look on Hancock's face that his commanding officer had been successful with Sherman.

"I want a letter sent to Major Edward Wynkoop," Hancock could barely conceal his disdain for the very sound of the name, "agent for the Cheyenne Indians."

Higgens produced pencil and paper, and sat down beside the General's desk.

Hancock began:

> "To Major Wynkoop. Please notify the Cheyenne Indians under your jurisdiction that I expect shortly to come into their lands, and that I will expect to meet with their chiefs. Tell them that I come fully prepared for peace or war. It will be up to them which it will be. I will insist on their keeping off the main lines of travel of settlers and stage coaches, where their presence will only bring about collisions with the whites. If they are not prepared to agree to this, I intend to march across the state of Kansas and destroy every hostile village and kill every hostile warrior that I can find."

At the last sentence General Sherman gave a slight cough, cleared his throat, and said. "Don't you think that's putting it a little strongly, General? We don't want the Indian Bureau thinking that we are deliberately seeking a confrontation."

Hancock glared at the floor for a moment before relenting. "Very well, General, you are right, of course. Strike that last sentence, Corporal. Instead write "If not,

I would expect you to be at my side as I visit the tribes to demonstrate to them the folly of their ways."

"Much better, Winfield, much better," Sherman stated. "Whereas I agree with you on the necessity of a show of force to keep the Indians in line, and to convince them on the necessity of abandoning the plains of Kansas, we must be careful not to fan the flames of rivalry that already exist in Washington between the Army and the Indian Bureau."

"Humph!" Hancock snorted. "I'd like to have some of those Indian lovers back east come out here and witness the atrocities committed by these "poor lost children of the plains." They'd be demanding protection from the U. S. Army soon enough, and forgetting all about their high ideals for nature's 'noble man.'"

Sherman chuckled. "Well, Winfield, I know how you feel, but I'm not convinced that the trouble is all one sided. For the Indians, I admit, it is as natural for a few braves to go off and make raids as it is for you and me to pull on our boots in the morning. I think most of the chiefs want peace with the white man, but they are unable to control their young warriors."

"On the other hand, for many of the gold miners and trappers, shooting Indians is just about like shooting wild beasts. It's a sport – a game. And it is my personal opinion that the ranchers and farmers are exploiting the rumors of hostility, hoping to get the Army to enlarge their garrisons so as to create a better market for their grain and cattle. You know full well that the settlers have always tried to profit from the Army by selling them supplies."

"Maybe so, Sherman, but whatever the reason, the fact remains that there are increasing signs of trouble and it is innocent men, women and children that are the victims. Why just in the past two months I've heard reports that the Cheyenne ran off stock from some buffalo hunters, that they compelled one poor old rancher to cook them a meal and threatened to kill him when he didn't have any sugar available, they stole 40 mules from a wagon train, and finally they killed two men and destroyed a wagon station at Chalk Bluff. You can thank the Cheyenne and that Roman Nose for that or I'll eat my hat. And there are reliable reports that there will be an all-out war this spring, just as soon as the grass is up for the ponies to feed on."

"Well, I've not found much truth in those rumors, Winfield. But go ahead, plan your expedition, make a show of force – just remember, I don't want you to be the one to initiate a war. If there is a fight, they must be the ones to start it."

"Understood, General," Hancock replied. "The Cheyenne are the real troublemakers, and that Roman Nose, so I'll begin with them. And I'll make sure their agent, Wynkoop, is right by my side. If trouble does come we won't have to listen to any more of his pious claims that his poor little Indians are being picked on by the U. S. Army."

Sherman chuckled again as he rose from his chair. "Well, General, I must be on my way back to the citadel in the east, and try my damnedest to convince one half of Congress that we are actively engaged in the protection of life and limb on the western frontier by relentlessly pursuing the Indians, while at the same time demonstrating to the other half that we are making every effort to make peace with the Indians and are treating them with the dignity to which they are entitled. Good luck on your expedition – and remember, don't borrow trouble if you can avoid it."

In the latter part of March, 1867, General Hancock left Fort Riley with 1,400 men, consisting of cavalry, infantry and artillery. He even brought with him pontoon bridges for crossing rivers. He reached Fort Larned on April 7. In command of the 7th Cavalry was a young officer of Civil War fame, who at the age of 23 had jumped from a

Lieutenant's commission to become a Brigadier General, George Armstrong Custer. There were several reporters on the expedition, including one from Harper's Monthly who would later gain fame in deep Africa, Henry M. Stanley.

Black Kettle was informed of the impending approach of this large military contingent, and remembering Sand Creek, moved his tribe's lodges further south from the Little Arkansas to below the Canadian River in what is now Oklahoma.

Wynkoop, as requested, sent messengers to the remaining Cheyenne, the Dog Soldiers, requesting that they come to Fort Larned and meet with General Hancock to discuss a new peace initiative. Tall Bull and the other Cheyenne chiefs were skeptical, but finally agreed to see what Hancock had to say, stating that they would be there on the 10th of April.

On the night of April 9th, a huge storm erupted across the plains, dumping eight inches of snow in the region. On the next day, which was set for the conference, the chiefs sent runners to the fort to announce that they were on their way, but were delayed by the snow. The Cheyenne camp consisted of 500 lodges, 35 miles distant from the Fort.

Hancock was beside himself, believing the delay to be an act of disrespect by the Cheyenne, and questioned whether they would show up at all. However, on the 12th, Tall Bull, White Horse, Bull Bear and Little Robe, the head chiefs of the Dog Soldiers, rode into camp.

Hancock received them in a belligerent manner, assembling the troops and cavalry to show the Indians the strength of the expedition. He also had the artillery fire the fort's cannons to impress the visitors, thus earning himself the nickname of Old Man of the Thunder. He demanded that a conference be held that evening, which was against Indian tradition. Council meetings were never held at night.

The Cheyenne leaders were wary, even though Wynkoop tried to assure them that Hancock meant well.

As the meetings got under way, Hancock expressed his displeasure that Roman Nose was not present, showing his ignorance of Cheyenne custom. Roman Nose was not a chief, but a war leader. It was not his role to participate in peace talks. Hancock said it was important that he meet with all the chiefs, and since they weren't here he would have to go to them. Tomorrow he would move his troops to the Cheyenne camp.

This was the very thing the Indians feared most. They remembered Sand Creek all too well, and were convinced that Hancock intended to attack the women and children in their village. Hancock continued his antagonistic harangue. "I've heard rumors that the Cheyenne are spoiling for a fight. If that is so, we are here and will be happy to oblige. If you want peace, however, you know the conditions. All of the chiefs must sign the Treaty of the Little Arkansas, and abandon the plains of Kansas. The white men are coming like a prairie fire in a strong wind, and nothing can stop them. What does the Cheyenne have to say?"

The chiefs sat in a shocked silence, not knowing what to make of the words of the Old Man of the Thunder. Finally Tall Bull, with great deliberation, lit his pipe, took a few puffs, and rose to face Hancock.

"Our agent, Colonel Wynkoop, told us you wanted to meet with us. We are willing to be friends with the white man. If you want to go on the roads in the Smoky Hills, you are free to do so. But your young men must not fire on us when they meet us on the road. You say you are going to our village tomorrow. I'll have no more to say to you there than here." Tall Bull sat down after these words and stared at the ground, avoiding the eyes of the white officers. Hancock twitched in his chair, making no attempt to hide his disdain for Tall Bull and the other chiefs assembled there. On this note the evening council with the Cheyenne leaders came to an end.

The chiefs camped that night with Hancock's troops just outside of the fort, but sent runners back to the village warning of the impending approach of the Army and cannon, and that Hancock wanted to meet with Roman Nose. Wynkoop tried his best to dissuade Hancock from marching to the Cheyenne lodges at Pawnee Fork, but Hancock would not listen.

"Major, I would remind you that you are here strictly as an observer. I will be the one to parley with the savages, and I don't need you as a go-between or to tell me what to do."

The next morning the troops were assembled and the march began. Hancock had been led to believe the Indian camp was only 25 miles away, and at the end of the day they had traveled this distance, only to learn the camp was still another 10 miles to the northwest. This did not improve his humor.

The people in the Cheyenne village, having been warned that Hancock was coming, were filled with fear. The chiefs debated whether it was better to leave the lodges immediately, or better to stay so as not to make Hancock any angrier than he already was. Many of the warriors wanted to fight the soldiers, but they were heavily out-numbered, and for the most part only had bows and arrows while the soldiers were armed with the latest repeating rifles. But they all vividly remembered what had happened at Sand Creek, and during the night the women and children began slipping away from camp, leaving their teepees and most of their belongings behind.

Roman Nose was highly incensed at being singled out by Hancock, and suspected Hancock meant to arrest or kill him. He stated that before this happened he would kill the General. Bull Bear, one of the Dog Soldier chiefs that Roman Nose greatly admired, was assigned to ride with him the next day to make sure he didn't do anything foolish. Nevertheless Roman Nose told Bull Bear "This officer they call Hancock is spoiling for a fight. I will kill him in front of his own men and give them something to fight about."

The next morning was cold and windy as the Army continued their march to the Cheyenne village. The warriors armed themselves for a fight and rode out to intercept the troops. They met about half way between the two camps.

There has never been a more dramatic and suspenseful moment in the lore of the west. On the one side were 1400 troops – foot soldiers, cavalry and artillery – and on the other 400 excited Cheyenne – shouting and singing and waving their weapons at the soldiers. Hancock ordered Custer to bring the 7th Cavalry to the front. They rode up to the line with swords drawn, ready to charge.

The two sides faced each other for what seemed like an eternity, each waiting for the other to make a move. The regiment flags snapped sharply in the wind as Hancock raised his hand to attack, but at the last minute he remembered Sherman's admonition not to be the one to start the fight. In the distance the Indians presented a wild sight, riding back and forth, shaking their lances high in the air. The wind all but drowned out their shouting, giving the whole situation a surrealistic feeling.

Wynkoop, sitting on his horse beside Hancock, thought, "My God, he's really going to do it. He's going to attack these people that he invited to talk peace." Without conscious thought he spurred his pony forward, proceeding slowly into the no-man's land separating the two sides.

"Major! What do you think you are doing? Are you crazy? Come back here." Hancock shouted after him.

"You might just let him go if he's that intent on getting himself killed," Custer said. "If they threaten him, you'll have your reason to attack."

Hancock thought about this for a minute, and a smile spread slowly across his face. "I reckon you're right, Colonel. If they murder their own agent, we'd be forced to take action. And it's not as if I sent him out there."

Wynkoop rode slowly towards the shouting, belligerent Indians, wondering if he had completely lost his mind. "I know Tall Bull doesn't like me," he thought. "And Black Kettle's not here." But there was no turning back.

The Cheyenne stopped their clamoring and watched the lone figure proceed deliberately towards them. Three Indians detached themselves from the rest, and with weapons held high over their heads raced to meet him. As they drew nearer Wynkoop recognized Bull Bear and two other chiefs, one from the Sioux tribe.

"These people know me," Wynkoop kept telling himself. "I know I can talk with them. If they will just listen."

Approximately 1800 pairs of eyes that morning were glued on the lone rider and the three Indians bearing down on him. When they met, the Indians surrounded Wynkoop and an animated conversation ensued. The soldiers could see arms raising high in the air, and weapons being shaken at Wynkoop. The wind picked up in intensity.

"Hancock does not intend to fight unless provoked," Wynkoop told the three chiefs. "He only wants to talk. Do not do anything foolish. For the sake of your women and children, hear him out."

As they talked, several other Indians rode out to join them, Roman Nose among them. At the same time Hancock and a handful of his officers approached from the other side.

When they met, the two delegations faced each other for a few minutes without a word between them. General Hancock easily picked out Roman Nose from among the other warriors. He was dressed in an officer's blouse that had been taken off of a dead cavalryman, and was wearing his famous war bonnet.

Hancock ignored all the others and rode directly up to Roman Nose. Without preamble he asked, "Do you want peace or war?" Roman Nose sarcastically replied that if he wanted war he would not have ridden out here exposed to all those army troops and heavy artillery.

"Why were you not at the council with the other chiefs?" Hancock persisted. Ignoring the fact that he was not a chief and that it was not his place to be in peace talks, Roman Nose simply replied that his horses were too weak to travel. Besides he was not sure what Hancock's intentions were towards him. Wynkoop tried to explain to Hancock once again that Roman Nose was not a chief, but Hancock ignored him.

Tall Bull, Little Robe and the other chiefs who had ridden with Hancock now joined the group. Bull Bear, hoping to defuse the situation, told Hancock that their women and children were frightened of the soldiers and big guns, and were running away from their camp.

This made Hancock furious. "You must not let them go," he said. "My words are for all the Cheyenne to hear. I demand that you go after those that have left and bring them back."

Roman Nose, who had been sitting astride his horse with great calm, pulled Bull Bear aside and told him to take the chiefs back because he, Roman Nose, was going to kill Hancock. Once again Bull Bear reminded Roman Nose that they were heavily out-numbered, and that if he were to do such a thing the soldiers would surely catch and kill all the women and children.

The wind seemed to pick up momentum, and blowing dust stung the faces and eyes of the soldiers and Indians alike, making it difficult to be heard or carry on a conversation. Abruptly Hancock announced that this conference was over, and he expected the chiefs to ride after the women and children and bring them back to the village. He would hold no further talks with the chiefs until this was done. He and his officers returned to the lines of the soldiers, and Hancock ordered them to make camp for the night.

The warriors rode off in the general direction that the women had taken, but never returned. They were convinced that Hancock wanted to trap them into another Sand Creek. They left behind their tepees, travois, blankets – everything they could not carry on their horses.

After two days of waiting for the Indians to rejoin them, a frustrated Hancock, over the strenuous objections of Wynkoop, ordered the abandoned village at Pawnee Fork to be inventoried and burned. Included were 251 tepees, 962 buffalo robes, 436 saddles, and hundreds of lariats, mats and articles for cooking.

Now Hancock felt that he had all the justification he needed for an all out war. He ordered Custer to give chase to the Indians. Custer and the 7th Cavalry rode after the fleeing villagers, but were never able to find them. In typical Indian fashion, they scattered into dozens of smaller groups and disappeared from view.

The end result of Hancock's peace initiative was that the Cheyenne and Sioux were once again on the war path over the burning of their village. The Dog Soldiers attacked settlements, railroad camps, and stage coaches all across the Smoky Hill, Platte and Republican River country, while to the south war parties from Black Kettle's camp made raids to the west into New Mexico.

"That was when old Custer got discouraged, and did something pretty stupid," Old Joe said.

CHAPTER 13

Custer and the 7th Cavalry crisscrossed Kansas and Nebraska for the rest of the summer hunting for the Cheyenne Dog Soldiers, but his campaign was a total failure. Even worse he was unable to protect the stage lines and railroad working parties from Indian attack. He led his troops from Fort Hays north to the Platte, then back to the Republican, and finally back to Fort Wallace. The only Indians he saw were when the troops themselves were attacked, and once when some non-warring Indians came in to parley.

The morale of his troops was low. Many had enlisted during the Civil War, and now that the war was over, decided that there were better things to do than be in the Army. The railroads were paying good wages for workers. As a result, the number of desertions from Custer's forces was on the rise. In frustration, Custer at one point ordered his officers to hunt down and kill six deserters. Three of them were shot, and one later died. The officers under Custer were sharply divided between Custer admirers and Custer haters, and the latter were beginning to make their views known to the upper echelons.

When Custer got back to Fort Wallace, he expected he would find a letter from his wife, Libby. He was upset when there was none. Whether from frustration over his failure to find and destroy any Indians, or concern for his wife's health, or dismay with the morale of his troops, or all of the above, Custer at this point abandoned his search for the Cheyenne raiders, and proceeded on a very personal mission to visit his wife. With only two days rest from their long march down from the Platte, he left the 7th Cavalry at Fort Wallace, and with some 72 men set forth on a forced march to Fort Hays, purportedly to escort a wagon train of supplies back to Fort Wallace. At Fort Hays he left the rest of his troops, and proceeded to Fort Harker, only to learn that his wife had left Fort Harker and now was further east at Fort Riley. Without hesitation, Custer caught a train to Fort Riley.

As a result, Custer was placed under arrest and charged with deserting his command at Fort Wallace, using government property for personal use, and mistreating the men under his command. He was found guilty, and was sentenced to one year's suspension from command, rank and pay. For the super hero of the Civil War, the boy wonder General, this was a devastating blow.

General Hancock was severely chastised for his impetuous actions against the Cheyenne, and was transferred to another post. By the end of the year it was obvious that the Treaty of the Little Arkansas was meaningless. The Cheyenne Dog Soldiers never signed it, and Washington failed to act on it. Now there was a growing recognition among the nation's leaders that they had to reach some kind of accord with the plains Indians.

A new peace commission was appointed in the summer of 1867, consisting of Generals Sherman, Harney, Terry, Augur, and Sanborn; the Commissioner of Indian Affairs N. G. Taylor; Senator John Henderson and Colonel Tappan. The group announced their intent to meet once again with the Cheyenne, Arapaho, Kiowas, Comanches and Prairie Apaches, and establish these five tribes on a large reservation south of the Arkansas River. In return, the Indians would be given cattle, and would be taught to till the ground to become farmers.

The runner sped through the outskirts of Black Kettle's camp, and directly to the tent of the Cheyenne chief. Black Kettle emerged from the teepee, and stood before the exhausted man.

"I have a letter for you, Black Kettle," he said. "A letter from Colonel Leavenworth, agent to the Kiowas and the Commanches."

He extracted a wrinkled envelope from his waistband, and handed it to Black Kettle. Black Kettle regarded the envelope for a few minutes, then slowly and deliberately opened it and removed the letter. He unfolded it, and studied the letter at length. Then, as the group of curious Indians that had gathered around him watched, he folded the letter and inserted it back into the envelope.

"Thank you for delivering this message so quickly," he told the runner, then turned and reentered the teepee. He went to the rear of the tent, knelt, and placed the envelope with his other valuables.

His wife, Medicine Woman Later, watched him. "What does the letter say?" she finally asked.

"I do not know. We must wait for George Bent to return from the raids. There is nobody else in camp who can read the white man's words."

Since Hancock had burned the Cheyenne camp at Pawnee Fork, the Cheyenne considered that they were at war with all whites. The Dog Soldiers and the Northern half of the tribe, under Tall Bull and Roman Nose, raided settlements along the Republican and Smoky Hill regions, easily eluding Custer. But Black Kettle, still hoping for peace with the white men, had led the Southern group to the banks of the Washita River in Indian Territory. In spite of

Black Kettle's objections, however, small groups of warriors frequently slipped north or west during the summer to make raids on wagon trains, stage stations and unwary settlers. George Bent had joined one such group, which had just completed a successful raid near Cimmarron Crossing on a wagon train coming up from Mexico. They captured around 40 mules and horses. But George Bent was beginning to have doubts about his future with the tribe.

On the trail back to the Washita, George forced himself to think about his life. It was not an easy task, for there were many diversions to pull his attention away. The soft song of a meadowlark, the blurred image of a wild turkey running through the tall grass, even the refreshing coolness of the prairie wind on his cheek, lured his mind away from serious thought.

"Eiee, man was made to feel, not think," he growled. "That's the trouble with the white man, he spends too much time thinking and planning and not enough in feeling and enjoying."

Still, George made himself ponder the things that were happening; the trouble between the Cheyenne and the white man, the building of the railroad and the ever growing number of settlers, and about Magpie and himself. He loved his life with the Indians. Although he and his brother, Charlie, had been sent to school in Westport, Missouri when they were young, and had learned to read and write, and study history, both boys had eagerly awaited the day when they could return to the tribe and the open prairie.

George guessed that he could never understand the white man's outlook on life. To the Indian the land, air, the streams, the buffalo – these were things that were placed in this world by the Great Father for all the people to enjoy. And the Great Father had created man to ride free across the plains, to be one with nature, and to enjoy his gifts. But the white man had a smallness of mind. To the white man the land was there to measure off, to be fenced in, and to be kept to oneself. Rather than enjoy the entire prairie with its rolling hills and hidden streams, and great cottonwood trees, the white man would pace off one little segment, and declare with pride "this is mine!"

What fools, George thought. Of what value is one piece of land without all the rest? Individual lots are worthless. It is only when they are all put together into a great expanse, where game can roam, and birds can fly, and man can ride on a sleek pony, that it has true meaning.

But in spite of all this, George knew that the white man's way of life would prevail, while the way of the Indian would soon disappear from the land. George did not hate the white man, as did his brother Charlie. White men and Indians are alike in one way, George thought. Some are good, some are bad, but most are a mixture of both, and are only good or bad depending on your point of view.

Even his own family was a mixture of the two cultures, George mused. On the one hand was Charlie, who rode with the Dog Soldiers and who had become hateful and cruel towards all white men, while his sister, Mary, had married a white man, Robert Moore, who was now a judge in Denver. Another sister was the wife of Edmound Guerier, a half breed trader and trapper. And myself, George thought, where do I fit? Am I an Indian like Charlie, or do I belong to the white man's world, like Mary?

Perhaps, George mused, I should take Magpie to visit Mary in Denver, and try living like a white man for a little while.

When Bent returned to Black Kettle's camp he read Leavenworth's letter to the chief. Colonel Leavenworth was inviting the leaders of the Cheyenne, Arapahos, Kiowas, Commaches and Prairie Apaches to come to the Wichita village at the mouth of the Little Arkansas to discuss peace proposals.

Black Kettle, always anxious to make peace with the white men, decided he would go, and asked George Bent to accompany him. The trip was not without its dangers, however. To get to the Wichita, they had to travel through several villages of the Cheyenne's enemies, the Osages and the Sacs - Fox. Moreover, a band of Cheyenne had recently killed a Wichita brave in a skirmish between two hunting parties. But Black Kettle decided that it was worth the risk. The Wichita chief, Buffalo Goad, sent word that Black Kettle would not be harmed if he came to talk peace with Leavenworth.

So Black Kettle, his wife, George Bent and a few others set out for the Wichita camp. They rode boldly into their enemies' camps, announced who they were and where they were headed, and were greeted warmly at each site. The buffalo were plentiful along their route, and times seemed good.

At the Wichita village Black Kettle found chiefs from the Prairie Apache and Arapaho tribes, along with the Cheyenne agent, Major Wynkoop, and the Kansas Superintendent of Indian Affairs, Thomas Murphy. Wynkoop and Murphy told Black Kettle about the new peace commission, and their desire to meet with the five tribes of the Upper Arkansas to reach a new agreement that would bring peace to the plains.

Black Kettle and the other chiefs agreed to the meeting, and selected a spot on Medicine Lodge Creek for the affair. The grass was good there, water was plentiful, and the buffalo were thick. The chiefs left with a great feeling of optimism and returned to their respective tribes to prepare for the conference.

By mid September the tribes began to converge at Medicine Lodge. On September 17 Wynkoop and Murphy appeared with several wagon loads of supplies to sustain the troops and Indians during the pow-wow. By this time there were over 500 lodges of Indians assembled along the creek bed from the five tribes. The Arapaho alone had 170 tepees.

But there were only 25 tents of Cheyenne, with Black Kettle the principal chief. Tall Bull and the other Dog Soldiers were camped on the Cimarron, abut 20 miles away. They refused to come in to the conference, still incensed over the burning of their village by Hancock. Black Kettle told Wynkoop that the Dog Soldiers were still on the warpath, and that the supply wagons should be closely guarded. He also stated that the Cheyenne were in the middle of renewing their sacred Medicine Arrows, and that it would be eight more days before the rest of the tribe could come in.

That afternoon, however, Roman Nose and about 10 Dog Soldiers rode into camp to confer with Black Kettle. When Roman Nose saw Wynkoop, he became angry, and brandishing his weapons, threatened to kill him. He blamed Wynkoop for leading Hancock to their village.

Some of the Arapahos who were present saw Roman Nose's intention, and grabbed the reins of his horse to pull him back. Wynkoop wisely decided to make a hasty exit. Superintendent Murphy explained to Roman Nose that Wynkoop had not been responsible for what had happened at Pawnee Fork. He also tried to convince the Dog Soldiers to attend the peace conference. Roman Nose said they would watch the proceedings from afar, and decide later if they wanted to come or not.

Meanwhile the Commissioners and their entourage were on their way. They arrived at Fort Larned on the 11th and at Medicine Lodge on the 14th. They were escorted by 200 troops from the 7th Cavalry under the command of Major Elliot, who had assumed the post after the court martial of George Custer, along with some165 wagons and 1200 horses. Reporters from the East were also present, including Henry M. Stanley. In all, there were roughly 600 persons in the peace group, and around 5,000 Indians, squared off along the banks of the Medicine Lodge Creek.

The main goal of the peace group was to get the Indians out of the land north of the Little Arkansas, and the main goal of the Indians, especially the Cheyenne, was to reestablish their claim to that same land. The peace effort seemed doomed from the start.

On the evening of the 14th a large number of armed Cheyenne, headed by Tall Bull and Grey Head, rode into the camp. They met with General Harney, who told them the Great White Father was unhappy with Hancock for what he had done, and invited the chiefs to attend a hearing into Hancock's actions which was going to take place the next day.

In the morning rations were issued to all the tribes, and the Cheyenne were there in full regalia. Later the chiefs sat in on the hearings Harney was conducting. Late in the afternoon Tall Bull, Grey Beard and the Dog Soldiers went back to their camp on the Cimarron.

Several days later Tall Bull and Grey Beard returned to sit in on more of the hearings regarding Sand Creek, and Hancock's burning of the Cheyenne village at Pawnee Fork. General Harney was an outspoken critic of Hancock, and apologized to the Cheyenne for the way they had been treated. The chiefs finally agreed that Wynkoop was not responsible for what had happened to their village, but were still suspicious of any peace treaty that the white men might want the Cheyenne to sign. That evening they returned to their own village, taking Black Kettle with them. The Dog Soldiers wanted Black Kettle to explain to the rest of the tribe why the Cheyenne should sign a treaty with the whites, and threatened to kill all of his horses if he didn't come.

Black Kettle and Grey Bear returned on the 19th, in time for the first general council meeting with all the tribes. Black Kettle said very little, letting Grey Beard do most of the talking. The commissioners discussed at length the need for the Indians to settle on reservations south of the Little Arkansas, where the Government would build houses and schools for them. The Indians in turn said that they would keep their lands north of the Little Arkansas, and that they had no desire to have the Government build them any houses or schools. They did not plan to change their way of life.

However, on the 21st, the Comanche and Kiowa chiefs signed the new treaty, and received provisions – boxes of soap, beads, tin cups, butcher knives, revolvers and ammunition.

The Arapaho waited to see what the Cheyenne would do. Black Kettle told the council that the Cheyenne needed four more days to complete their religious ceremony before deciding whether they would sign or not. The commissioners reluctantly agreed to give the Cheyenne until Monday the 28th, but no longer.

On the 25th, the Prairie Apaches signed the treaty, and the camp settled into an uneasy wait for the decision from the Cheyenne. Tension mounted in the Commissioner's camp with each passing day. The Arapaho were nervous, and said they did not know what the unpredictable Dog Soldiers might do.

On Saturday one of the Cheyenne chiefs, Little Robe, rode into camp and said the rest of the tribe would be coming soon. He told the commissioners that they would be fully armed, and would probably fire their guns in the air, but that they would mean no harm. This did little to settle the growing tension that was building in the camp. On the next day a Cheyenne runner came into the camp and announced that the Dog Soldiers were on their way.

The word spread quickly. Arapaho and Kiowa braves mounted their horses and readied their weapons. Major Elliott put all the troops on alert, and everyone checked the status of their firearms.

General Harney remained calm, and told the commissioners to walk down to the river edge to greet the Dog Soldiers, displaying a show of confidence and authority. The delegation was nervous about being out in the open, but finally agreed to go along with him.

Then the Dog Soldiers were there, seen through the trees, racing their ponies towards the encampment, bodies painted and in full battle dress, chanting and yelling. They burst through the underbrush, and appeared on the shores of the river, now firing their guns in the air and shouting wildly.

General Harney kept his composure, telling the other commissioners that he had never known a Cheyenne to break his word. As the line of warriors came over the bank of the river, a bugle sounded from their ranks, and the first row of braves turned their ponies towards Harney in perfect military execution. The other rows of shouting Indians followed suit. Now they rode at a full gallop directly towards Harney and the commissioners. Four to five hundred warriors bore down on the small group, who nervously awaited them.

The Indians brought their ponies to a halt directly in front of the delegation, showering them in a cloud of dust. Black Kettle, Tall Bull, Grey Beard and other chiefs dismounted, and greeted their hosts with boisterous enthusiasm. The Cheyenne had just put on an impressive military performance, one that would make even the cavalry proud.

The next morning the commissioners and Cheyenne and Arapaho began their meetings. The Cheyenne came to the conference fully armed, and by their demeanor let it be known that they were the master of the plains, full of pride and dignity.

Buffalo Chief of the Cheyenne was their chosen spokesman. He told the commissioners that the Cheyenne had no intention of giving up their lands north of the Little

Arkansas. "You think you are doing a great deal for us by giving these presents to us, but we prefer to live as formerly. If you gave us all the gifts you could give, yet we would prefer our own life, to live as we have done. You give us presents and then take our land – that provokes war."

The meetings lasted all day, and broke up at sunset with little progress. Later Senator Hendrickson, who had been the chief architect of the peace plan, met with the chiefs to try to persuade them to accept the proposals. He told the chiefs that they would not be required to leave their hunting grounds while there were still buffalo to hunt. When the buffalo were all gone, then the Cheyenne could come south to live on the reservations allotted to them. Hendrickson may have believed the buffalo were already near extinction above the Arkansas, so in his mind the Cheyenne would be moving south immediately. But the Cheyenne felt that the buffalo would be there for many more moons, in spite of the wanton slaughter by the whites.

It seemed to the Cheyenne that the white men were agreeing with them that they could retain the lands above the Arkansas to hunt and live as they had always done. And so the next day the Cheyenne chiefs, along with their Arapaho brothers, signed the Treaty of Medicine Lodge, by which they gave up all claim to the lands in which they had always lived and hunted.

Many at the conference were convinced that the Indians didn't know what was in the treaty, believing only what they had been told. Henry M. Stanley reported that the chiefs had no idea what they were signing. Bull Bear and Buffalo Chief, even while they put their mark to the paper, said: 'We will hold that country between the Arkansas and the Platte together. We will not give it up yet, as long as the buffalo and elk are roaming through the country.' Major Elliot also filed a report to Washington that the Indians didn't understand what the treaty said.

The participants on both sides, however, left the conference believing that they had achieved their irreconcilable objectives.

CHAPTER 14

"Yup, there was a misunderstandin' all the way around at Medicine Lodge," Old Joe said. "But even so, for a while there it looked like peace had been obtained. There were no immediate problems between the settlers and the tribes, but the differences were still there, just waiting to explode. The Indians continued to roam the prairie, concerned that the railroads were being built across their land. And they were upset that they had not received the supply of guns and ammunition for hunting that they thought had been promised to them at Medicine Lodge. The settlers in turn were disturbed over the fact that the Cheyenne were still there, when they had supposedly agreed to stay south of the Arkansas."

"General Sheridan took over command of the Military District of Missouri from Hancock. But he wasn't much better in his outlook on the Indians. He met with Black Kettle and some of the other Cheyenne chiefs late in the spring." Old Joe chuckled to himself. "That was pretty much of a stand-off."

The pungent smoke filled the teepee and stung Wynkoop's eyes, causing them to water. He wiped his arm brusquely across his face, and then studied the others seated around the circle. To his right was General Philip Sheridan who was on a tour of all of the Indian camps. Sheridan

117

made no attempt to hide his hostility to the Cheyenne chiefs seated around him. He was particularly annoyed to find that Tall Bull, White Horse, and Bull Bear and a large number of braves had broken their winter camp at Fort Larned, and had ridden off to the Smoky Hill region to join with Roman Nose and his renegades.

Black Kettle spoke. "We felt that our White Father had reached out his hand to us at Medicine Lodge. The Cheyenne were happy, and took this hand in good faith, and have held it close to our heart. Many times we have listened to our white brother's promises, only to see the words disappear, like smoke in the wind. But this time we believed the Great White Father's words were straight, and we have done as he has said."

"This winter my people have made their camp here at Pawnee Fork, and we have been at peace with the troops at Fort Larned." Black Kettle didn't mention Roman Nose and the growing trouble with the Dog Soldiers. "The food which we were promised, however, has not been delivered. Our women and our children are hungry. Our braves are restless. Many of our people have ridden off to our old camping grounds to hunt for food. They have left in an angry mood at the broken promises of the White Father."

Sheridan muttered an oath under his breath and shifted his body in barely subdued irritation. Wynkoop was quick to respond to Black Kettle before Sheridan could speak.

"Black Kettle, my brother, you know that we have brought what food and goods we could during the winter months. Five or six times I have ridden here to bring you supplies from the fort. The reason there has not been more is that the Great Council in Washington is still debating the treaty signed last fall. Most of the white chiefs say that it is a good treaty, and should be accepted. But some few argue that it is not good, that the white man has promised too much to his Indian brothers. Until this debate ends, the

Great White Father cannot give us money to buy the food and clothing that was promised."

Stone Calf, who was every bit as belligerent as Sheridan, responded. "The white man also promised us guns and ammunition so that we can hunt the buffalo and obtain food on our own. Give us only this. Give us only the guns and we will look after our own needs."

Wynkoop stole a glance at Sheridan. This had been a burning issue between them. An issue, in fact, that was hotly contested at the highest levels of Government between the Indian Commissioner and the Department of the Army. Sheridan's face turned red with anger, but he knew well that the arms had been promised.

"Give them the arms," he finally thundered, "and if they go to war, my soldiers will kill them like men."

"If they wish to fight like men," Stone Calf retorted, "let your soldiers grow long hair so that we can have some honor in killing them."

Sheridan gave a harsh laugh. "Sorry, I can't do that," he responded, "If I did I fear that the long hair would become infested with lice." As he said these words he stared contentiously at Stone Calf's hair.

The council fell silent. Black Kettle and Wynkoop looked at each other in despair as the others sat in a smoldering rage.

"Our white brothers are pulling away from us the hand they offered at Medicine Lodge," Black Kettle finally said, "but we will try to hold on to it. We were promised guns and ammunition for our buffalo hunts. If you will but give us these we would not need other presents from the Great White Father to keep our people happy and fed."

"I will do everything I can to get you these guns," Wynkoop replied, not looking at Sheridan as he spoke.

When the council broke up Sheridan rode away from camp, his demeanor stiff and unbending, convinced that the Indians were up to no good.

Several days later Wynkoop was able to send a limited supply of arms to the tribe, but they were mostly outdated. After they had been dispersed, Black Kettle and George Bent rode into the fort to talk with Wynkoop.

"There will be trouble this summer," Black Kettle said. "The Dog Soldiers and many Cheyenne are in an angry mood. The people who stay with me, however, want to avoid trouble. We will move tomorrow far to the South, to the banks of the Washita, where we will be away from the troops of the Army."

Wynkoop nodded. It was the best thing. "Are you going with Black Kettle, George?" he asked.

"Only as far as the Arkansas. Magpie and I are going to Colorado to visit my sister Mary. I'm not sure when we will join the tribe again."

Wynkoop nodded again. George Bent and the old chief avoided looking into each other's eyes. Both knew George would likely never rejoin the tribe, opting to live in Denver as a white man.

"Let's see," I said, "this was taking place in the spring of 1868 wasn't it? Just a year before the massacre of the settlers in Lincoln County?"

"Yup," Old Joe replied, "That's just about the time table."

"Didn't I see something on that Kansas Historical Marker just east of town about some depredations about this time?" I consulted my notes. "Here it is. 'In 1868 three women who had been captured and maltreated by marauding Indians were found several days later half dead on the prairie.' Do you know anything about that?"

"Sure do. That was Mrs. Bacon, Mrs. Shaw and Shaw's sister, Miss Foster. The marker doesn't say anything about those that were killed, though. Or about the two children."

Trouble had been brewing all spring, and came to a head the following summer when a war party of 200 Cheyenne set out for a raid on their traditional enemies, the Pawnee. They insisted that there was no threat to the white men in the area, but the young braves were full of fight, and incensed over the lack of guns and supplies that had been promised them. On August 10, 1868, a group of about 30 warriors were fired on when they approached a settlement in the Spillman Creek area, which increased their hostility and resentment.

Simmering with rage, they came upon the home of a settler named Bacon and his wife, Janie, who was 27 years old, and their two year old baby. The Bacons, hearing the Indians coming, fled from their home, seeking shelter in the woods. Mr. Bacon, although in his bare feet, was able to make it and hid out in a hollow log. His wife, however, was not so fortunate, maybe because she was carrying their baby. She was overtaken and felled with a blow to the head.

She was repeatedly raped by the Indians, even though she was seriously wounded. When the braves finished with her, they placed her on a horse along with the baby and rode off. Later in the day they spotted soldiers riding over the hills. Although the detachment was unaware of the atrocity committed by the Indians and in fact were unaware of the presence of the group, the Indians were afraid the captives might slow them down if they were chased, so Mrs. Bacon and her child were abandoned on the prairie.

Mr. Bacon stayed hidden until dark, and then proceeded barefoot to the home of Mart Hendrickson, where he alerted the settlers to the presence of the Indians.

Meanwhile the main contingent of Dog Soldiers descended on the home of Simeon Shaw who lived with his wife and her sixteen year old sister, Miss Foster, just a few miles north of what is now Denmark, Kansas. The Indians came early in the morning, and spent the entire day mulling around the cabin and surrounding area. They were surly, and soon began taking things from the Shaw home. Mr. Shaw was helpless to stop them.

Late in the afternoon the party of Indians that had abandoned Mrs. Bacon and her baby on the prairie returned and took her and the baby into captivity once again. They returned to the Shaw home, and although Mrs. Bacon was still in a daze from her head wound, continued to violate her.

When darkness came, and the Indians showed no sign of leaving, Shaw decided he and his wife and sister-in-law should try to get away. They were able to obtain three horses, and took off at a gallop. However, 30 or 40 braves took after them, yelling and shouting. They overtook the three, and one of the braves smashed a war club into Shaw's head. He fell from his horse, seriously wounded. The Indians pulled Mrs. Shaw and Miss Foster from their horses, tore off their clothing, and repeatedly raped them.

The next day they placed the three women, with Mrs. Bacon clutching her baby, on horses and turned them loose on the prairie. Mrs. Bacon hardly knew what was happening, and repeatedly fell off her horse trying to hold on to her baby. Eventually the other two decided it would be best to leave Mrs. Bacon and ride on to find help.

Not many miles away Thomas Alderdice headed out to look at some land to the north and west of his and Susanna's homestead. The property had been abandoned by a settler who had pulled up stakes the week before due to the Indian scare. It was a beautiful August day in 1868, and the heat of the previous few weeks had abated slightly.

Thomas had been out of the Army for several years now. He never mentioned his prior service with the Confederacy to anyone other than his close family. On this particular summer afternoon he figured that things were going along just about perfect. He and Susanna had gotten married shortly after he first met her and had a young baby boy of their own, in addition to his two step sons from Susanna's previous marriage. It was a family in which Thomas felt a great deal of pride. Susanna was a wonderful wife, and they were very much in love. Still, the dark cloud of Indian trouble always hung over them – something they could never completely forget or ignore.

As Thomas rounded the crest of a rolling hill, he saw a rider coming his way, coming at a full gallop. Something wrong, judging by the looks of that fellow, Thomas said to himself. When the man drew nearer, Thomas recognized Phil Lantz, who lived on the other side of Spillman Creek.

"Thomas – am I glad to see you," Phil gasped as he reared his horse to a stop. "I was comin' to warn you. Indians been sighted over your way. They got the war paint on – probably Cheyenne. Took three women captives already. Mrs. Shaw and her sister, single lady named Foster. And they got old man Bacon's wife, too, along with her baby."

Thomas's heart sank. He had left Susanna and the children at home alone. "Oh dear God," was all he could say.

"All the families are gathering at Hendrickson's house, just like we planned in case of trouble. Better get Susanna and the kids and get over there pronto. I got to get over to the Erhardt place to warn them." Lantz turned his horse around and was off at a gallop.

Thomas felt fear like he had never known in his life as he raced back to his home and Susanna. Oh dear God

– please- please- he muttered over and over, as he sped back along the trail. As he neared their cabin he slowed to a walk, and then stopped altogether. Partially hidden by cottonwood trees surrounding the clearing, he surveyed the scene before him. There was no sign of life.

He waited a few minutes more, studying the farm and surrounding area. A dozen crows were in a tree on the south side of the cabin, squawking noisily. Finally Thomas proceeded down the hill into the clearing. It became obvious there was no one there. The front door of their home was open. Thomas rushed in, calling for Susanna, but there was no response. Everything looked in order, except for a cake that had been dropped on the floor. Thomas examined it. It had been freshly cooked. He checked the oven, which was still warm to the touch.

He rushed back outside, calling for Susanna over and over. Where was she? Had she been captured by the Indians? Was she hiding in the creek bed with the children? Thomas criss-crossed the property looking for any sign that might tell him what had happened, but he could find nothing. They only had the one horse that John was riding, so she had no way of going anywhere except on foot

Not knowing what else to do, Thomas mounted his horse and turned towards the Hendrickson place. As he approached the home he saw several men milling around outside. He recognized Fred Erhardt, Mart Hendrickson, and Phil Lantz, who had brought him the warning. Also John Strange. They were huddled around another man who was bandaged and badly bruised. Old man Shaw. As he dismounted from his horse, he spotted his brother-in-law, John Alverson, coming out of the cabin. Thomas called to him. John, seeing his brother-in-law, rushed over.

"Thomas – am I glad to see you," John said. "We were getting pretty worried about you. Have you seen any Indians?"

"Susanna – is Susanna here?" Thomas asked, his voice quivering with anxiety.

"She's here – she's safe," John replied. "She's inside with the rest of the women. And all the children. I went by your place with the wagon when I heard there were Indians in the vicinity. You weren't there, so I brought Susanna and the boys and baby here with me. Mary and my children were already headed over this way."

"Thank God – thank God" was all Thomas could say, as he ran inside the house to embrace his wife.

Later Mart Hendrickson filled Thomas in on the Indian problem that had brought all of them together. "The Indians raided Shaw's house," he related. "Raped his wife and her sister, Miss Foster, and then rode off with them. Shaw was pretty badly beaten up, but managed to get down here later that night.. They also hit Bacon's place. Raped his wife, too, and made off with her and her baby."

"Everyone gathered here just like we planned. Then I got one of those visions I sometimes get. I knew the three women were out there, alone on the prairie, so I went looking for them. I found the Shaw and Foster women first, and brought them back here, then went looking for Mrs. Bacon. When I found her, she was wandering senseless and naked on the prairie, still clutching her child. I brought her back too. Don't know why the Indians turned them loose. Maybe because they thought the Army was hot on their tail."

The Indians stayed in the vicinity, eluding the cavalry that was now trying to track them down. Two days after their assault on the Bell and Shaw homes, 50 Dog Soldiers descended on a home near the present community of Beloit, shared by two families; David Bogardus and his wife Hester, and Hester's brother, Braxton Bell and his wife, Elizabeth. There were two men, two women and five children in total. The Bogardus's had two boys, aged 7 and 8 years old, and the Bells had a 9 month old baby. They also had two other children staying with them, Esther and Margaret, the daughters of Aaron Bell, brother of Hester and Braxton. They were six and eight years old.

The Indians appeared to be friendly, and the women prepared a meal for some of them. However, when Elizabeth served coffee to the Indians in a tin cup, they became angry and threw it in her face. They didn't like eating or drinking out of anything metal.

The Dog Soldiers now became belligerent, and forced the two men, David Bogardus and Braxton Bell outside, and made them run around the house while beating them as they ran. Then they shot both men. As they got ready to leave, the Indians decided to take Elizabeth Bell and her baby captive, but every time they put her on a horse, she jumped off. Finally they shot her, and speared the baby in the neck. Then they took the two smaller children who were visiting their aunt and uncle, and rode off, leaving Hester Bogardus and her two sons unharmed.

Later Captain Benteen and his troops found the trail of the Indians. Realizing they were being followed, the Indians abandoned the two little girls on the prairie. Benteen was not able to catch up with the Indians, and was unaware of the children left alone on the windy plains without food or water.

I reached down to the knap sack I had brought with me and pulled out a bottle of Avrian water. I guess thinking about the children being out on the prairie without anything to drink made me thirsty. After taking a few swallows I offered it to Old Joe.

"No thanks, Sonny," he said. "I never drink anything from a bottle. Only what falls fresh from the sky."

I gave him a sharp look to see if he was laughing, but he seemed totally absorbed in cleaning the tobacco out of his pipe. "From what I know about Kansas summers," I replied, "a body

*could get pretty dried out between showers if that was all he had
to quench the old thirst buds."*

*"Yup. Mighty dried out," he said, still concentrating on his
pipe.*

*I decided Old Joe liked to pull my leg with that dry sense of
humor of his, and I was just too dense to realize it.*

*"Remember I mentioned those visions that Mart Hendrickson
used to get?" Old Joe said. "How he seemed to know that those
three women who were captured and then abandoned by the
Indians were wanderin' out there on the plains, abused and
bedraggled? Well, he had another one of those peculiar insights a
few days later."*

The settlers and their families remained at the
Hendrickson place for several days after the rescue of the
Shaw, Bacon and Foster women, with no sign of Indians.
The men were getting restless and wanted to go out on
scouting parties, but the women strenuously objected.

One day while they were eating their noon meal, Mart
Hendrickson began to stir in his chair. Where he had been
eating vigorously a moment ago, he now aimlessly pushed
the food around on his plate with his fork, staring at it with
unseeing eyes.

John Alverson noticed the change that had come over
his friend. "What's the matter, Mart? You look like you just
saw a ghost."

"Maybe I have," Mart replied. "A ghost whispering in
my ear."

Then he looked up and announced in a loud voice,
"Someone out there needs our help. I've got to go find out
who it is."

Everyone stopped what they were doing and looked at
Mart. No one questioned him, for Mart was known to have
visions that were amazingly accurate. And just a few days
earlier he had demonstrated his amazing powers by sensing

the distress of the three women left on the prairie, and riding out and finding them. If he said someone was in need of help, it was probably so.

"Well, if you're a mind to go looking for trouble, guess I'll be going along with you," Fred Erhardt stated.

"Count me in" Tom Alderdice and John Alverson chimed in unison.

"No," Mart replied. "Fred and I will go, the rest of you better stay close to the women till we know the Indians are gone for sure. Anyway, I don't sense any kind of danger, except to those that need our help."

Mart and Fred saddled up and headed out.

"Which way?" Fred asked.

"I think we need to head over to the Spillman," Mart replied.

They rode for several hours with no sign of Indians anywhere. Then, coming over a hill, they saw an old abandoned house near the creek.

"I think I saw something move by that house," Mart stated.

Fred pulled his Colt revolver from his waistband, but Mart rode boldly on to the cabin. There they found two small girls, aged six and eight, dirty and haggard and in tattered dresses.

The older of the girls looked at Mart and said without emotion, "Do you have any bread? We haven't had anything to eat for two days."

Mart dismounted and dug some food out of his saddlebag, which he fed to the two ravenous children.

"The Indians got us," the older of the two told the two men. "Then they were afraid the soldiers were going to catch them, so they turned us loose. We have been waiting for someone to come."

Fred and Mart took the two Bell girls back to Mart's home.

"These events made a big impression on John Alverson and Thomas Alderdice," Old Joe remarked. "What feelings they might have felt for the Native Americans before was now completely gone. Like most of the other settlers in the area, they felt there was only one solution to the Indian troubles. The same solution that was shared by many of the bigwigs back east, including General Sherman."

Old Joe looked off into the distance, like he was seeing something in the fields of corn. "I think the way Sherman put it was somethin' like this, and I'm quoting him direct, 'My opinion is, if fifty Indians are allowed to remain between the Arkansas and the Platte, we will have to guard every stage station, every train, and all railroad working parties. In other words, fifty hostile Indians will check-mate three thousand soldiers. Rather get them out as soon as possible, and it makes little difference whether they be coaxed out by Indian commissioners or killed.'"

"That was pretty much the sentiment of the people in Lincoln County. They were riled up. And before the month was over they got their chance to hunt down the Indians involved in this raid and, as General Sherman recommended, either kill them or drive them out of the country for good. Ever hear of Forsythe's Scouts?" he asked.

"You bet," I replied. "Anyone interested in frontier history knows about them, and the battle at Beecher's Island. Was Thomas Alderdice part of that group?"

"Yup. Him and his brother-in-law, Eli Ziegler. They got a little more than they bargained for in that little expedition, though."

CHAPTER 15

I was anxious to hear all about Tom Alderdice and Eli and the Forsythe Scouts. That was a major event in the history of the west. But I was also curious about what had happened back in Germany.

"What about that German couple you were telling me about?" I asked. "George and Maria. They must have gotten out of Hanover without any trouble. Did they come directly to Kansas?"

"Not directly," Old Joe replied. "They ended up going to Bern, Switzerland. But George was pretty restless. He kept hearing about the wonders of the west. The thought of a new land and new opportunities was gettin' under his skin."

Maria stood in front of the mirror and surveyed herself with an appraising eye. All in all, she thought, the year and a half of marriage to George and living here in Switzerland had agreed with her. Her dark hair had a rich sheen to it that went well with the pink color in her cheeks and the red of her lips. Her eyes had a twinkle that reflected her vitality, and her figure, now displayed to good advantage by a new purple and white lace gown, drew an appropriate number of admiring glances whenever she appeared in public.

It had been a happy eighteen months, although she sensed restlessness on the part of her husband. They were married in February, 1867, and moved to Bern. George had invested in a new brewery with the profits from the sale of the one in Germany. Fred Meigerhoff had come with them and helped to manage their business. They had prospered, but George was not altogether happy.

As for Maria, she enjoyed living in the city – the music festivals, the grand balls in the winter, ice skating in the heart of the city. Perhaps George would be less discontent once she had given him a son, but so far their union had not been blessed with a child. Maria thought that maybe she should see a doctor.

But tonight – tonight was for fun and dancing. She surveyed herself one last time as she heard George bounding up the stairs, and then gave a happy twirl for his approval as he entered the room.

"Ah my little flower, you look wonderful," he exclaimed. "Have I not told you that yet today? So beautiful that I fear I cannot allow you to be seen in public because it would surely create a riot."

Maria laughed and pressed into his waiting arms. "And you, my lover," she said, "you would not protect me from this riot? What is a poor girl to do?" The ardent kiss that followed indicated that George knew exactly what the poor girl should do, but Maria broke away.

"Now George, we must remember Herr Gamble's party. What would people say if I were to appear in a gown that was all wrinkled and crushed?"

"I have a simple solution for that. Let's just stay home and have our own party – and we won't worry about what gets wrinkled and crushed. Ah well – that's what I get for marrying such a young girl. Come on, if we must, or we will miss the whole affair."

Hand in hand the lovers went down the stairs to the waiting carriage.

As Maria and George entered the ballroom Maria spotted their good friends Helena and Werner Gottch, who were also originally from Hanover. The orchestra stopped playing for a short intermission, and all of the guests milled about in animated conversation

."Maria – oh how pretty you look," greeted Helena. "We were afraid you weren't going to show up. And George – how very handsome." Laughing, Helena gave George a peck on the cheek, much to his red-faced embarrassment.

Greetings had hardly been exchanged before Helena was dragging Maria off to meet some new friends who had just arrived from Germany.

"Well, George," Werner asked, "How are all of your business affairs going? Well, I hope,"

"Yes, yes – everything is well," George replied. Then after a moment, added, "What do you hear from your friends who have moved to America?"

"Most of them have settled in a place called Pennsylvania, and they seem very happy with their move. Seems that quite a few of our countrymen are living in their community so they feel right at home."

"Pennsylvania – yes I hear that the land is good there. But pretty well settled, too, I understand. Now if it were me going to the new land, I would go further west – to a place called Kansas. They tell me there are miles and miles of open prairie there just waiting to be farmed. And the Homestead Act that their government has passed makes it easy to obtain land. They encourage you to claim it."

"Bosh! You can have your Kansas," Werner replied. "From what I hear it is nothing but a region of savages and whirling dust that couldn't grow anything but a few blades of meager buffalo grass."

"Yes, that is what most people think," George laughed. "And perhaps it is partially true. But I wager that a scientific farmer could make a pretty good life there. With my experience in growing hops for my brewery, I think I could do well. And I dare say that most of the homesteaders that are going there and filing claims aren't farmers, and they are not going to be successful. Their land will probably be up for grabs within a year or two. I have been in touch with a German who has moved there, a Fred Erhardt, who tells me that the land is very fertile where he lives."

"Well, you may be right. It sort of gives a man an itch just to think about it."

"It certainly does," George replied, somewhat wistfully.

Later that night Maria awoke to find George gone from their bed. She sat up to see him standing by the window gazing out in the cool night.

"George, what is it? Why are you not in bed?"

"Nothing – nothing is wrong, my love. It is only that I cannot sleep. And I have been thinking."

"Thinking? Thinking of what?"

"Oh nothing – and everything. About our future."

Maria felt a tremor start in her chest and spread slowly throughout her body. She remembered the night in Hanover two years previously when George had proclaimed his intention to go off to fight the Prussians. She sensed another major decision was near – one equally as important as the one that had driven them from their homeland. She tightened her grip on the bed covers as she waited for George to continue.

"Maria, I know that you have been happy here," he finally said, "and would be happy to live here for the rest of our lives. But this is not a life for me. It is too staid – too settled. I do not think that I am meant to be a merchant living in the middle of a city."

"Oh, George – I know you have not been content here. You know that I will gladly go wherever you want and do whatever you want, but you really haven't given this new life here a fair chance."

George walked across the room and sat down on the edge of the bed, taking hold of Maria's hand.

"Maria – I have a plan that has been playing in my head for many months now. I try to put such thoughts away, but they keep coming back. Maria – how would you like to go to America?"

"America? The United States? So far from here?" Maria turned pale, shocked at what she had just heard. Whatever she might have been expecting, it wasn't this.

"Oh my dearest – listen to me. America is a new country where a man with ambition can do anything or be anything. There are vast areas of land just waiting for someone to tame them. I can be that someone, Maria. We can go to America – to the western plains to the place they call Kansas – and we can start up a brand new colony for German immigrants. There are dozens of Germans right here in Bern who are wanting to go to the new country. I have talked with many of them – and they are looking for someone to go ahead of them – to investigate the land and find a suitable place. Oh Maria – we can be the vanguard of an entire new community in the new world."

Maria was silent for a moment. She was having difficulty in grasping the significance of what George was saying. America? A new colony?

"But, George, the Indians," she said. "I hear such stories of the savages and the horrible things they do to the settlers. Surely we would not go to such a wild, uninhabited place?"

George laughed. "Oh my dear, if that is your only worry, do not fear. The Indian problem has been settled. The Indians signed a treaty at a place called Medicine Lodge over a year ago, and agreed to move south to a land set aside for them, and not to bother the settlers anymore. Oh, I admit, there are still some stories of troubles here and there, but these are being worked out. And I promise – I will take extra care to make sure that no savage will be allowed to frighten my little one."

Maria giggled, although she could not keep her heart from pounding at the prospect George held out for them. America – Kansas – could such a thing be? What would it be like? And what would their fortune be in such a remote place – so far from anything she had ever known? But did it matter? If George wanted to go to the new world, she would follow as a faithful wife should. And she would never complain if things were hard and the life uncertain.

For the past 30 minutes I had been watching the clouds build up in the west. At first they were white and billowy, but now they were turning into an ominous dark color that covered the entire sky. As I studied their progress, a large rain drop hit on the porch with a loud splat. Then a second followed, landing on Old Joe's rocking chair.

He scrutinized the heavens. "I reckon you'd best be heading out of here, Sonny. These Kansas storms can be pretty wicked this time of year. And when that driveway gets muddy, it's dang near impassable."

I didn't need a whole lot of urging. The drops were starting to fall closer together and with greater frequency. "Joe, can I come back tomorrow?" I asked, as I gathered up my notes.

"I'll be here," he replied.

I made a dash for the car as the rain started to come down in earnest. As I drove out of the drive I looked back. Old Joe was still sitting in his chair, staring at the clouds. The house looked forbidding against the sober background of dark skies. Old Joe couldn't possibly be living in that old wreck, I thought to myself. First thing tomorrow I intend to ask him about that. But tomorrow turned out to be longer than I thought.

CHAPTER 16

It was three days before the dirt road into the house dried up enough to drive in. There were no new ruts, so I knew Old Joe hadn't been in or out with any kind of vehicle. When I pulled into the yard, Old Joe was nowhere to be seen. I parked, got out of the car, and walked onto the porch. I hadn't really noticed before, but the front door was off its hinges, just propped up in the doorway. I peered in through a window, and saw what I had suspected. There wasn't a speck of furniture inside. Nothing but dust and cobwebs, except for one corner where it looked like the rain had seeped in through the wall.

I was about to go around to the back when I saw Old Joe coming out of the corn field just to the east of where the creek ran. He waved, and I waved back, watching him stride up to the porch. He moves pretty spry for an old man, I thought.

He climbed the steps and sat down in the old rocker, pulled out his pipe, and filled it with Prince Albert.

"For a bit there I didn't think you were around." I said. "Been over to a neighbor's house?"

"Oh, no. Just inspecting a place down there on the creek where the brush hangs over the water. Kind of a special place, if you know what I mean. Got some memories attached to it."

"You don't really live here, do you, Joe?" I asked.

"Well now, I never claimed I did nor said I didn't," he replied, as he lit the tobacco in the pipe. "Why do you ask?"

"I guess since this is where we always met I just assumed this was where you lived. But now that I've looked inside, it's plain to see that no one has been living here for quite some time. In fact I wouldn't be surprised if this whole building just collapsed any day now."

"This old place and me have a lot in common," Joe observed. "We're both a little on the dilapidated side, but we've both seen a lot in our time. Why this old house probably has more stories to tell than I do."

We sat in silence for a while, Old Joe rocking back forth in his chair. It was obvious that he wasn't going to enlighten me any about where he lived. Finally he seemed to come back to the present, and asked. "Now where were we in talkin' about that there massacre of yours?"

I snorted at the question. "I don't recall that we've talked about the massacre," I replied. "Only about all the things you say led up to it. Let's see – first of all the Sand Creek attack, then General Hancock burning the Dog Soldier village at Pawnee Fork. I know all about Black Kettle, Roman Nose and Tall Bull. But we've hardly discussed the settlers."

"Well now as I recall I told you about Thomas Alderdice coming out west with the Army, then marrying the widow Susanna Daily. She was a Ziegler. They were a pretty big family. Her younger sister, Mary, latched on to John Alverson, who was a really early pioneer. Her brother, Eli, played a large part in the affairs of those days. Then there's the Germans – George and Maria Weichel. I told you about them."

"And I think I described some of the events that happened right here in Lincoln County that were just about as bad as your massacre, even though they happened a year earlier. The settlers involved might have said it was a massacre. Several killed, and three women left out on the prairie after being mistreated by the Indians, and the two children who were taken captive and

then abandoned. Those things really stirred up the anger in the community."

"You mentioned Forsythe's Scouts. Were they related to any of these things?"

"Yes, sir. Directly related. These depredations had the local citizens ready to wipe the Indians off the face of the earth. Or at least off the plains of Kansas and Colorado." The far-away look came into Old Joe's eyes once again as he began to talk.

In the raids during the summer of 1868, 15 settlers in Kansas were killed by the Cheyenne and a few Arapaho who had joined with them. General Sherman announced that these raids amounted to a declaration of war by the Indians, and vowed to destroy the marauders and drive them well below the Kansas line.

But he realized that the Army simply didn't have enough men to chase after Indians while trying to protect the increasing number of settlers, the workers building the new railroad, and stage coaches and wagon trains headed west. Custer had proved that the regular Army was inadequate in hunting down and punishing marauding bands of Indians. A new approach was needed.

It was then that Sherman hit on the idea of raising a small volunteer force of frontiersmen who could move swiftly, live off the land, and knew the ways of the Indians. A small group of scouts such as this – 50 in number – if they were unencumbered with wagons and field artillery - could track down raiding war parties and deal them a severe blow where the regular Army had failed.

This plan was greeted with a great deal of enthusiasm in Lincoln County, Kansas, where the settlers were still in a rage over the recent Indian attacks.

"Heck, John, I don't see why you won't sign up with Tom and me and chase the Redskins out of Kansas once and for all," Eli said. Eli Ziegler had grown into a strapping young man now 16 years of age.

Eli, Thomas Alderdice and John Alverson were sitting around a wooden table in Thomas's cabin. Thomas's step son, John, five years old, was leaning on the table listening with rapt attention to the men talking about fighting Indians.

Mary Alverson and Susanna Alderdice were busy baking apple pies, half listening to the men and half engaged in their own conversation. Susanna's other son by her former marriage, Willis, a four year old, was playing with Thomas's and Susanna's newest baby now one year old, and just beginning to learn to walk.

"Well," John Alverson replied to Eli, "guess I've been hunting and trapping too long on my own to be wanting to join up with the Army again. I did my share with the 17th Kansas Volunteers four years ago. That's just about enough for me."

"But it's not the regular Army," Eli countered. "This is a special bunch of volunteer scouts made up of people who live out here, guys like you and Tom and me. Heck, John, you're just the kinda guy that oughta sign up, seeing as how you know the Indians and country so well. And there's only going to be 50 of us. All experienced frontiersmen – trappers and farmers who know how to travel light and can forage for grub on our own."

John smiled. "I just don't cotton to taking orders from some Army Lieutenant who's probably not dry behind the ears, and never saw an Indian in his life. Shucks, Thomas, you've been in the Army before. You know what it's like."

"There's only going to be three regular Army men," Thomas replied. "Colonel Forsythe will be in charge. He's been proven under fire at Shenandoah Valley from what I hear. Men all seem to like him. Call him "Sandy" in informal settings. And Lt. Beecher's been in most every battle the Union's fought in. Got wounded at Gettysburg. Left him with a limp. And if you can believe it, the Sergeant is a fellow name of McCall, who was a doggoned general in the war. Sounds like a pretty savvy group to me." Thomas made no mention of the fact that he had fought on the opposite side of these gentlemen in the Great War.

"Well, you two go ahead, and I wish you all the luck in the world. But I think I'll just stay close to home and look after the women," John replied, and turning to study the pastries that were now cooling by the stove, "and keep testing these here pies to make sure the women don't lose their touch while you're gone."

"You are the only one here with any sense," Susanna chimed in, more harshly than she intended. "I don't see why Thomas has to go charging off to do the Army's job. I already lost one husband to the Army – I don't want to lose another. Why not let the regular Army do it?"

"Well, you know the Army's undermanned and too darn slow and cumbersome to catch any Indians," Eli told his sister. "Old Custer proved that last summer."

Mary put her arm around her big sister. "Don't worry, Susanna. John and I will watch out for you. Anyway, this bunch of galoots probably won't be any more successful in finding Indians than Custer was."

Susanna forced a smile, and after dabbing at her eyes, said "Oh, I know. I shouldn't worry. It's just that I hate being left alone with the children. And I can't help worrying." Rubbing her swollen belly, she added," Guess I'm just a little over- emotional right now with the baby coming on."

Susanna couldn't help remembering that she had been pregnant with her second child when her first husband had ridden off with the Army and never came back. Now she was pregnant with her second child with Thomas, and here he was volunteering to head off to the Army, just as James had done.

Thomas guessed what she was thinking. He got up from the table, went to her side, and gave her a quick kiss on the cheek. "You know why I am doing this," he said. "I just can't stand the thought of anything happening to you or the children. This last raid and what happened to those three women has made me realize that none of us are ever going to be safe till we drive those devils out of the country."

Nobody spoke for a moment, then Eli said, "Well, I guess old John's got it right on one account anyway. How about us testing some of that apple pie we been smelling for the last hour?"

Susanna wiped away her tears and gave her brother a grateful smile. "It's nice to know someone around here appreciates our cooking skills," she said. She and Mary cut several slices of warm pie for their men-folk, and poured fresh coffee from the stove.

"By the way, Eli," John mumbled between bites, "just what are you going to use as a horse on this Indian chase?"

"The Army is furnishing mounts for anyone that needs them," Thomas answered. "You get paid $75.00 a month if you provide your own horse, or $50.00 if the Army gives you one to use. You've got to admit, that's pretty good wages."

John did some quick arithmetic. "That means the Army thinks you boys are worth twice as much as a horse." With a wink at the women he added, "I guess that's just about right for a bunch of idiots that don't have any more sense than to go chasing across the hills looking for trouble. But just make sure you live to collect them wages. Watch your backs. I know those tricky devils, and I don't go along with the thought some have that 50 well armed men could take on 200 savages and beat them."

The group of volunteers assembled for this task was known alternately as the Solomon Avengers – avenging the Indian raids on the Solomon and Saline Rivers over the past several months – and as Forsythe's Scouts. Major George A. (Sandy) Forsyth was chosen by General Sheridan to raise this militia and lead them after the Cheyenne raiding parties. Forsyth had ridden with Sheridan in the Shenandoah Valley campaign, and had requested this assignment. Lt. Beecher, nephew of the famous clergyman Henry Ward Beecher, had also distinguished himself in the Civil War at Fredericksburg and Gettysburg. W. H. H. McCall, a brevet brigadier general during the War, won acclaim in the battle of Petersburg. He drifted west after the war, and now signed on as Sergeant of the group.

Twenty-three of the volunteers, almost half the group, were from the Saline Valley, where feelings still ran high over the ravages of the Bell, Shaw and Bacon families.

The scouts were outfitted at Fort Hays. Each man was given a Spencer rifle with 140 rounds of ammunition and a Colt revolver with 30 rounds. Additional ammunition, equipment and medical supplies were loaded onto four pack mules.

On August 29, 1868, Forsyth's Scouts set forth on their search for Cheyenne war parties. Counting the officers, there were 53 men, composed of hunters, trappers, and farmers, many of them veterans of the Civil War. They were an undisciplined, hard bitten, independent group of men, but they all shared a common desire to clear the renegade Indians from the western prairie.

Eight days later they rode into Fort Wallace near the Kansas-Colorado border without having seen any sign of Indians. Here another scout joined the group, and they replaced a couple of the volunteers who felt they had had enough, and replenished their supplies. On September 9, they headed out once again, this time in response to a report that a large Indian war party had struck a wagon train just three miles to the east. Four men had been killed, and a large number of horses driven off. Each of the scouts was issued rations for a seven day march.

For several days they had little luck in picking up sign of the Indians, but on the fifth they found tracks heading for the Arickaree Fork of the Republican River. Forsythe followed this trail, which increasingly grew wider as a large number of Sioux and other smaller groups of Cheyenne and Arapahoe joined the caravan.

As the days went by, Forsythe estimated that the 50 volunteers were on the trail of around 1,000 Indians. This would mean anywhere from 200 to 400 fighting braves.

Running low on supplies, and increasingly fearful of the size of the Indian party they were following, several of the party petitioned Forsyth to return to Fort Wallace. But Forsyth was determined to fight the Indians, and would not hear of turning back just when they had been located.

Eli didn't know which he hated the most; the merciless heat beating down from above, the choking dust from riding at the rear of the column, his tired and aching muscles that cried out from days in the saddle, or the elusive Indians that they could never quite find. He decided that it really didn't matter, and rattled off a three minute string of expletives at the whole world in general, every word spoken with great vehemence. It didn't seem to make him feel any better.

"What's the matter, Eli?" Thomas said. "Sorry you signed up?"

"Just anxious for a little more action and a little less riding. Didn't know I was volunteering to ride this darn horse all across creation."

"Well, I reckon we'll be getting our fill of action soon enough. Signs indicate that we've stumbled across a pretty sizable raiding party. Maybe more than we bargained for. But that Forsythe is a determined one. I'll say this for him, though. He doesn't ask anyone to do anything he's not willing to do himself. And he cares about his men. Reckon he's a good one to go into battle with."

"Yeah, and Beecher seems like a decent guy," Eli responded. "I hear he got that limp of his at Gettysburg. Guess that must have been some fight."

"Over there is a man to get friendly with, in case you ever have a need for him," Thomas pointed to a distinguished looking man riding beside Forsythe. "Doc Mooers, one of the best there is this side of the Mississippi. Lives in Hays City now. He's the company surgeon for this expedition."

"And the fellow riding up to Forsythe right now. That's Sharp Grover, one of the best scouts the Army ever set eyes on. Knows the territory, and knows the Cheyenne, too."

"Guess we got us a pretty savvy bunch of men," Eli said. "Just hope they don't go and get us all killed."

Roman Nose, Tall Bull, White Horse, Bull Bear and Ice Bear, along with several other Cheyenne, rode into the Sioux camp at dusk. Already numerous fires had been lit throughout the village in preparation for a big feast for their Cheyenne brothers. The camp was alive with activity - women chatting excitedly around the cooking fires, children and dogs racing between the tepees, and the men gathered in groups discussing the day's events.

The Cheyenne were greeted by Pawneee Killer, Bad Yellow Eyes, and Two Strikes, chiefs of the Sioux lodges. "Welcome my friends," Two Strikes greeted them with a raised hand. "We are happy that you can join us. There is much food, and afterwards there will be much dancing."

"We are pleased that our Sioux brothers have asked us to eat with them," Tall Bull replied. "The Cheyenne and Sioux have always been as one. May it be so forever."

The Cheyenne dismounted, and several Sioux led off their horses.

"Before we eat, there is a thing that we must discuss." Bad Yellow Eyes motioned to the visitors to have a seat around the fire in the center of the camp. When they were settled he continued, "Some of my people have sighted a troop of white men searching for your trail. My scouts are watching them now. The White Eyes are following the signs of your war party that attacked the wagon train several moons ago. Soon they will find the path left when your village moved to the waters of the Republican."

"How many of the white men?" Roman Nose inquired.

"My scouts report there are about 50 men. They are not dressed in the clothing of the cavalry. They appear as trappers and hunters, but they ride as soldiers. Also there are no wagons, so they move swiftly."

Roman Nose laughed. "Then let them move swiftly – into our hands. We will be ready. It will not be as it was at Sand Creek or at Pawnee Fork when our villages were burned."

"Our lodges will ride with you," Two Strikes said. "Together we will crush this war party like an ant beneath our moccasin."

Tall Bull sent a messenger to the Cheyenne camp to warn the Dog Soldiers to make preparations for a fight, while the Cheyenne and Sioux chiefs made their plans for the attack. "It is well," Tall Bull finally concluded. "And now we shall forget the White Eyes and enjoy the hospitality of our brothers."

Later in the evening, Ice Bear became worried. He didn't know what triggered the gnawing feeling within him, or why he was uneasy. Everything seemed to be as it should. But he felt something was wrong. A sub-conscious voice was trying to be heard.

He drew apart from the circle of men watching the Sioux dancers and studied the faces of those around him.

They all seemed intent on watching the dancers. Nothing wrong here that he could see.

Ice Bear wandered through the camp. A group of noisy children came running past, chasing one of the camp dogs. Some of the older men of the tribe were retiring to their lodges. Here and there several groups of young girls were talking and giggling, and casting sly glances at young men who pretended not to notice. Everything seemed normal.

At the far end of the village some of the older women were still cooking, knowing that the feast and dancing would last far into the night. Ice Bear watched them stir the pots with a big Army-issue metal spoon, and dish up a few bowls for those still hungry. He started to move on when he suddenly realized what was wrong.

He rushed to the women, asked a few abrupt questions, and with a low moan dashed off to find Roman Nose.

Colonel Forsythe called the column to a halt, and pulled out his watch. It was 4:00 in the afternoon on the 16th day of September. For two days now the troop had been riding hard on the trail of the Cheyenne. They had crossed the Republican River in the northwestern part of Kansas earlier in the day, and now had come to a small tributary in eastern Colorado known as the Arickaree. For the most part it was a dry creek bed, with only a trickle of water.

Sharp Grover pulled his horse alongside that of the Colonel.

"Well, what do you think?" Forsyth asked.

"I think we're in for a fight," the scout replied, "and it could come most any time. The Indians have been watching us for several days now. They know we're here, and from the look of the trail we can't be very far from their camp."

Forsyth surveyed the surrounding terrain. They had entered a large, flat valley, with a ridge of hills about three miles to the East. The valley was mostly barren with only a few willows and thick buffalo grass along the creek bed. At this particular juncture in the Arickaree a small island had been formed, rising several feet above the sandy bed surrounding it. A trace of water trickled on each side of the island. In all it was about twenty feet wide, and sixty feet long. A solitary cottonwood tree punctuated the south end.

Forsyth studied the valley and the island. Although it appeared that everything in the surrounding plains could be seen for miles, Forsyth knew that it was full of depressions and ravines in which Indians could be hiding. He had pushed the men hard, and he knew both they and their horses were dead tired. It was not a good way to go into a fight, he thought.

"Lt. Beecher, pass the word that we will make camp here alongside the creek bed for the night," he finally said. "Double the guard, and warn every man to be ready for a scrap at a minute's notice. Likely we won't have any trouble till tomorrow, but we will be prepared none the less. Tell the men to sleep light, and best keep their boots on."

Eli was riding alongside a young man about his own age when the command came to dismount. He had struck a friendship with Jack Stillwell who seemed wise beyond his years in the ways of the Indians. Eli was always anxious to get Jack's assessment of things.

"We've been out here six days now," Eli said as they unsaddled their horses. "Only have rations for seven. If we don't find the Redskins tomorrow seems to me like we're gonna have to give it up and high tail it back to Fort Wallace."

Stillwell grinned. He was young enough to share Eli's excitement, but experienced enough to know that they had ridden into a situation where the only way out now was likely a fight for their lives.

Eli glanced at Stillwell when he didn't respond. He knew enough of the situation to read Stillwell's thoughts. It sent a stab of apprehension through him, in spite of his outward show of cockiness and confidence.

"How many do you figure there are?" he asked in a more subdued voice.

"Well, old Garver estimates as many as two hundred braves. Four times as many as we have. 'Course with these new seven shot Spencer rifles that more than evens the score. We can get seven shots to their one."

Eli found comfort in that thought, as he hustled off to find his brother-in-law, Thomas. Only later would he discover that Jack's estimate of the number of warriors they were to face was woefully understated.

That night, several miles to the West, the Cheyenne and the Sioux held their final war council.

"When the moon gives us light we'll move into position behind the hills," Tall Bull reiterated. "With the dawn we will sweep down on the camp without warning, while they still have sleep in their eyes. We will come from three sides, and leave the only way open to them to the east."

"At least it will appear to be open," Two Strikes said. "But when they retreat in that direction, they will run into our ambush. We will kill all of these soldiers who do not dress as soldiers."

The other chiefs nodded in agreement.

"What of Roman Nose?" Pawnee Killer finally asked. "Does he not ride with us?"

There was an awkward moment of silence. All knew that Roman Nose had unknowingly broken one of the taboos placed on him when he had received his famous war bonnet. He had eaten food at the Sioux village dished out by a metal spoon. Ice Bear, the Medicine Man, had been most adamant when he made the war bonnet, that its magic would fail to protect Roman Nose if he ate food touched by metal. Even worse, he would surely be killed in his next battle. This was known to all, even to the Sioux, and they felt great dismay that they had been the cause of trouble for their good friend.

"Roman Nose is still undergoing purification rites," Tall Bull said. "Our medicine man, Ice Bear, works to restore the magic of the war bonnet, and to cleanse his spirit. However, such things take much time. He will not ride with us at the dawn."

All of the chiefs sat in reflective silence. Roman Nose was the leader that all the young braves admired and wanted to follow into battle. His absence was not a good omen.

"It is of little importance," White Horse finally said. "We have almost six hundred braves to ride against fifty pale faces. It will be over before the sun warms the sand."

"One final thing," Tall Bull admonished. "We must all make sure to hold our braves in check so that we attack in unison. Do not let any become overly anxious, and alert the white men before we are ready. We do not want them to have time to get organized before they flee to the east."

"You worry too much," Pawnee Killer said. "Our braves will do as they are told."

"We hope that will be so," Tall Bull replied. "But too many times in the past our plans have been spoiled by young men who are anxious to count the first coup and who strike before the trap has been set. It must not happen in this attack."

Again the chiefs nodded their agreement.

A few miles from where the leaders were holding their conference, another group of young Dog Soldiers and Sioux were holding a meeting of their own.

"It would be a good thing if we could drive the horses off before the main attack," Little Hawk told the group.

"Then we could be sure that none of the White Eyes could escape."

"Aiye," Starving Elk replied. "It would be a thing of much honor."

Without further discussion the small group mounted their horses and rode off to the east.

CHAPTER 17

The first glow of a new day began to light up the eastern sky, although it was still dark around the camp at the Arickaree.

Eli and Jack Stillwell had been among those drawing the final night watch, and were lying in the grass several hundred feet from the sleeping scouts. They talked very little, spending most of their time straining their ears to catch the many night sounds, and trying to pierce the darkness with their eyes. At various times throughout the night they had seen small fires, probably torches, waving back and forth in the distant hills.

"Most likely signaling to each other," Jack had commented.

Neither had any lingering doubt that the coming dawn would bring the most exciting and dangerous time of their lives. As they lay in silence, a twig snapped behind them, and both men whirled around with rifles cocked.

"Easy boys," Colonel Forsyth said. They recognized his voice and saw the faint red glow from his cigar.

"Good morning, Colonel," Stillwell said in what sounded like a calm voice. Eli struggled to get his heart back to normal from the sudden scare.

"You're up early, Sir," Stillwell continued.

"Yes. Well, guess I'm a little too antsy for sleep right now. You boys OK?"

Both men nodded.

"Looks like we may be getting that action we been looking for," the Colonel continued. "Been a lot of activity over in those hills all night."

"Yes Sir. We've been watching them," Stillwell said.

The eastern sky brightened by the minute. Eli glanced across the open valley and saw that it was light enough to see objects previously hidden by the night. As he started to turn back to the Colonel, he saw movement out of the corner of his eye. He stared intently into the receding darkness, and made out two shadowy figures moving towards the camp.

"Indians!" he shouted. At the same instant Stillwell's rifle barked at his side. The next few minutes blurred with noise and confusion as both he and Stillwell fired into the semi-darkness, while the Colonel yelled to the bugler to sound the alarm. The breaking dawn came alive with reverberations of wild war whoops and guns blasting away on all sides.

The scouts soon realized it was not a major attack, however, but only a small group of Indians trying to drive off the horses by waving blankets and firing rifles. The horses had been tied and for the most part were secure, though a few broke loose, and together with the mules, stampeded off to the north.

Within minutes the entire camp was ready for action: bed rolls hastily packed and horses saddled. It was now daylight on the morning of September 17, 1868.

Forsyth's Rough Riders stood by their mounts, ready for the command to saddle up. An eerie silence descended on the troop. Following the noise and confusion of the preceding minutes, the world seemed to come to a standstill. Eli, standing beside Thomas and Stillwell, was dimly aware of a crow complaining in the distance. Then one of the men behind him exclaimed, "My God! Look at the Indians!"

Eli scanned the surrounding hills, his heart pounding. On all sides except to the east, row after row of brightly bedecked Indians appeared. It was an awesome sight; even from a distance a sea of color and movement.

The warriors were stripped for battle; bodies painted in vivid hues with hair braided behind them, entwined with feathers and ornaments - sea shells and beads. The chiefs were in full war bonnets, with long trailing feathers blowing in the morning breeze alongside their horses. Lances were tipped with rawhide, bones and bright ornaments. Multi-colored ponies were ridden by braves up and down the lines, encouraging their brothers to fight bravely.

The wind shifted slightly, and for the first time sounds drifted across the valley: war songs and chants, ear piercing shouts, and the steady beat of drums. Within seconds, the Indians raced down the hills in a thundering charge.

Forsyth, with Beecher and Sharp Grover by his side, studied the situation "The only way open is to the east," Grover remarked, "which means that is where they want us to go."

"Reckon you're right," Forsyth replied. "Worst thing we could do is get ourselves strung out in a retreat, anyway. Lt. Beecher," he turned to his second-in-command," move the men onto the island, quickly, and set up a perimeter defense."

Already under fire from the Indians on the far bank, the volunteers raced pell mell onto the island, dragging their horses with them, and trying to salvage what supplies they could. Eli tied his horse to a small willow, then dove into the grass beside Thomas.

Colonel Forsyth strode over from the right side of the island. "I've just had young Stillwell take some men to the lower end," he told Beecher. "Instead of stopping there, however, they went on over to the far bank and are hiding in the grass. Ought to give someone a surprise."

The first wave of Indians crossed the valley floor and charged down the river bed. Breaking into a cold sweat, Eli had a fleeting fear that his finger might become so sweaty and slippery that he wouldn't be able to pull the trigger on his carbine. He glanced over at Thomas, who gave him a reassuring grin.

Standing tall and erect, Forsythe walked behind his men, giving encouragement and issuing commands. "Don't fire till I give the order," he barked.

"For God's sake get down, Colonel!" Sharp Grover cried. Bullets filled the air, hitting horses and ricocheting off the rocks and ground, but Forsyth continued to stand in the face of the charge. One of the volunteers cried out in pain, and then yelled, "I'm hit! I'm hit!"

Eli focused his attention on the hordes of Indians bearing down on them. Nothing would keep the savages from overrunning the island and killing them all. He tried to calm himself, and vowed to die bravely, fighting with his comrades to the end.

"Fire!" He heard the Colonel's command. Spencer repeating rifles barked all around him. He trained his rifle on a weaving Indian riding nearly naked on a spotted pony, waving a rifle high in the air. As Eli squeezed the trigger, the Indian leaned forward, unhurt, and seemed to merge with the horse.

With the first volley of fire from the volunteers, however, a number of horses in the lead charge staggered and fell. One Indian was blown out of his saddle as if he had been ejected, but the charge continued in full force.

"Fire!" He heard the Colonel yell again. The scouts blazed away with their repeating rifles. The Indians were startled that the white men did not need to reload their guns, but they continued to bear down on the small island.

Some stopped to pick up their friends who had horses shot out from under them, another group veered off to the north, but the main line of warriors, some on foot, some going different directions, inexorably bore down on the small group of volunteers.

Eli fired rapidly, but tried not to waste shots. The Indians were almost to the island, and Eli made sure his revolver was close at hand.

Then the front edge of the Indian attack wavered and divided, and instead of riding over the island the charge broke to either side and circled the beleaguered scouts. Soon the attackers were milling around in confusion and disorganization, shocked by the new Spencer rifles that never seemed to run out of bullets no matter how many rounds were fired. The attack became less frenzied as many of the Indians pulled back. Eli took the opportunity to dig a pit in the sand for better protection.

Thomas Alderdice crawled over to where Eli was digging. "The man on my right has been wounded and is in pretty bad shape," he said. "I'm going to find Doc Mooers." He rose to a crouch and disappeared into the tall buffalo grass. Most of the Indians had withdrawn from the dry creek bed now, but sporadic firing continued from snipers on the ridges above.

Within minutes Thomas reappeared and slid back into his rifle pit, his face set in a hard look.

"Where's the Doc?" Eli asked.

"Shot in the head," Thomas muttered. "Still breathing but he won't last long."

"What about the others?"

"Not too good." Thomas paused, and then continued, "Forsyth has been shot twice in the leg. One of the shots broke the bone. Lt. Beecher is near death. Two others that I know of. About half the men have been wounded one way or another. And all of our medical supplies were on those two mules that skedaddled when the Indians were attacking. Only good news I guess is that we still have plenty of ammunition."

Eli stared at the ground, tried to think of something to say, but no words came.

"Some of the men are already calling this Beecher's Island after the Lieutenant," Thomas continued after a long period of silence. "Seems appropriate that it should have a name. A man shouldn't die fighting on some unknown, nameless strip of land. Ought to have a name."

"Beecher's Island," Eli muttered. "That's as good a name as any. Reckon I wouldn't mind defending an island by that name."

Eli peered out from the pit he had dug in the soft sand. The Indians had re-assembled on one of the distant hills. One, probably a chief, rode up and down the line giving instructions. A few minutes later they started towards the island once again, slowly at first, then increasing in momentum.

Eli heard someone yell out "Here they come again, boys. Better get ready."

For a short time the Indians disappeared behind a small rise in the river bank, but   dust from their progress could be seen rising to the sky. They reappeared upstream in the creek bed, and charged towards the island, hitting it from the point where Stillwell and some of the scouts were hidden in the grassy bank.

Eli watched with chilling horror as the wild, yelling mass of painted warriors descended on them. Shooting erupted once again, and the scene of an hour earlier repeated itself.

On and on the Indians came even as their lead ponies stumbled and fell under the barrage laid down by the defenders. The chief who had been rallying the warriors on the hillside led the charge and seemed immune to bullets flying around him.

At the last possible moment the Indians wavered under the continuous round of fire and once again broke on either side of the island rather than swarming over it. However the chief leading the attack continued straight towards the island. Weaving and yelling and brandishing his lance he reached the lower end of the island, rode through the perimeter of defenders, then wheeled around and charged back the way he had come. But as he rode close to the far bank of the river where Stillwell and the men were hidden, small puffs of smoke erupted from unseen rifles. The chief slumped forward on his horse, which halted, then moved slowly back up the dry creek bed.

The attack once again broke off, and the fighting slowed to a few isolated skirmishes. Eli stole a quick glance towards Thomas and was relieved to see him smiling, indicating that he was alright. Eli said a little prayer of thanksgiving, and wished that John Alverson was here with them. Somehow old John would know what they should do. Without conscious thought Eli recited the 23rd Psalm to himself. "Yea, though I walk through the valley of the shadow of death, I will fear no evil, for Thou art with me..."

It was 11:00 in the morning.

I was fascinated by Old Joe's account of the battle. He was telling it like he had been an eye witness to the attack.

"That chief who got shot – was that Roman Nose?" I asked.

"Nope – that was an old chief named White Thunder. Roman Nose was off trying to cleanse his spirit for breaking the taboo about eating food touched by metal."

"So Roman Nose didn't participate in the Beecher Island affair?"

"Oh yes," Old Joe said. "He participated."

Several miles away from the fighting, on the far side of a rolling hill, a solitary figure squatted on the ground, drawing strange figures in the dirt with a willow branch. He sang a soft chant, punctuated occasionally by a piercing, supernatural-like yell. So intent was he on the ritual that he didn't notice the band of riders until they were almost upon him.

Roman Nose halted his chant and raised his eyes to the horsemen: Tall Bull, White Horse and Bull Bear, with a half dozen Dog Soldiers.

Roman Nose knew why they had come. He asked, "How does the fight go?"

Tall Bull paused before answering. He seemed uneasy.

"The white men are well fortified. And they have rifles that do not run out of bullets."

Roman Nose nodded. He had heard the sound of the fight; the rifle fire, the yells of the warriors, the shouting of commands. He knew that there had been two major attacks and that neither had been successful.

"White Thunder gained much honor," White Horse said. "He led the second charge, and the white men's bullets bounced off him like sticks. Twice he rode on the island, but the other braves did not follow. One bullet found its mark, however, and he is wounded in the shoulder."

There was another pause in the conversation before White Contrary gave voice to their thoughts.

"Well, here is Roman Nose, the man that we depend on, sitting behind this hill." He waved his arm in a half circle, and then pointed to the sound of the rifle fire. "You do not see your brothers falling out there? Two more fell just as I came up."

Roman Nose laughed.

"All those people fighting out there feel that they belong to you," White Contrary continued, "and they will do all that you tell them to do, and here you are behind this hill."

Roman Nose ignored White Contrary and spoke directly to Tall Bull. "What the old man says is true." He rubbed out the sketches he had made in the dirt and went to his pony. He removed a bundle from the horse's back and laid it out on the ground. He extracted a small pouch, opened it, and began painting his body for battle.

"How is it with the ceremony of purification?" Tall Bull asked.

"There was no time," Roman Nose replied. "It is of little consequence," he continued, "because I know that this is the day that I shall die."

Roman Nose unfolded his war bonnet, the one that had protected him from the white man's bullets, shook it out to its full size, and after performing the required rituals, mounted it on his head.

"Let us now see this island that six hundred braves cannot overrun," he said.

It was 2:30 in the afternoon when Roman Nose led the third attack.

He urged his horse forward at a slow trot, then increased speed as he approached the island until he raced at a full gallop, brandishing his lance high over his head. The Dog Soldiers followed with greater confidence than they had felt in the previous two charges.

On the distant hills Indian women and old men from the village gathered to watch this final assault on the white men.

"The breeze feels cool on my face," Roman Nose mused. "This evening there will be rain. It is good." The island and the puffs of smoke erupting from it drew nearer, but his mind was detached, as if he were watching the charge from some distant place.

"It is a good day to die," he thought. "The sun of the Cheyenne is already setting. It is just as Sweet Medicine predicted many seasons ago. The white man will prevail, and the Indian will be scattered and homeless. It is a good time to die."

Now Roman Nose forced himself to concentrate on the attack. As he rode close to a thick stand of grass on the bank of the river he thought he saw rifle smoke coming from the grass. He turned back to look, then felt a hard jolt in the small of his back. He lost control of his horse, which stumbled, turned around, and started back up the river bed away from the firing. He slumped forward, feeling tired and weak. He was not conscious when he fell on the sand of the dry creek bed.

As quick as it started the attack on the island stopped. The Indians disappeared, with only an occasional shot from the high banks keeping the scouts under cover.

"I think we got one of their main chiefs," Thomas whispered.

A great silence descended on the island. In the distance a line of storm clouds filled the western sky, with a faint rumbling of thunder. Then a chilling, mournful wail arose from the distant hills, and filled the valley floor. Women and children who had watched the battle could be seen swaying back and forth, arms in the air, crying in grief and sorrow. It was a sight none would ever forget.

Far upstream a group of Indians on foot formed a column and trotted towards the island. As they got within rifle range the front row dropped to their knees and fired, then those behind rushed forward to do the same, continuing in leap-frog fashion. They had come to retrieve the body of their fallen leader.

The scouts sporadically returned the fire, but without much enthusiasm. The Indians reached their chief, lifted him from the sand, and made their retreat in the same manner in which they had come.

"One thing you can say about the Indians," Thomas observed, "they don't leave their dead behind. Especially their leaders. You know, I wouldn't be surprised but what that was old Roman Nose himself. Did you see that fancy war bonnet he was wearing? Guess it didn't help him much this time, if that was him."

"The real question," Eli answered, "is not whether that war bonnet helped him, but whether getting him will help any of us."

CHAPTER 18

It was late afternoon, and Eli realized with some surprise that he hadn't eaten since sunrise. With the realization came a ravishing hunger.

The Indians had withdrawn, and the men were now moving carefully about the island. Likely the Indians wouldn't try anything more on this day.

Eli looked for his horse, and found it dead on the ground where he had tied it. In fact, as he surveyed the island, not a single horse was left alive. "Looks like we'll have plenty of meat for awhile," Thomas remarked. "At least until the sun starts to turn it rancid."

Eli shuddered, and pulled the last of his hardtack from his saddle. Horsemeat was not his idea of a feast.

He and Thomas moved across the island to where Colonel Forsyth lay propped up in his rifle pit. Although his leg was shattered, Forsyth still seemed calm and was in complete command. At the moment he was receiving reports from McCall and Grover on the dead and wounded.

"We've lost four men, and Lt. Beecher and Doctor Mooers are in bad shape. They won't make it," McCall said. "We got nine others in critical condition, and many have wounds of varying severity. Bottom line, we have twenty-three killed or wounded, leaving us with just thirty able-bodied men. Most of the damage was done on the first charge, before we got dug in. We didn't get hurt much on the next two attacks."

"Well, Grover," Forsyth asked, "do you think the devils will be able to muster up anything worse tomorrow than they did today?"

"Not in my opinion," the scout replied. "I think they gave it their best shot today. Still, that's the most Indians I ever did see gathered together in one spot."

"Umm," Forsyth muttered. "Well, better get a burial detail going. And tell the men to salvage what meat they can from the horses, and then move the carcasses in front of their pits. It'll give them some protection."

Later in the evening Stillwell and the others who had been hiding in the grass on the bank of the river slipped back to the island. They joined the circle of men that always seemed to be around the Colonel. It seemed to give everyone comfort and reassurance to hear the Colonel discuss the situation. It was a circle of camaraderie rather than that of military command. Many of the scouts bragged about shots they had made, or close calls they had lived through. Others joked about the fine fare they had scraped up for supper.

"You boys did a great job on that river bank," Forsyth said to Stillwell. "Which one of you was it that got that big chief?"

Stillwell laughed. "Reckon we'll never know, sir. We were all trying to get him. Do ya think that might have been Roman Nose?"

"We can hope," the Colonel replied.

"What's our prospects look like, Colonel?" one of the men asked.

"Well, I guess you would have to say it wasn't the best situation we could have thought up. Half the command wounded, all of our horses killed, no medical supplies and down to our last meal. The savages don't have to make any more charges, they can just keep us pinned down till we starve to death."

After a pause he continued. "On the positive side, however, we still have plenty of ammunition, and we can dig down in the sand for enough water to keep us going. And we seemed to have killed one of their big chiefs. Maybe Roman Nose. And horsemeat's not all that bad. Just takes a little getting used to is all."

Forsyth looked at the circle of men gathered around him, studying their faces. They all knew what had to be done.

"Reckon we need to send someone for help," the Colonel said.

A number of men volunteered without hesitation, including Eli and Thomas. All of them knew their chances of getting through would be slim, and if caught their death would be slow and painful. Sharp Grover also volunteered, but Forsyth quickly turned him down, telling him he would be needed here to take command in case Forsyth was no longer able. McCall, the only regular Army man not wounded, understood that this situation called for someone of Grover's skills rather than relying strictly on the military chain of command.

Forsyth gave the matter some thought, then called for Stillwell and an older frontier scout, Pete Trudeau. Both men had been among those who volunteered to go. Both were knowledgeable of the plains and of Indians.

"You know the risks." Forsythe said. "Are you willing to give it a try?"

"Yes, sir," both men replied in unison.

"Then God be with you. I guess I don't need to tell you to be careful."

Later that evening as the two scouts said their good-bys, Eli took Jack Stillwell's hand in a last firm handshake.

"Good luck, Jack." And then added, "And don't spend too much time sight seeing along the way. OK?"

Stillwell answered with a grin and a friendly jab to the shoulder. The next minute Stillwell and Trudeau disappeared into the darkness.

Eli wandered around the island, trying not to make too much noise. Though exhausted, he found sleep hard to contemplate. The wounded had been placed at the base of the lone cottonwood tree. Eli paused beside Lt. Beecher, who was delirious and in great pain. Someone had to be at his side at all times to keep him down. Periodically his mumbling would cease, and then in a loud clear voice he would call out "Won't someone please shoot me? Oh God, please kill me." Then he would fall back into his painful comatose. As Eli moved away he heard Beecher cry out, "Mother! Mother!" It made the hair stand up on the back of his neck.

Doctor Moores was about as bad. Though blind and speechless from the bullet in his forehead, his motions seemed to indicate that he knew where he was.

Eli returned to his rifle pit and talked with Thomas about home, and their plans for next year's garden. They both kidded that they sure would like some of Susanna's apple pie about now.

Shortly after midnight the storm that had been building in the west moved in, the cool rain a refreshing respite from the day's heat. Eli soaked his handkerchief in the moisture and placed it across his forehead.

Just before he fell asleep he heard someone telling Thomas that Lt. Beecher had died. He thought about Stillwell, and how long it might take them to reach Ft. Wallace.

When Eli awoke in the morning he was surprised to see that most of the Indian wounded and dead had been retrieved by their brothers during the night. However, three braves who had actually reached the shores of the island still lay lifeless where they had fallen, near the scout's rifle pits.

During the day the Indians resumed their attack, but not with the same determination they had shown on the first day. Nevertheless, the defenders were kept close to the ground by rifle fire from the banks. Periodically a group of Indians on horseback appeared in the river bed and charged towards the island, but they always stopped when they got within rifle range, shouting and taunting the defenders to come out and fight.

That night Forsyth selected two more men, Jack Donovan and A. J. Plily, to try to slip through the Indian lines for help. They left just before midnight, but returned several hours later saying the Indians had the island surrounded and they couldn't get through. Everyone wondered if this meant that Stillwell and Trudeau had been caught. Eli shuddered when he thought about the torture they would have faced before a merciful death rescued them.

On the third day Doc Mooers died, and the horse meat turned rancid from the blistering September heat. But it was also a day of hope, because several of the scouts saw Indian women leaving on the far hills. For a short time the volunteers thought the fight might be over. But sporadic bursts of rifle fire soon let them know they weren't to be so fortunate.

That night Donovan and Plily tried again to sneak through the Indian encirclement. This time they didn't return, and there was hope that they might have gotten through.

Little happened the next two days, except that the swelling and pain in Colonel Forsythe's leg became excruciating.

"Boys, I need someone to dig that blasted bullet out of my leg," he pleaded. "McCall - how about you?"

McCall examined the wound. The bullet was lodged next to the femoral artery. One slip and the artery would break and Forsythe would bleed to death.

"I can't do it, Colonel," he said. "It's too risky. I can't take the responsibility."

"Someone else then," Forsythe replied. "Find someone to do it. If it gets to festering, the artery's going to bust wide open anyway."

But nobody wanted to be the one that might cause the Colonel's death.

"Then by jiggers, I'll do it myself," Forsythe exclaimed. "Bring me a knife with a sharp point on it."

"Best use a razor, Colonel," Sharp Grover commented. "Won't hurt as much and you'll get a cleaner cut." He dug a razor out of his saddle bag and brought it to Forsythe.

"Well, if you're so doggoned intent on doin' yourself in," McCall said, "guess the least I can do is to help."

He knelt beside Forsythe and pulled the skin apart at the wound. Forsythe took the razor, and cut into his leg at the point the bullet had entered, his face contorted with pain, but not uttering a sound. Perspiring heavily he kept at his task, stopping several times to brush away tears from his eyes. Finally he pushed the razor in deeper, and with a groan pried the bullet loose.

"By Jove, you've got it!" McCall yelled.

Forsythe managed a weak smile before falling back on his bed in exhaustion.

Each day now seemed much like the one before. The horse meat was putrid, but was still being eaten by the desperate scouts. One evening a coyote wandered onto the island and was killed by one of the men. This provided a little fresh meat for the group, but not much. The volunteers were able to move around the island with greater freedom, being careful, however, not to expose themselves unnecessarily.

The surrounding banks still contained Indians who would occasionally fire a volley into their midst. There had been no more charges on horseback, however.

The days dragged slowly by, with no relief in sight. Afternoons were blistering hot under the blazing fall sun with no clouds to provide relief. As soon as the sun went down, however, it cooled off, and by midnight the scouts shivered under flimsy blankets, staring at the myriad of stars in the sky, wondering if they would ever see their loved ones again.

Eli had a dream. It was a pleasant dream in which he and his two sisters, Mary and Susanna, were playing house. When he was younger, he had often been coaxed into playing his sister's games, though he would vigorously deny it today.

Susanna was pretending to bake a blueberry pie. Except that somehow it wasn't a make believe pie but a real one. Eli could smell the tantalizing aroma as she removed it from her pretend oven.

The eagerness must have shown on his face, because Susanna admonished, "Not yet mister. You must wait till it cools." With that she and Mary took the pie into the back bedroom, which was always closed off and shut up to keep out the hot summer wind.

Eli waited for them to return, but the minutes went by and they didn't reappear. He walked over to the bedroom door, but could hear nothing inside. He opened it and walked inside, and was aware of an eerie coldness and dampness in the room.

He saw no sign of either Susanna or Mary in the subdued light, but thought he heard a whimpering sound in the corner. Was it one of his sisters? And where was the other one? He felt a cold chill run through his body, and although scared to the bone, started towards the corner.

Out of nowhere he felt a hand clasp his shoulder and a voice whisper his name. He whirled around and blindly struck out with his arms.

"Eli – take it easy. Wake up. Are you alright?"

Eli opened his eyes to see Thomas hovering above him. "Wake up," he repeated. "Colonel wants to talk with us."

Thomas moved on to awaken the others, and Eli slowly sat up. He rubbed his hand over his whiskered face, and shook his head to clear the cob webs. It took several minutes to move out of his dream and to shake the awful premonition it brought.

Eli shuddered in the cold, bleak morning air. Rain had fallen during the night, and was now mixed with light snow.

"Too darned early for snow," he thought as he rose to his feet and stamped the ground to get his circulation going. But at least it would bring relief from the hot afternoon sun.

Eli didn't need anyone to tell him their situation was desperate. They had no food, and hope of rescue dimmed every day. He thought about his new friend, Jack Stillwell, and wondered where he was, and if he was still alive. Surely he must have been captured, tortured and killed, or help would have been here by now.

Eli picked up his Spencer rifle and moved over to the cottonwood tree where the Colonel lay. He sure was hungry. The aroma of the blueberry pie in his dream had been so vivid that he thought he could still get a whiff of it now and then.

The Colonel was propped up against a big boulder, Sharp Grover and McCall by his side. Eli looked at the men who had gathered in a circle around their leader. Their gaunt, bewhiskered faces, along with their dirty and sweat-stained clothes, didn't make for the most handsome troop he had ever seen. The light snow had ended and the day began to warm up.

"Boys," Forsyth began. His voice was husky, and he had to clear his throat and start again.

"Boys, we've been trapped on this island for six days now. You've all performed admirably. I can't think of a finer bunch of men I'd want to ride with."

Forsyth surveyed the faces around him. Some were looking at the ground with a sheepish grin, some turned away, and some met his gaze with a steady eye.

"I guess you all know our situation without me telling you," he continued. "I think the main contingent of Indians have pulled out. Oh, they're probably not too far away, just waiting to come in for the kill. But there might be a chance that those of you who are healthy and haven't suffered any wounds might be able to get out of here."

This brought an immediate murmur of protest from some of the men. But Forsythe raised his hand to silence it.

"Now don't answer too quickly," he admonished. "You all know there's no way you can carry out those of us with bad wounds. On the other hand, I don't see any reason why you should stay here just because of us, to die of starvation."

"Don't talk that way, Colonel," one of the men called out. "Likely Donovan and Plily got through to the fort even if the first two didn't. Why, I bet help's on its way right this minute."

Several of the volunteers seconded this thought.

"Besides," another said, "the Redskins will know we're leaving. If we divide our forces, and leave the safety of this island, and get strung out there on the prairie on foot, why I figure we'll all be goners for sure."

Forsyth held up his hand again. "OK, OK," he said. "I just want you to think about it seriously, and discuss it amongst yourselves. If any of you want to leave I want you to know that it will be with my blessing and Godspeed, and an eternal gratefulness for the bravery and courage you have shown on this expedition. Now talk it over and let me know your decision."

The scouts broke into small groups and engaged in animated discussion. Eli and Thomas exchanged questioning looks.

"What about it, Eli," Thomas asked. "Want to make a break for it tonight?"

Eli looked at the ground. The thought of escape was certainly tempting. But he thought about the Colonel, and the other wounded they would be leaving to a certain death, and he knew he couldn't do it. He raised his eyes to look into Thomas's face, and saw a twinkle there that he hadn't noticed before.

"Reckon it's not what John would do," Eli replied, referring to their brother-in-law, "and reckon it's not what I would do either."

Thomas slapped him on the shoulder with a grin, and replied "And I reckon I didn't need to ask."

There was a consensus among the men to stick it out, and Sergeant McCall acted as their spokesman. "Colonel," he stated, "We rode out here together, and fought together, and by thunder we'll ride back out of here together. We're not leaving you and the other wounded behind, and that's it."

A round of cheers and yells seconded McCall's words.

"Very well," Forsyth responded, his voice husky once more. "Better get back to your posts then. And God be with you."

Forsyth lowered his head, and picked up a book he had brought with him, Oliver Twist, and ostensibly began reading from it. Only Sharp Grover saw the tear trickle from Forsythe's eye and run down his cheek.

Eli and Thomas returned to their rifle pits without speaking. The hills to the east appeared deserted. Eli scanned the horizon in all directions without seeing any sign of life. Then three rifle shots broke the morning quiet, and Eli heard a bullet whiz close to his ear. He dropped to the sandy ground and thought about the pie that had been in his dream.

The next two days were a sullen nightmare for Eli. For awhile his stomach complained constantly over being so badly neglected, but then seemed to subside into an unfeeling, nothingness thing. The cold, wet weather of a few days ago had given way to an unbearably hot, late autumn sun. Water dug from the holes in the sand was brackish, and each endless hour stretched into the other without any sign of relief. It was now the 25th of September, nine days since their ordeal had started, and hope of rescue was fading.

Eli awoke from a fitful sleep and rolled on his side. Thomas, propped up in his rifle pit, was concentrating on a letter he was writing. Eli knew without asking that it was for Susanna.

Fletcher Violett, another of the volunteers from the Saline valley, came over to where Eli lay. Fletch was a tall, dangling youth with a shock of red hair and 52 freckles, by his own count, sprinkled across his face . "Eli," he said without preamble, "I need to talk with you."

"What's up, Fletch? Figured a way to get us out of here?"

"Well, just maybe I have. Or if not how at least when - one way or the other. It's today."

Eli studied Fletch's spotted face to see if he was delusional, but he seemed rational enough. "Just how did you come by this bit of knowledge?" he asked.

"I've had a dream," Fletch responded. "Or maybe more like a vision, it was so real. That's what I want to talk about with you. Somethin's gonna happen today, for sure."

Eli sighed. "I never knew you to be a man who had visions. Not like old Mart back home. OK, Fletch, but first let me go to our grocery store here and see what I can dig up for breakfast." He strolled over to the remains of a putrid horse, cut off a slice, and cooked it over a small fire burning nearby. Somehow he kept from gagging when eating it.

He and Fletcher meandered up a small hill. The scouts now were able to move freely about the island. As they approached the rim, Eli studied the hills to the East. There had been no sign of activity for several days, but just now Eli thought he saw movement.

"Fletch," he muttered, "looks like the Indians are over in the hills again. Do you think they're getting ready for another charge?"

Fletcher studied the horizon where Eli pointed. He, too, saw something moving. "Looks like horsemen. I knew it! This is my vision. Today's the day we either get rescued or meet our maker."

They both strained their eyes to make out what was happening.

Then Eli exclaimed, "Hey that looks like a wagon. That's a wagon coming over the hill!"

"You're right!" Fletcher yelped. "By God, it's an Army ambulance! It's the Army come to rescue us sure enough!"

A wild cheer erupted from the island, from others who had been watching. Men stood and danced up and down. Some dropped their rifles and ran towards the oncoming troop of cavalry, Eli among them, running, laughing and crying at the same time.

The rescuing soldiers were from Troop H of the Tenth Cavalry, a black regiment headed by Brevet Lieutenant-Colonel Louis H. Carpenter. Stillwell and Trudeau had gotten through to Fort Wallace, and word had been sent to Carpenter, who was already on patrol in the area. On their way to the Arickaree the troops ran across Donovan and Plily, both safe and unhurt.

Carpenter guided his horse through the milling, cheering mob of volunteers. He, along with others in his troop, handed out what food they carried on their horses to the starving men, and now he sought out Colonel Forsyth. He spotted Sharp Grover, whom he had met before, and rode over to him. Dismounting, he took Grover's hand in a firm handshake, and asked about Forsyth.

"He's over there," Grover indicated with a jab of his thumb.

Both men stared at Forsyth. Unwilling to trust his emotions in the midst of the wild jubilation, he was propped against the cottonwood tree, outwardly appearing to read his book, Oliver Twist.

"There's a man I would follow to Hell and back," Grover muttered.

Eli and Thomas walked the length and breadth of the island one final time before the contingent pulled out.

"Guess this is a place I'll always remember," Eli mused. "I can hardly wait to get back home and tell John about it."

"Yes, it's been quite an experience," Thomas agreed.

"How many Indians would you say we killed here?" Eli wondered.

Thomas thought a moment. "Kinda hard to say. You see a horse go down, but you're not sure about the rider. I'd guess somewhere between 35 and 70, though."

After the Battle of the Arickaree, as it came to be known, many of the Cheyenne decided to head south to join the Cheyenne camps on the Washita River, in Indian Territory. Black Kettle, who strongly disapproved of their raids in Kansas and Colorado, nonetheless welcomed them back to the tribe.

Tall Bull and the Dog Soldiers remained in their old hunting grounds, and continued to wage war on the Army and on the settlements. In October Tall Bull and about 200 braves attacked a troop led by Major Royall, killed two soldiers and ran off 26 horses. A company led by Colonel Carpenter was attacked on Beaver Creek, and was under siege for about six hours before the Indians withdrew. There were no casualties on either side. On October 25th Major Carr attacked a Cheyenne village on the Solomon River, killing from 10 to 20 warriors and capturing a large number of horses and supplies from the village.

It was the settlers, however, who were hit hard during this period. By some estimates there were157 people killed by Indians in the latter part of 1868, another 57 wounded; fourteen women outraged and murdered; and one man, four women and twenty-four children taken into captivity.

None of the actions taken by General Sheridan had in any way reduced the danger to the farmers in western Kansas and eastern Colorado. For families like John and Mary Alverson or Thomas and Susanna Alderdice, the frontier remained a dangerous place.

CHAPTER 19

"Did you grow up around these parts?" Old Joe asked.

"Yes, petty close. A little to the southeast. Newton, Kansas."

"How about your folks, they been there for a while?"

"Since 1868. My grandfather and his family came from Illinois in a covered wagon after the War. He liked the land, and decided to stay. We've been here for almost 140 years."

"I kinda figured that might be the case," Old Joe remarked. "Ever consider that part of you was living way back then when all these events we been talking about was taking place?"

I studied Old Joe carefully, but saw no sign of laughter in his face. He was serious. "How do you figure that?" I responded.

"Well, you didn't just appear out of nowhere, you know. No bolt of lightening hitting the ground, and when the dust cleared there you was. That only happened once in all creation, millions of years ago. No, sir. You were created by your Mommy and Daddy. They took some of their cells that was living back then and made you. So isn't it right that part of you existed back in their period of time? And the same is true for your parents. They were created from living cells from their folks that lived back in the 1800's. So the way I figure it you have cells in your body from way back then. In fact cells that have existed every since creation."

I could never get used to Old Joe's wild ideas. The problem was that I wasn't smart enough to adequately refute them. I decided that I needed to read up on things like mental telepathy and human cells so that I could put Old Joe's theories to rest.

"That's why you're so interested in these here events we been talkin' about. It's because part of you was alive way back then, and that part of you has this hunger to learn more about them."

I shook my head in denial. I wasn't buying any of it. "Joe, where in the world do you come up with these weird ideas?"

"I guess I just hear people talkin' about things and then I kinda reason them out to a logical conclusion. Pretty simple, really." Joe had a smug look, like he had just won a school spelling contest.

"Well, I think my interest in these events is because they make a good story," I said. "Lots of drama, a little love interest, and plenty of action. I didn't realize that it was because I was alive back then. But whatever the reason I sure would like a little more information about that raid in 1869. Was the death of Roman Nose the reason the Indians attacked the settlements?"

"I guess that might have been part of the reason. The Cheyenne were mighty upset over his death, and things were getting more desperate by the day. But there was another even more powerful event at the end of 1868 that contributed to the attack. The Battle – if you can call it that – of the Washita."

Samuel J. Crawford was elected governor of Kansas in 1864, the year of the Sand Creek massacre. He was a big man, and his facial features stood out in strong profile; a prominent nose, eyes set wide in a broad forehead, and a determined set to his jaw. True to the style of the day he sported a substantial mustache, the ends of which came well below the corners of his wide mouth. The mustache helped to compensate for the baldness on the top of his head.

The main highlights of his administration were in the continued settlement of the state by people from all over the world; the expansion of the railroad from the eastern border of the state almost to Colorado; and the increasing difficulties with Indians all across the western frontier. It was the latter problem that occupied most of Governor Crawford's attention. He was vitally concerned over the safety of the families who had been encouraged to settle in the state, and who braved the sun, wind and drought to do so. Having to face the danger of attacks from Indians was asking too much.

Being essentially a man of action rather than words, Crawford could hardly restrain himself during the raids of 1868, following the complete collapse of the Treaty of Medicine Lodge. In August of that year he traveled to Salina and placed himself in charge of a company of volunteers organized to track down Indians who had been raiding in Ottawa, Mitchell and Republic counties.

Returning to Topeka he sent a telegram to President Johnson stating; "The savage devils have become intolerable, and must and shall be driven out of the state."

The pressure for putting an end to the Indian problems in Kansas was mounting in the military as well. General Sheridan, Commanding Officer of the Army of the Missouri, was totally frustrated by the Army's lack of success in engaging the Indians during the long, hot summer. The only confrontation of any significance was the Battle of the Arickaree at Beecher's Island, and that had been with a bunch of volunteers, and was of little consequence, except for the death of Roman Nose.

With the blessings of General Sherman and the Department of the Army, Sheridan determined to make an unprecedented move – he would carry the attack into Indian Territory, where the peaceful Indians had set up their lodges in conformance with the Treaty of Medicine Lodge. He had become convinced that the only way to deal with the Indians was to hit them hard in their villages rather than trying to track down individual raiding parties. Sooner or later, he believed, the warring Indians always returned to their peace loving brothers and were welcomed back.

Sheridan decided to carry the attack into Indian Territory during the winter months, when the Indian ponies would be weak and the Indians sedentary and unsuspecting. He reasoned that this would have the additional benefit of making the Indians now raiding in Kansas come back into Indian Territory in order to protect the villages there.

There were some who objected to this decision on the grounds that it would be impossible to distinguish between those Indians who had been living peacefully in the lands set aside for them, and those who had been north participating in raids during the summer. But for Sheridan this was not a problem – he considered the entire Cheyenne tribe to be hostile and in need of punishment.

On September 24, 1868, Sheridan sent a dispatch to his protégé, General George Custer, who was still sitting out his year's suspension from command in his home in Monroe, Michigan, asking him to return to active duty and join in the proposed winter campaign.

Custer was overjoyed, and without waiting for official approval from Washington for cutting short his suspension, proceeded at once to Fort Hays along with his personal horses and his two Scotch staghounds, Blucher and Maida.

On the 10th of October Governor Crawford issued a proclamation authorizing the creation of the Nineteenth Kansas Voluntary Cavalry:

"With scarcely an exception all the tribes of Indians on the plains of Kansas or contiguous thereto, have taken up arms against the Government, and are now engaged in acts of hostility. The peace of the exposed border is thereby disturbed, quiet and unoffending citizens driven from their homes, or ruthlessly murdered, and their property destroyed or carried away. In fact children have been carried into captivity and in many instances barbarously murdered; while many women have been repeatedly violated in the presence of their husbands and families. Besides these instances of individual suffering, great public interests are being crippled and destroyed by this savage hostility. The commerce of the plains is entirely suspended. The mail routes, and the great lines of travel to the territory and states beyond us, are constantly being blockaded, and are sometimes completely closed for the space of several days."

"Longer to forbear with these bloody fiends would be a crime against civilization, and against the peace, security and lives of all the people of the frontier. The time has come when they must be met by an adequate force, not only to prevent the repetition of these outrages, but to penetrate their haunts, break up their organizations, and either exterminate the tribes or confine them upon reservations set apart for their occupancy. To this end the Major-General commanding this department has called upon the Executive for a regiment of cavalry from this State."

Nearly 1200 men were mustered into the 19th Kansas Volunteer Cavalry at Topeka on October 20. Included in the group were A.J. Plily and Jack Stiwell, fresh from the Battle of the Arickaree. General Sully at Fort Hays had 11 troops of the 7th Cavalry, now under the command of Custer, and five companies of infantry. Sheridan's expedition into Indian Territory was about to begin.

The tall cottonwood was about 30 feet inside of the perimeter formed by the other trees at the bend of the

Washita River. It looked out of place, as if it shouldn't have been there. It spoiled the symmetry of the half circle formed by the oaks and elms, huddled closely together on the creek bank. It was unique in yet another way as well. While all of the other trees had lost their leaves to the autumn chill, the cottonwood still retained almost a third of its bright, yellow color. But this was a distinction it would not hold for long. Even now a dozen leaves broke loose from the limbs in a gust of wind, and floated lazily to the ground.

Black Kettle watched one exceptionally large leaf settle near his feet. He picked it up, studied it carefully, first one side and then the other, before laying it back on the grass.

"The snow will come early this winter and will be heavy," he observed to the white man at his side.

Major Wynkoop made no reply. He wasn't sure whether the leaf had anything to do with Black Kettle's observation, or whether it was just a statement in general. At any rate the autumn leaves and winter snow were not really at the center of his thoughts.

"Will you be gone long?" Black Kettle asked.

"I don't know," Wynkoop replied. He did not meet Black Kettle's gaze, which answered the Chief's question more truthfully than his words. Wynkoop absentmindedly touched the pocket of his shirt, once again feeling the telegram folded inside.

"My mother has said that my father is not expected to live long. I must return to the East to see him once more before he dies, if God is willing. Then I will need to look after my mother and my sister. It will be some time."

"I do not think we shall see each other again," Black Kettle said with finality. "It is as it should be. You have done much for my people, but now you must return to your own and tend to their needs. It is as the Great Spirit wills it."

Wynkoop studied the old chief's wrinkled face.

"Black Kettle, I am afraid there will be trouble this winter. The Army plans on a winter campaign to punish the Indians who have been on the warpath this summer. You must not let Tall Bull or the Dog Soldiers stay near your camp when they come south. You must send them away."

"Yes, I have heard of this winter campaign by the angry Sheridan. It will be hard to send our brothers away. We are all of the same family, you see. Yet I will try to do so, and maintain faith with the white man's treaty."

"Good," Wynkoop replied. "And keep in close contact with the new military commander for this area, General Hazen, at Fort Cobb. Let him know where your camp is."

"It will be done," Black Kettle replied.

Wynkoop studied his friend's face once more. Black Kettle looked tired, he thought. But then I'm tired, too. Sick and tired of this whole darned mess. What did Sheridan think he was doing?

Wynkoop forced his thoughts away from the Army's planned winter campaign. He knew it was going to mean trouble, but he had done everything within his power to dissuade such an expedition. As his last official act as the agent to the Cheyenne, he had written a letter to Washington and to General Sheridan pointing out the shortages of food, arms and ammunition among the Cheyenne, and the failure of the U.S. Government to live up to its treaty obligations. It was these shortages that caused the wilder elements in the tribe to become incensed and want to drive the white men out of the country. But his entreaties had been to no avail. For Major Edward Wynkoop, the Indian problem was ending.

Wynkoop took Black Kettle's hand in a strong grasp. He searched for the words to express his feelings, but looking into Black Kettle's eyes, realized that none were necessary. Black Kettle had become like a brother, and each knew what was in the other's heart.

Without another word or a backward glance, Wynkoop mounted his horse, and rode away.

The autumn breeze that had blown the leaves at Black Kettle's feet had come from the north, and earlier in the day had cut across the banks of Bluff Creek in western Kansas. George Custer felt it whip across his face as he strode to the assembly area where his officers were waiting. Although not a cold wind, there was a coolness about it that foretold the coming of winter. This didn't bother Custer. Winter was what he was waiting for, when it would be to the Army's advantage, and when the Indians would be hunkered down in their teepees.

Custer walked under the canopy covering the briefing area as his men snapped to attention. He studied his staff, deliberately delaying the command to put them at ease. Finally he spoke.

"Be seated, gentlemen." Again he paused before continuing.

"This regiment is going to make history in a few very short weeks. We are going to strike the Indian in his winter camp, when he least expects trouble, and we are going to thoroughly punish those who have been raiding and murdering innocent women and children this past summer."

There was not exactly an outburst of applause, but the sudden light that sprang into the eyes of his officers, and the smiles that cracked their sunburned faces, were testimony enough to their enthusiasm.

"I have brought the regiment into this camp for two purposes. The first is to reorganize and renovate this command to prepare for the coming expedition, and the second is to refrain from further movement against the Indians until the full force of winter is upon us. We have crossed weapons with the savages in the summer months, when the buffalo and the grass are plentiful, and in so doing have yielded the advantage of movement and terrain to the enemy. Now we will be the ones to choose the circumstances of our meeting. When winter has pressed fully upon us, we will seek out the camp of the renegades and strike them hard while they are immobile and unsuspecting. We will end the Indian problem once and for all."

"But first, gentlemen, we have a task before us. It is all too evident to me after the past few weeks on the trail that this command is not ready for action. I realize many of you are comparatively new, and the officers and men have not served long together. But by God in the next few weeks we – you and I, gentlemen – are going to whip this regiment into the best group of fighting men the west has ever seen."

"Until I tell you otherwise, the companies will be marched beyond that hill behind you twice each day for target practice. I want a record kept of each bullet fired by each man. Also I want daily drills on the horses until this group of ragamuffins begins to look like a cavalry worthy of the U. S. Army. All horses will be newly shod and each trooper will carry extra shoes and nails in his saddle bag."

"As an incentive, you may tell your men that I expect to select 40 sharpshooters at the end of our stay who will be the pride of the 7th. These men will be marched as a separate company independent of the rest of the column, will not have to stand picket duty, and in battle will be stationed in a position of special responsibility and honor. Any questions? Very well, then. My adjutant will go over the details of the plan."

Over the next few weeks, as the north wind grew steadily cooler, Custer was true to his word. Well before sunrise the troops were rolled out of their warm blankets, fed, and started on their various training exercises, not ending until the only light left was from the evening camp fires. Over the groans and protests of tired muscles and aching bones, the 7th Cavalry slowly solidified into a toughened, cohesive, fighting group.

During this time Major Joel Elliot became Custer's favorite senior officer. He had an enthusiastic, reckless abandon that matched that of Custer, and they both shared the same belief that a company of 50 well trained cavalry could easily defeat 500 undisciplined Indians in battle.

"Well, General," Major Elliot remarked after one particularly grueling day, "what do you think of your men by now?"

"They are coming along, Major. Coming along. But they still need something a little extra to give them that special pride in themselves. I think it is time that we color the horses."

Elliot stared at his commander with a puzzled look. "Color the horses, Sir?"

"Yes, Major. I want all the horses gathered together and redistributed to the companies based on their color. The troop commanders, in the order of their rank, will select the shades they desire for their company. Put all the grays in one group, the bays in another, the chestnuts and blacks in another, and so forth."

During this time Custer also procured thirteen Indian scouts from the villages of the Osage Indians to help find the Cheyenne villages. The Cheyenne and Osage were traditional enemies, and the Osage were happy to participate in this expedition.

On the 12h of November, General Sully, Custer and his forces broke camp, and with a large train of almost 400 wagons, loaded with clothing, food and supplies, forded the banks of the Arkansas and headed south to establish a camp closer to Indian Territory. Approximately six days later a site was selected at the juncture of Wolf Creek and Beaver Creek, which together formed the north fork of the

Canadian River. The name given to the new base was Camp Supply. Here General Sully awaited the arrival of the Nineteenth Kansas Volunteers.

However, this ill fated contingent had run into a disastrous march trying to get there, which delayed their arrival by a week or more, and when they did arrive they were hardly in any condition to be going into battle.

On the 5th of November the 1200 members of the Nineteenth Kansas Volunteers, under the command of Governor Crawford, marched out of Topeka with crowds cheering them on, and started west. On the 14th they crossed to the south side of the Arkansas, and from here on they were in territory that was pretty much uncharted by white men. They had expected to be greeted along the way with fresh supplies from Sheridan, but these failed to materialize. They soon ran out of grain for the horses, and had to depend on grass for forage. By the 21st, they realized that they had no idea where they were.

Then came the blizzard. Hopelessly lost and floundering in the snow, their progress came to a complete standstill. By the 22nd they ran out of food, with only a few sugar cubes left to suck on. Their horses were weak from lack of forage, and many died. Crawford decided to send a group on ahead of the command to let Sheridan know they were in need of supplies. Plily led a contingent of 50 men into the snow-covered terrain, looking for Camp Supply.

By the 25th, they were in desperate straits. Crawford divided the command into two segments. Those who were still well and strong, and had horses that could carry them, about 500 men, would push on for help, while the remaining group, more than 600 volunteers, who were sick or without horses, would stay behind with the few supplies they had left. They named this encampment Camp Starvation.

The 500 men under Governor Crawford trudged ahead, and eventually ran across the trail of Plily and his 50 men. On the 26th of November, the 500 volunteers stumbled into Camp Supply, sick and weak from their ordeal. Plily had reached the camp the previous day, and supplies were already being assembled to send back to the troops that had been left behind. This last group, together with their rescuers, staggered into Camp Supply a few days later.

The 1200 man Nineteenth Kansas Volunteer Cavalry had arrived at Camp Supply, half frozen and half starved, with no supplies and half their horses dead or lost, and in no condition to launch an attack into Indian Territory.

Meanwhile, on the 21st of November, General Sheridan had arrived at Camp Supply to see his operation set into motion. He was disappointed to find the Nineteenth Kansas Volunteers had not arrived, but Colonel Custer probably did not share his concern. Custer was anxious to redeem his reputation, and didn't need to be burdened by a bunch of undisciplined volunteers, commanded by a Governor.

On the 22nd, Sheridan gave Custer authorization to proceed into Indian Territory and look for any sign of an Indian trail leading to or from the north that they could follow back to the south, to the Indian camp from which they came. The next morning, with snow drifts two feet deep, Custer and the 7th Cavalry set out.

Several days prior to this, Black Kettle and Little Robe, and two Arapaho chiefs, met with General Hazen at Fort Cobb. Black Kettle knew about Sheridan's winter campaign, and, following the advice of Wynkoop, wanted to bring his village closer to Fort Cobb for the Fort's protection, as had the Kiowa and Comanche. General Hazen, however, was well aware of his superior's plan to attack the Cheyenne Indian villages, and turned down their request. He told them they should go back to their lodges, and seek out

General Sheridan at the newly established Camp Supply to discuss their situation.

On the 26th, Major Elliott's company, which had been sent out ahead of the main body, discovered a large Indian trail of from 100 to 150 Indians, headed south. They assumed that this was a war party, now coming back to the Cheyenne villages to spend the winter. Elliott sent a messenger to Custer with the news, which was greeted with great enthusiasm. Custer sent word back to Elliott to follow the trail till 8:00 that night, and then wait for Custer and the main group to catch up with them.

Custer had his men shed all unnecessary equipment and clothing, left the wagon trains with a detachment of 80 troops to guard them, and hastily struck out to find Elliott and his men. Each man had 100 rounds of ammunition, and a small supply of hard tack. The march was hard and unrelenting, but at about 9:00 that night they came upon Elliott, awaiting Custer's arrival as ordered. After an hour's rest, Custer pushed the regiment on, with the Osage scouts well in advance.

Around midnight the scouts came upon a sleeping Cheyenne village. Custer and his officers scouted the encampment from a high ridge, and formulated their attack plan. The regiment was divided into four groups, and each proceeded into position for a dawn attack. The exhausted men, once in position, tried to get a few hours sleep before the winter sun would brighten the eastern sky.

Black Kettle had arrived in the village earlier in the evening from Fort Cobb. He gathered the village leaders together, and told them that in the morning he would set out for the new Camp Supply, to try to find General Sheridan, and assure him that Black Kettle's group had been peaceful, and had been following the instructions of their white brothers.

Black Kettle's camp, consisting of about 70 lodges, was the western most village of a large number of Indians camped on the Washita. Just below his camp, there was a village of Arapaho, and further down two other large Cheyenne villages. Most of the Indians whose trail Custer had been following had gone on to the other Cheyenne camps.

As dawn approached, Custer and his men waited, anxious for the order to attack the village. Custer placed the 40 sharpshooters on foot in the trees near the village where they could fire more accurately than on horseback. When the first rays of sun came over the horizon, a rifle shot rang out from somewhere in the Indian camp. Without hesitation, Custer sounded the charge. Bugles blared and the regimental band struck up "Garryowen," Custer's personal battle song.

Black Kettle did not sleep well that night, in spite of his long journey returning from Fort Cobb and his meeting with General Hazen. He was troubled by Hazen's words. Black Kettle had assured the General that his people were peaceful, and abiding by the decrees of the white chief. He wanted to move his people closer to the fort for their protection, but Hazen had denied this request. Why had he done this? Black Kettle did not have a good feeling about this man. Something about him reminded Black Kettle of the mad dog Chivington, and of their meeting just before the treachery at Sand Creek.

Black Kettle thought once again about the words spoken by Hazen. The white chief's promises were evasive, and he would not look Black Kettle in the eye when he spoke them. All he would say was that Black Kettle should see General Sheridan at some place he called Camp Supply. Sheridan believed that all Cheyenne were hostiles, Hazen had said, and Black Kettle should go and tell him that his people were peaceful.

Why can't the white man understand that not all Cheyenne are alike, Black Kettle thought? It is mainly the Dog Soldiers, the wild young men of the tribe, who are causing all the trouble. Just as there are white men who are for war, and others who want to live in peace. But those who want peace often are hurt because of the actions of those who are angry and discontent. This was true for both the Indian and the white man. Why should all be punished for the actions of a few? We Cheyenne and the whites, he thought, we are not too different.

Tomorrow without delay he would take some of his men and try to find this Camp Supply before something bad happened. A few hours before dawn Black Kettle finally fell into a deep sleep.

He was awakened abruptly by gun fire and bugles blasting across the cold morning's fog. With a sinking heart he looked outside to see soldiers racing into the camp, firing at everyone in sight. It is happening again, he thought in quiet despair. My people are being attacked again for no reason – just as at Sand Creek. Black Kettle had never known such sadness and anger as swept over him at this instant.

He called for his wife, Medicine Woman Later, and together they ran outside to Black Kettle's horse which was tied near the teepee. Swiftly Black Kettle leaped on the horse's back, and pulled Medicine Woman Later up in front of him. With a shout he brought the horse to a gallop, heading towards the creek bed.

He never felt the bullet that plowed into his back, as he slipped off the horse into the mud of the creek bank. Medicine Woman Later also received a fatal wound, and fell beside the body of her husband. The cavalry raced in pursuit of the escaping Indians, riding over the bodies of

Black Kettle and his wife, who lay trampled in the soft earth beside the creek.

For the first few minutes of the attack the village was a scene of utter chaos and confusion, Indians dashing from their tepees with rifles in hand, fighting the charging cavalry as best they could. Many were killed immediately; others were able to make it to the river banks and grove of trees, where they fought off the soldiers with great courage. The soldiers were everywhere, choosing targets where they could.

Within an hour Custer gained control of the camp. While various elements of the cavalry continued to fight Indians on the outskirts of the village, and to round up women and children prisoners to take back to Camp Supply, Custer set about to inventory and destroy the village itself.

Major Elliott, meanwhile, noticed a number of Indians coming out of the creek bed downstream. Probably these were women and children trying to escape to the south, but Elliott decided that he would either round them up if that was the case, or disperse them if they were braves assembling for an attack. He charged after them with 16 men from his company.

Around 10:00 in the morning, Custer became aware that the Indian resistance along the creek banks and in the trees was growing stronger. He also noticed large numbers of Indians gathering on the high ridges off to the south. These were warriors from other villages downstream on the Washita, the Arapaho and Cheyenne. They had become aware of the attack on Black Kettle's village, and had come to survey the situation. At this point they had not joined the battle, but their presence was threatening.

The Army rounded up all of the Indian ponies that had been left behind, around 830 of them. The choicest of these were divided among the Indian scouts and the officers, and the rest, almost 800 horses, were killed. The bloody execution took most of the morning.

The 70 Indian lodges were burned, and the contents of the village were gathered in a huge pile and destroyed by Custer's men. In addition the Indians lost their winter supply of buffalo meat, corn meal flour, and most of their clothing.

By noon the 7th Cavalry was running short of ammunition and supplies. Custer began to worry over the increasing Indian resistance. The village was now surrounded by small numbers of Indian fighters who were harassing the troops from a distance. But a wagon with supplies that Custer had arranged for was able to break through the ring of Indians, and reinforced the troops.

It was now late afternoon and the number of Indians gathering on the distant hill side was increasing. Custer was concerned that they might attack. He was also worried that they might discover the location of the wagons and supplies which he had left behind, and which were defended by only 80 soldiers. He decided to start an advance down the Washita towards the other Indian villages that he had now learned were there, and then when the sun went down, make a hasty retreat under the cover of night to their supply base.

He assembled the troops and their prisoners, some 53 women and young children, and started on the march. Notably missing was Major Elliott and the 16 men who had last been seen riding after a bunch of Indians up a grassy draw. Custer did not send anyone to look for them, or to try to determine their fate. His main concern now was for the safety of the main force.

When the Indians saw the 7th heading for their villages, many rode off to warn the women and children to get away. Custer advanced unopposed till night, then under cover of darkness turned the troops around and headed back to their supply wagons. The expedition made tracks for Camp Supply.

Custer claimed 103 Indian raiders had been killed. The 7th lost four men, including Captain Hamilton, plus the 17 men in Major Elliott's command. The Major and his men, chasing Indians they had seen leaving the river bed downstream, rounded a bend of the river and riding up a draw, found themselves surrounded by a group of Cheyenne who had fled from the village earlier and a band of Arapaho who had come up from the east to assist their brothers. Elliott and his men dismounted and formed a circle in the tall grass of the draw, but were quickly overrun by the Indians. They were all killed. Two weeks later, Custer and the 7th would return to the scene of the battle to discover the fate of his men.

General Sheridan praised the efforts of Custer and the troops, calling the fight the most complete and satisfactory battle ever waged against the Indians. Many others, however, called the attack on Black Kettle's village a wanton massacre of innocent Indians, and likened the battle to the Sand Creek affair.

People on the frontier were elated to learn of the death of Black Kettle. There were few Indian names actually known to the settlers, but the two that were most prominent on everyone's lips were Roman Nose and Black Kettle. These two were blamed for almost every instance of Indian brutality on the Kansas plains. Few of them realized that Black Kettle had become a great peace chief. He sought to avoid trouble with the white man and find a safe place for his people, even though he was continually betrayed and deceived. And he was belittled by many of his own tribe. He paid the ultimate price for his faith in the white man's pledges.

The 53 Cheyenne prisoners were later released and returned to the remnants of their village. Little Robe was elected as the new chief for what remained of Black Kettle's followers.

General Custer, in his official report of the battle, said that the body of a white woman was found, who had been murdered by the Cheyenne before she could be rescued by the troops. Also other soldiers described seeing an Indian woman leading a white boy by the hand, trying to escape the soldiers. When she found herself surrounded by troops, she pulled a knife from her dress and before the startled soldiers could move, stabbed it into the chest of the boy. When Custer and his troops returned to the Washita a week later, they found another murdered white woman in an Indian camp further downstream, apparently killed lest she be found and released by the soldiers. These acts made it obvious that the Cheyenne did not intend to have any of their prisoners rescued alive.

"So Black Kettle was killed at the Washita" I said. "That was tragic all right; after all he had done to try to find a way to live with the whites. But I still don't understand. All I really wanted to know about was the Cheyenne raid of 1869, and here you've told me about Lean Bear, Roman Nose and Black Kettle – and all of them were already dead by then. They had nothing to do with the raid."

"Well, Sonny, you remember that old song about the hip bone connected to the thigh bone, and the thigh bone connected to the shin bone, and the shin bone connected to the ankle bone, and so on? Same thing with history. Every event is connected to the next. The massacre of Cheyenne in their winter home made the Dog Soldiers pretty mad, let me tell you, and thirsty for revenge."

"At the same time," Old Joe continued, "the news was heralded by the settlers up in Kansas, and it made them even more determined to deal out frontier justice to any Indians threatening their homes. That led to the Mulberry Creek incident."

CHAPTER 20

Eli Ziegler was chopping wood in the side yard of his parent's home. Although it was a brisk February day, he was sweating heavily, had shed his coat, and was down to his rolled up shirt sleeves. Eli, now 17 years old, had filled out considerably since the battle at Arickaree the previous fall.

As he paused to wipe his brow, he saw a wagon coming up the road, and recognized his two brothers-in-law, John Alverson and Thomas Alderdice. His sisters, Mary and Susanna, and all their children, were riding in the back, Susanna holding their newest baby tight in her arms. Two other horses, tied to the wagon, trotted briskly behind. Something was wrong. Eli lay down the axe, slipped on his jacket, and walked to the front of the cabin to greet the visitors.

Thomas, who was driving, pulled up in front of the house, jumped down and tied the horses to the hitching post. "What's happening?" Eli asked. John, who had also leaped from the wagon, answered. "Indians. About 20 of them over at old man Skinner's house."

"Anyone hurt?" Eli asked.

"Not so far," John answered. "Unless you count terrifying an old man and his wife for several hours as being hurt,"

Thomas said. "Made them cook up a meal and hung around awhile, and then left."

"Cheyennes?"

"No – Pawnee. On foot. Left their reservation up in Nebraska – likely out to raid some horses from the Kaw or Cheyenne, or from some unsuspecting settler." While they talked, Thomas helped the ladies and children out of the back of the wagon.

"Oh, Eli," Mary was nearly in tears. "We were so worried. Aren't we ever going to be safe here? When will these Indians ever be gone and leave us in peace?"

"I shudder to think of being captured by them," Susanna added. "Why, Thomas was gone all day yesterday to look at some property. I was at home all alone with the children. What if they had come to our house? A woman with no man around? I get weak just thinking about it."

Thomas tried to reassure her. "Well, Pawnee are mostly friendly. Still, you never know what might get in those heathen's minds. It makes me furious to even think about them coming around to our place."

Eli's father, Matt, came to the door and held it open. Mary and Susanna ushered the children into the house while trying to answer questions from Matt and his wife.

The three men stood by the wagon for a short time in silence, each absorbed in his own thoughts. Overhead a line of crows flew closely over the trees, headed for the grove where they roosted nightly. Their sharp cries echoed across the country side, as the sun sank lower in the west.

"I don't think I ever saw Mary so upset," John finally said.

"Yeah, Susanna too," Thomas replied. "Ever since she's had the new baby she's been pretty excitable."

"Well, who can blame them?" Eli suggested. "We've got to do something about these Indians. The Army can't seem to do anything."

"Seems like the darn savages didn't take any heed about old Custer killing Black Kettle and his band," John muttered. "I guess we just need to keep on punishing them till they get the idea straight that they need to stay on their reservations."

"I think what we should do," Thomas said, "is to get a bunch of us together and go after them. We need to teach them it's not a smart idea to come poking around our homes and scaring our women."

"You got that right," John answered. "We need to make the rounds anyway to warn everyone to get their women to a safe place. Susanna and Mary and the children likely will be safe here with your Dad around to look out for them."

"Let's do it," Thomas replied. "John, if you want to let the settlers know there's Indians about, Eli and I will ride over to Schermerhorn's store. There's usually some Army camped out there. Maybe someone we know from those that rescued us at Beecher's Island. We'll see if we can get them to join us."

"Good. Meet here at 8:00 in the morning?"

The three nodded in agreement. John untied his horse from the rear of the wagon, mounted, and without another word headed out. Eli saddled his own horse, while Thomas went inside to tell everyone their plans. Soon he and Eli headed the other direction to Schermerhorn's store in search of the Army.

The next morning started off cold and dreary. The settlers, about a dozen of them, stomped their feet to keep warm as they milled in the yard outside of Matt Ziegler's cabin. Thomas pulled out his pocket watch and checked it for the third time in the past few minutes. "Almost 8:30," he said.

"Where do you think the Army boys are?" John asked. "They for sure said they'd be here, didn't they?"

"They'll be here," Thomas answered. "The Lieutenant promised. Reckon they're just a little slow getting around."

"Well, I'm not waiting around any longer," Eli stated. "I'm going on over to Skinner's place and see if I can pick up their trail. I'll leave plenty of sign so's you can follow me when the Army gets here."

"I'll go with you," Ed Johnson stated. "I'm pretty good at tracking. Twenty of them on foot ought to be easy to follow."

"OK," Thomas agreed. "But be careful. Don't start anything till we get there."

"We won't," Ed answered. "We weren't exactly born yesterday." He stuffed a large wad of tobacco in his mouth, turned to Eli, and declared "Let's be off, young 'un."

Fifteen minutes later a Lieutenant and a dozen soldiers arrived. "Sorry to be late," he said to the group waiting for them. "We got a little mixed up in our directions. But we're ready to ride. Which way do you think the Indians went?"

"We've got a couple of men tracking them now," Thomas replied. "We'll head over to Skinner's place and pick up their trail there."

Eli and Ed had little trouble in finding the path the Pawnee had taken. Coming to a grove of trees they saw the remains of a campfire, and evidence of where the Indians had spent the night. Eli got down from his horse and stirred the ashes of the fire. "Still warm," he said. "I bet they aren't far ahead."

Eli jumped back on his horse and they continued following the trail. A few minutes later they came to a cabin with smoke pouring from the chimney. "Who lives there?" Ed asked.

"That's Charles Martin's shack," Eli replied.

"Reckon they've got Martin cooking for them, just like they did with Skinner's wife," Ed observed.

Eli and Ed crept to the cabin door and listened to the sounds from within. They heard voices speaking in guttural accents. Eli called out "Hey Martin! You OK in there?"

Charles Martin, sounding relieved to hear another white man's voice, replied, "OK so far. They've got me cooking them up a meal. Reckon I'm OK till that's done anyway. Sure could use some company, though."

The door swung open and several Indians started to come out. Eli shoved his rifle into the belly of the lead man, and growled "Get back in there. You ain't going no place till the Army gets here."

The Indian backed into the cabin, but another pushed past and into the doorway. Again Eli stuck his rifle in the man's guts, and pushing him back, pulled the door shut.

Eli called out once again, "Charles! There's help on its way. Army boys and some of us locals. I'm going to go get them. Ed here will keep the savages inside till we get back. You just go on a'cookin for them."

Eli took off in a cloud of dust. The Army and the rest of the settlers weren't far behind. Eli raced to the Lieutenant's side, whirled around and shouted, "Come on. We've got them cornered in Martin's place." He rode off at a gallop. The soldiers and settlers gave a short yell, and followed.

When they got back to the cabin there was no sign of Indians.

"Durn, I just couldn't fight the whole bunch," Ed complained. "They started pouring out of the cabin, and there was too many of them for one old man to start shooting. They'd of just run all over me. As it is, no one's hurt and we know which way they went."

Eli, John and Thomas rode alongside some of the soldiers as they took up the chase. "I heard that Sheridan told Congress that the only good Indian is a dead Indian," John said. "When we catch up with this bunch I'll tell you for sure there's going to be some good Indians. Mighty good."

One of the soldiers gave him a funny look, and said, "Heck, we won't do them no harm. Our orders are not to shoot unless they fire first. Just round them up and return them to the reservation."

John stared at the trooper. "You mean you're just going to ask them to go back to their home, nice and polite like? After they terrorized and bullied settlers? "

"'Course if someone other than the Army was to start something with the Indians," the soldier continued, "and the Indians started firing back, we would sure have a right to come in and protect him, if you get what I mean."

John turned to Eli and Thomas. "Seems like I read somewhere that our Governor declared that any Indians not on their reservation are to be considered hostile. Far's I'm concerned, these are hostile Indians, and I intend to treat them as such."

The sun broke free of the early morning clouds and began to warm the winter day. John and Eli shed their coats and tied them to the rear of their saddles.

Coming around a bend in the river they saw the Indians.

"There they are, boys," John shouted, and took off at a gallop. The Pawnee scattered and ran to the banks of the creek where they hid in the grasses and bushes. The soldiers held back as the settlers rode in, trying to rout them out.

"Beats me how there can be twenty goshdurned Indians here one minute," Ed Johnson muttered," and then disappear right before your eyes." Even as he spoke four rose from the grass directly in front of his horse. Ed quickly swung his rifle around to fire. But he saw that the Indians were not raising their weapons. One held a paper for them to see.

"What's this?" Ed asked, keeping a steady bead on the lead Indian with his rifle. He took the proffered paper and studied it. "It's a discharge paper from the Army," he said at last. "Says this Indian was honorably discharged as a scout from the U. S. Army." He passed the paper to Thomas.

While this was going on, John Alverson slid from his horse unnoticed, rifle in hand, and took careful aim at the leader of the Indians. His finger tightened on the trigger, but at the last minute he paused, and lowered his weapon. Then he thought about Mary, and Susanna, and all of the other women and children that had been captured and terrorized by Indians. His anger surfaced once more. Taking careful aim he fired, and the Indian who had produced the discharge paper was blown backwards into the creek bed.

With a surprised yell the other three Indians raised their weapons, fired wildly and tried to get away down the creek bank. The settlers were quick to respond. Bullets filled the air and moments later the three Indians lay dead on the ground beside their companion. "That's four of them that won't be bothering our women anymore," Eli shouted. Aware of a stinging sensation in his leg, he looked down, and saw blood soaking through his pant's leg.

"Well I'll be durned," he exclaimed. "Here I survive Beecher's Island and all those Cheyenne without a scratch, and then get shot by a no-good Pawnee." The wound was superficial. Eli pulled a handkerchief from his pocket, tied it around his leg, and returned to the fight.

The rest of the Indian group, about 16 in number, broke from their hiding places and fled downstream, firing at their pursuers as they ran.

The Lieutenant and soldiers rode up, and joined the settlers in chasing after the Indians. The Pawnee, racing downstream, found a cave along the creek side and took refuge in it. The pursuers circled warily, trying to figure how they could get the Indians out. One of the soldiers, trying to get a good look into the cave, exposed himself momentarily, and was shot through the chest.

"Damn," the Lieutenant muttered. "The rest of you stay put and keep your heads down," he shouted to his men. To John and Thomas, who were by his side, he said, "We're going to have a hard time getting to them now. It'll take forever to starve them out."

"Best way is to smoke them out," John Alverson declared. "That land behind the creek bank has been farmed, and I see some old hay stacked up there, and lots of old dried brush. Thomas and myself will circle around to the backside of the cave, and toss some of that debris into the entrance. When we get enough, we'll drop a torch and burn them out."

The Lieutenant considered this suggestion for a minute, then said, "Go ahead. We'll keep the front covered for when they decide to make a break for it."

Thomas and John scooted back, being careful to keep a low profile. When they were far enough away, they made a wide circle and came out above the Indian hideout. As soon as the Indians saw the brush dropping into the cave entrance, they knew what their pursuers planned. With a loud shout they erupted from their shelter, meeting a barrage of fire. All but three fell, mortally wounded. The three remaining Indians ran off down the creek bed.

Several of the farmers mounted their horses and rode after them. From their vantage point they fired repeatedly at a range of about 150 yards. Two of the Indians fell. The third, seeing the settlers closing in on him, lay down his weapons and raised his hands in surrender. He was the only survivor, and was later returned to Fort Harker.

Eli, John and Thomas rode back to the Ziegler homestead, contemplating the events of the day in silence. The excitement of the chase and shooting of the Indians had left them emotionally drained and withdrawn.

"Don't know if we did right or not," Thomas finally said. "I reckon these particular Indians weren't out to hurt anyone. Not like the Cheyenne. It kinda gets to me that they were Army scouts."

"Thomas, just you remember how terrified Mary and Susanna were," John replied. "I couldn't stand the thought of those devils getting their hands on them or the children. And it could happen, easy as pie. Won't none of us feel safe until all these savages are gone for good."

"I think that's just about right," Eli responded. "Our families can't live in constant fear of being raped or killed or, even worse, being captured. These Indians left their reservation where they belonged. They got exactly what they deserved."

The other two nodded their agreement, somewhat reluctantly, as they rode quietly on.

While these events were unfolding in Kansas, a passenger ship from Europe docked in New York. Standing on deck were three people from Germany; George and Maria Weichel and Fred Meigerhoff.

"Oh George," Maria exclaimed, "Isn't it exciting? A brand new country. We are going to have such adventures, I just know it."

Both George and Fred smiled. "Yes, Maria," George answered. "Here we will find our fortune. It will be a new life for all of us."

"How long will it take us to get to this – what do you call it – Kansas?" Maria asked, probably for the tenth time.

"Several months, I think," George replied. "We have much to do between now and then. We will take a train to a town called Salina which is at the end of the settlements, and then we will survey the lands to the west to see where we would want to start our homestead. I am told the ground is very fertile there."

"Our English is still not so good," Fred interjected. "And Maria, you have not learned even to say one word. Do you think we will find anyone out there that can understand German?"

"Oh I'm sure we will," George reassured them. "I am told many Europeans have come to this country. This new law, the Homestead Act, enables anyone to file a claim on 160 acres of public land. Fred and I can claim 320 acres between us. And I think many who come here are very poor, and are not able to stay for the 5 years to improve their land. So someone with money can buy more land very cheaply. I think we will end up with a very large farm in this country."

"And," Fred chimed in, "I think many who want the land do not know how to care for it. They are not scientific and will not do well. With our experience, we should be the best farmers in the whole west."

"But what of the Indians," Maria protested. "Are they still not a threat to the settlers?"

"Bah – the Indians will not bother us. The Army even now is chasing them to the south of where we go. Our timing couldn't be better. I think we will do very good in this new world. And we don't have to worry about the Bismark, and being conscripted to fight in his army. Here we are free. Here we will prosper."

CHAPTER 21

"That was a pretty awful thing the settlers did to those Pawnee," I said.

"Yup," Old Joe replied. *"But you gotta consider – they were worried sick over their families. I guess there were enough bad things and tension on both sides to keep from pointing fingers. But it shows just how riled up everyone was. Indian and settlers alike."*

"You said that Tall Bull was upset about the massacre at Washita. Did he go on the war path?"

"Not right at first. Remember it was winter, and their ponies were weak from lack of food. Not a good time to start raiding. But he was mad all right. He camped that winter on the Republican River way up In Nebraska."

Tall Bull opened the flap of his teepee and strode into the brisk February morning. The sun was rising over the trees to the east. He could see his breath in the air, but knew that the day would warm quickly. The grass, however, had not yet started to grow, and the horses were thin from the long winter.

Tall Bull thought of his brothers who had stayed in Indian Territory in the south. He was furious over the treachery of the soldiers at the Washita, but also thought

Black Kettle had been a fool to trust the white men. Black Kettle and his people had paid dearly - once at Sand Creek and again now at their winter camp. He had not been a good leader. The only way to deal with the whites, he thought, is to destroy their homes and families until they have no fight left.

Still, it might be a good thing to see his southern brothers again before the battles of the summer. The Dog Soldiers had many family and friends among those who had moved to the reservations. Little Robe had been chosen as the new chief of the people after Black Kettle's death. Little Robe was a good man. He would not make the same mistakes that Black Kettle had.

And maybe the government had issued supplies to the tribe. It would be good to visit their brothers to the south once more, and maybe they could share their provisions with Tall Bull and his followers. The grass would be much greener and the ponies could be fattened. And maybe a few young braves from the southern tribe would join Tall Bull and his Dog Soldiers.

Yes, it would be good to travel south.

Little Robe sat on the bank of the Red River, thinking about his new responsibilities as a chief for the tribe. Although he had ridden often with the Dog Soldiers, he had been a great admirer of Black Kettle, and thought to follow his policy of trying to live with the whites. He had been to Fort Cobb and met with General Hazen, and later with the General Sheridan. He told them his tribe wanted peace with the white men, and asked what he should do to ensure their safety, and to obtain the release of the prisoners that had been taken at the Washita.

A large oak tree just across the river, alive with the bright-green, new growth of spring, shimmered in the bright mid-day sun. Little Robe reached to the ground and picked up a dry, brown leaf from the previous summer. He remembered how Black Kettle always studied the leaves. Our tribe, he thought, is like the mighty oak, and our people are the leaves. Here on the ground are yesterday's leaves. The last leaves of autumn. Black Kettle, Roman Nose, Lean Bear – and myself. But on the tree are new leaves, bright and promising and glowing in the spring breeze. It is for these leaves that he must be concerned, to make sure that they could grow and blossom and make the tree strong.

Hearing noise and shouting in the camp, he arose, and proceeded back to the village. He hadn't gone far before he saw what was causing the commotion.

There on a magnificent white and brown spotted horse, surrounded by the village people, was Tall Bull, followed by several hundred Dog Soldiers. Everyone was talking and shouting at once, greeting old friends and exchanging news of loved ones.

Little Robe watched the proceedings for a few minutes, and knew what had to be done. He strode up to Tall Bull, who had now dismounted and was patting the backs of those surrounding him.

"You are not welcome here, my brother," Little Robe said without preamble. "You make war with the whites, with whom we are at peace. You must not come to this village, or the whites will follow you and attack us all."

Dumbstruck by this greeting, Tall Bull did not at first reply. Then, with anger building, retorted, "Is this the way in which we are welcomed? Your brothers who have been fighting for our tribe's freedom, while you stay down here where the white men tell you where you can go, like a puppy dog with your tail between your legs?"

"You and the Dog Soldiers bring trouble wherever you go," Little Robe maintained, "and you will bring trouble here if you stay."

"And was it I who brought trouble to your village on the Washita?" Tall Bull demanded. "Was it the Dog Soldiers that attacked your camp, and killed your people? Bah! It is the white man who is your enemy, and we are your brothers who fight them. Are we not welcome in your village then?"

Little Robe responded. "We have made peace with the white men. They have promised to release our women and children taken prisoners at the Washita if we remain peaceful. We are going to move our village to the new Camp Supply, as the white father has requested, and there we will be issued rations and live in peace. And our children will be able to play and grow without fear of war and attack."

"They will grow up to be rabbits, not warriors as the Cheyenne have always been," Tall Bull said with great sarcasm. "What good is it to live if we can no longer roam the prairie and hunt the buffalo? I do not accept your way of peace. Peace will come when we have driven the whites away, and torn up their railroads. Then the white man will respect our land, and leave us alone."

"It will not happen," Little Robe responded. "We cannot defeat the whites. We must learn to live with them. Our children must learn their ways."

"Bah!" Tall Bull said.

"You are not welcome here," Little Robe repeated. "You and the Dog Soldiers must leave. We do not want any trouble here, and you bring us nothing but trouble. You must go!"

"I cannot believe that you are my brother," Tall Bull shouted. "You, who once were a great fighter, have become the white man's camp dog. You have no honor. You do not know a warrior's blood. You are more worthless than an old woman!"

"Go," Little Robe said, "and if you do not, our people will join with the whites to hunt you down and destroy you!"

Tall Bull glared at Little Robe for a full minute, then with head held high, retorted, "Then we shall go. If we are no longer welcome here, we will ride to the north and join our cousins, the Northern Cheyenne, and the Sioux, who are not afraid of their shadows and still remember how it is to be a fighter."

He shouted to the crowd who had gathered around them, "Come with me, all of you who would be warriors! We go to our hunting grounds to hunt the buffalo, and kill any who would get in our way! And to drive the white men out of our country. Afterwards we will join our relatives to the north, who still know how to be men."

A wild cheer erupted from some of the young braves, who ran to get their things to join the Dog Soldiers.

Little Robe watched them go with a great sadness.

Tall Bull, seething inside with the greatest anger he had ever known, led his followers north to Beaver Creek, a tributary of the Republican River in northwest Kansas. Here they planned to hunt the buffalo before preparing for the long journey to the north to Wyoming and Montana, where the Indians still dominated the plains.

CHAPTER 22

"Ever hear of Schermerhorn's Store?" Old Joe asked.
"Nope – can't say that I have."
"It was a meetin' place for everyone around here," Old Joe said. "One of those places you go to for supplies and to get caught up on all the local news. It was located on Elk Creek, about two miles east and three miles south of here.

Lon Schermerhorn had been a merchant most of his life. For a number of years he operated a general store in Leavenworth, where he supplied wagon trains heading for the Northwest on the Oregon Trail. But the heavy traffic of the 40's and 50's had brought too much civilization to Schermerhorn's point of view. The earlier excitement and bustle of "wagon's west" had given way to a more settled and staid city trade.

"Too many people," was Lon's main complaint. "A fellow needs to be where he's got a little elbow room. Where he can sit by his front door and see the sun go down without any other houses around. And hear the singing of the birds and the quiet of God's creation. And where people ain't so close but what you're glad to see them comin' instead of wishin' they were going."

So Lon Schermerhorn packed up his things one day in 1867, sold his belongings in Leavenworth, and headed west with his wife of 30 years. He gave a lot of thought as to where he would build his new store, talked with settlers in the area, and did a lot of surveying. He finally decided on this location on the Elkhorn Creek, where there were a number of new farms in the making.

Some had urged him to build on the Solomon River a few miles to the northwest, as that seemed like an area that was going to fill up rapidly in the coming years. But an old buffalo hunter, who knew western Kansas like it was his own back yard, warned against it. "The Solomon still belongs to the Indians," the old timer had said. "Don't make no difference what the treaties say, or what Old General Sherman says, the Solomon and the Saline are the Cheyenne's favorite hunting grounds and they ain't goin' to take kindly to anyone settling down there, mark my words."

Lon Schermerhorn decided to follow the old timer's advice. He found just the place he wanted, filed a Homestead claim, and built a solid building out of logs brought from Missouri – half store and half house. From the very start he did a brisk business, providing the necessities to the settlers moving into the surrounding countryside, and saving them the longer trip into Salina. It quickly became a hub for the people moving into the region. The Army built a stockade nearby and camped there whenever they were in the vicinity.

On a warm and sunny day early in May, Lon Schermerhorn sat on a chair in front of his store and watched a wagon approaching. Two people, a man and a woman, sat at the front. A second man rode a horse alongside the rig.

Lon studied the load on the wagon. "Folks must be pretty well to do," he thought, based on the amount of baggage and goods stacked high above the rim of the wagon.

As the team drew near, the man driving the wagon yelled out a "Hello," and waved a greeting.

"This is the Schermerhorn Store?" the stranger asked in heavy German accents.

"Yep, this is it," Lon replied, "and I'm him. Get down and light a spell."

The man in the wagon hopped to the ground, tied the horses to the hitching post, and helped the woman down. Lon could see she was very pretty. Dark hair showing from underneath her bonnet, a generous mouth which was turned up in an impish smile and a sparkle in her eyes that could be seen even from this distance. Also very young. Probably only about 20 years old. She was dressed in very fine traveling clothes.

The other man dismounted and tied his horse to the wagon.

The one that seemed to be in charge took off his hat, wiped his brow, and then in halting English said "We look for man named Ferdinand Erhardt. You know him, yes?"

Schermerhorn nodded his head. "Yep, I know Ferdinand. Has a claim not far from here." Lon surveyed the bags and equipment on the wagon, and remarked," Looks like you might be interested in homesteading yourself."

"Yes – homesteading we are. We not speak much English, but look for Mr. Erhardt. He is German from Wurtenberg. We are to stay with him while we look for land. My name is George Weichel, and this my wife, Maria. This is my friend, Fred Meigerhoff," he added, indicating the other man who had joined them. The men all shook hands, and Maria gave a short curtsey.

"Well, you don't have far to go," Lon replied, and with many interruptions to make sure they understood, told them how to get to Erhardt's spread. George Weichel nodded eagerly as Lon talked, and relayed the information in German to his two companions.

"They don't speak the English so good," he explained to Lon.

A few days later Thomas Alderdice and his step-son, Willis Daily, rode into the Schermerhorn place to buy some grain. Dismounting, they tied the horses to the hitching post and ambled into the store. Once inside Thomas noted that Timothy Kine and his wife, Bridget, neighbors of the Alderdice's, were in the store also. Mrs. Kine, a spinsterish looking woman with a sharp nose and jutting jaw, was looking at yard goods, holding up a bolt of white cloth with red polka dots on it.

When Timothy saw Thomas, he hurried over to shake his hand. After exchanging a few pleasantries, Timothy jabbed his finger on Thomas's chest and said, "Did you know that Alan Smith, old Conrad's son, has filed claim to the land next to us?" he asked.

"Alan?" Thomas replied. "Why, he's just a kid isn't he? Not old enough to be filing a claim on his own."

"My point exactly," Timothy replied. "Old Conrad has been eyeing that land for a long time now, but he already has that homestead over on Bullfoot. So he's trying to pull a fast one and get the land under his son's name."

"Well, that's not right," Thomas surmised. "Plenty of land to go around. People shouldn't start getting greedy."

"My point exactly," Timothy agreed.

A clatter outside announced the arrival of another wagon. Thomas looked out to see Ferdinand Erhardt and three others, speaking in German, arriving to buy supplies. Thomas watched as they tied up their horses, and came into the store.

Seeing Timothy and Thomas, Ferdinand ambled over to say hello, while the three Germans went to work picking out food supplies. Ferdinand identified them as the Weichels and Fred Meigerhoff, who were staying with him temporarily.

The Germen men soon moved to the back of the store to inspect some of the farm tools, while Maria sorted through the clothing goods. She held up the bolt of polka dots that Mrs. Kine had just been looking at, and then put it back down with a soft giggle. Suddenly she saw a buffalo head mounted on the wall, and pointed to it with great excitement. The men all laughed, and Ferdinand explained that Maria had just seen her first live buffalo the previous day.

"How are they doing on their land search?" Lon Schermerhorn asked Ferdinand.

"Very good," Ferdinand replied. "I showed them a claim just above mine on Bullfoot Creek, which they're going to take. That George seems to be a pretty scientific fellow. Got a tool to stick in the ground and draw up a sample of the soil. They are pretty particular."

Two more wagons drew up to the front of the store, and in a few minutes several men came in, laughing and talking in German. They were Danes who had homesteaded on Spillman Creek, north and west of the store.

Thomas nodded to the new arrivals. He vaguely recognized the two men, Erskild Lauritzen and Otto Petersen. The two greeted Ferdinand Erhardt in German. Maria's face lit up as she heard her native tongue being spoken, and called for her husband who was still in the back of the store. She and George engaged the new arrivals in animated conversation in their native tongue. Thomas watched them talk on for 30 minutes or more while he and Willis loaded up their wagon. The Danes and Germans seemed to be discussing something very important, arms now and then waving in the air, or pointing one direction or the other. Ferdinand Erhardt joined the exchange, and Thomas could tell he was displeased with the way the conversation was going, finally shaking his head and walking away.

"What's that all about?" Thomas asked.

"The Danes there are talking my new German friends into filing a claim up on Spillman Creek, where they are. Said the land is much better than down here. I tried to tell them it just ain't safe up there. That's where the Indians like to camp, and they'll probably be there again. But I don't think I convinced them. There are several Danish families up there now, and the lady is very excited to think she could have neighbors, other than just me, that she could talk to."

"I sure wouldn't recommend anyone settle up there," Schermerhorn said.

"We'd best be on our way," Thomas said. Turning to Timothy Kine, he added, "Probably we need to go to Junction City before too long and file a protest over Smith's claim. I can't stand someone that doesn't play by the rules."

"My point exactly," Timothy replied.

George and Maria Weichel, and their friend and partner, Fred Meigerhoff, liked the land Lauritzen showed them on the Spillman, and were delighted to be in a community that spoke German. On May 10th, they traveled to Junction City to file their claim on the lands that they had settled on, and also to take out citizenship papers. They would return to their claim sometime around the end of the month.

CHAPTER 23

In May of 1869, Tall Bull and 165 lodges of Dog Soldiers, consisting of 200 warriors and their families, were camped at Beaver Creek, a tributary of the Republican River in northwestern Kansas. They were joined by a small band of Arapaho and Sioux Indians who had wintered in the vicinity. Unknown to Tall Bull, General Carr and the 5th Cavalry were also encamped on the river, further to the west. They were enroute to Fort McPherson in Nebraska in response to fears that there might be a major uprising with the Sioux and Northern Cheyenne that summer.

It was a warm spring day in the sheltered confines of the Dog Soldier village. Tall Bull and White Horse, the two primary leaders of the Dog Soldiers, were inspecting the tribe's herd of ponies.

"The horses are fattened from their long winter fast," Tall Bull said. "Soon now it will be time to begin our journey to the north. We have no brothers in this country to hold us," he added bitterly. "Our only brothers are far to the north, riding with Red Cloud and the Sioux in Montana."

"It is as you say," White Horse replied. "Many of our men are still angry over Little Robe's words. I think it is best that we leave this place and join our cousins. Together we will be much stronger against the whites than if we fight them separately."

A clatter of horses charging straight for Tall Bull's teepee in the center of the village interrupted their talk. Tall Bull could see that it was the small group of braves that had gone on a hunting trip earlier in the morning. The leader of the pack, seeing Tall Bull and White Horse near the horse corral, turned his pony and raced towards them, stopping only a few feet in front of them in a cloud of dust.

He was gasping for breath as he slid from his horse, and exclaimed, "Soldiers! Many of them just to the west." He struggled to catch his breath, then continued. "We were coming back from our hunt when we spotted a small scouting party. They have found our trail. We attacked, but they retreated before we could do much harm. We followed them, and saw a large group of soldiers. Not many miles from here."

Tall Bull responded without hesitation. "We must move our camp. The soldiers will be here. Quickly, spread the word. We will break into small groups to avoid the soldiers, and meet again on the Solomon."

The next day, while the village was still being torn down, the cavalry attacked. The Cheyenne fought a delaying action while the women and children escaped. The battle raged for most of the afternoon, with the Indians slowly moving downstream. At dusk the cavalry broke off and returned to their camp, but it was a great victory for the troops. Only four soldiers had been killed, compared to 25 Indians, with 25 lodges captured and destroyed.

That night Tall Bull and his men regrouped, and buried their dead.

"The soldiers will be back," Tall Bull said. "We must be ready for them."

Shortly after sun up Carr started in pursuit of the Dog Soldiers once again, sending a small scouting party ahead.

This group soon ran across a half dozen warriors, and the two sides once again took up the fight. But when Carr's full command came into view, the Indians turned and fled into the hills, with the cavalry in hot pursuit.

Tall Bull watched all of this from a deep ravine, where he and the rest of the Dog Soldiers were hidden, waiting for the Army to ride into the ambush. The warriors that had acted as a decoy came over the ridge and joined their brothers, ready to charge back into the ranks of the cavalry which were now spread out as they tried to catch the six Indians. But just before reaching the hill, a bugle sounded and the soldiers, seeming to realize it might be a trap, reined in their horses. They dismounted, and formed a skirmish line.

Tall Bull, realizing his ambush wasn't going to work, attacked with the full force of the Dog Soldiers. The ensuing battle was fierce but not as deadly as the previous day. Tall Bull finally broke off the attack, and the Cheyenne disappeared over the hills as quickly as they had come.

Carr, satisfied that he had dealt the Cheyenne a serious blow, assembled his troops and continued, as ordered, to Fort McPherson.

Tall Bull and the Dog Soldiers were infuriated. They had lost many braves, and their women and children had been in grave danger of being captured or killed. This was on top of the fury they were already feeling over Little Robe's rejection. The mood was one of great frustration and anger.

Tall Bull, White Horse and several other leaders of the tribe held a council shortly after the fight. "The horse soldiers have moved on to the north," Tall Bull said, "but our losses have been great."

"If the soldiers are gone," one of the men observed, "who is there to protect the railroad workers and settlers from our wrath?"

"It is a wise thing that we go to join our cousins to the north," another said. "But I think the white man must be taught one final lesson before we go. He must pay for the attack on our village. He must be made to realize that we do not go in fear or humiliation, like our brothers to the south, but with pride and defiance. He must be punished for attacking our village, and for his treachery at Washita, and for threatening our women and children."

Others voiced their agreement.

Tall Bull nodded. "These words are true. The white man has killed our people and burned our lodges at Sand Creek. The old man Hancock burned our lodges at Pawnee Fork. The yellow-haired one killed our people at the Washita and burned more of our lodges. All of this when our people were at a truce and doing as the white men had commanded. Now this Carr attacks us, and our people are once more on the run, terrified for their lives. Yes, this all must be avenged before we move to the north to join our cousins."

"Let us ride south to the settlements once more," White Horse stated, "and remind the whites that we are Dog Soldiers, the most respected and feared warrior society in the Cheyenne Nation."

"We will avenge the loss of our brothers," others echoed Tall Bull's words. "Let our wrath be felt before we travel to the northern plains."

Tall Bull listened to these emotional outbursts. The need for revenge was great, and must be satisfied. The next day he and the Dog Soldiers moved south and planned their assault on the settlers along the Spillman and Saline rivers.

"Well, Joe, I guess we're finally going to talk about the massacre that the monument was erected for in town," I said. "I was beginning to think you'd never get around to it. But I must admit everything you've told me has been really interesting. I guess I can understand the frustration the Indians felt when they swooped down on the homesteads. But still, to attack innocent women and children...."

"You got to look at it from the Indian's point of view," Old Joe interjected. "I'll grant you that the raid was cruel and vicious, but it was the "innocent' women and children that were at the root of all the trouble. It was the settlers that was driving the Indians off their land, not the Army."

"Guess you got a point there." I glanced at the setting sun. "Only problem is, it's getting late again. Why don't we call it quits for tonight and take it up again in the morning when we're both fresh?" I had noticed Old Joe's voice sounded tired, and his words had taken on a slight slur.

He didn't answer right away and I turned to look at him. He seemed agitated, like something was bothering him. "Anything wrong?" I asked.

"No, no. Just get a little riled up I guess thinking about the raid." He looked around at the lengthening shadows, and listened to the frogs croaking down by the creek. The sky, a bright orange from the sun sinking in the west, was beginning to take on a purplish hue.

"I reckon you're right, Sonny. Let's call it quits for today." He brought out his pipe and began to clean it, although he had just done this a few minutes earlier. I was a little concerned, but didn't say anything..

"O.K., Joe. I'll be here first thing in the morning."

CHAPTER 24

The next morning I was back to the ramshackle old house at 8:00 sharp. Old Joe was there waiting for me. I brought along some donuts that I had bought in town, and offered him one.

"No, thanks, Sonny," he said. "I never eat anything on an empty stomach."

It took a minute for what he had said to sink in. "Joe, that doesn't make sense," I said. "If you never eat anything when your stomach is empty, then I guess you'd never eat anything ever."

"Well, that's what I said wasn't it? When I was young I used to eat a lot, but as you get older you kinda lose your appetite."

I studied Old Joe carefully, but he didn't seem to have any idea how absurd his statements were. Trying to reason with him was like reasoning with a wart hog, and not worth the attempt. I decided to change the subject.

"You feeling better this morning?" I asked. "Last night I thought you sounded kind of tired."

"Oh yes. Feel fine," he answered. "I just seem to get a little upset whenever I think about that day. Not only about what the Cheyenne did to the settlers, but what they did to themselves as well. It was the end of an era. And the beginning of a new one." His voice choked up slightly. For a few moments there I wasn't sure he was going to be able to talk about the raid, but he finally cleared his throat and began.

"The day was beautiful," he said, "bright and sunny, just like a Kansas day can be in the springtime."

Susanna Alderdice watched the wagon, loaded with corn, oats and provisions for an extended trip, pull to the front of their cabin, recognizing her brother, Eli Ziegler and brother-in-law John Alverson.

"Hello Eli – John," she said as they drew near. "What brings you two up this way?"

"Land," Eli replied. "Land that's already been cleared and just waiting for someone to claim."

"Fellow staked a claim on Bacon Creek, just north of the Danish Settlement," John answered, "then got Injun scared, and lit out back east. It's an abandoned claim, and Eli and I thought we might as well be the ones to pick up where he left off. Going to go up there and plant some corn and oats."

Susanna frowned. "You know, that fellow who lit out might just have had good reason to be scared. That's beyond any of the other settlements. Puts you right on the leading edge. And I hear tell that the Indians are back. Some talk about a raid on a railroad working party just to the west of here two days ago. Two men killed."

"Well, guess it's good news they're to the west and not to the north," John replied. "But anyway, I reckon the Army's chasing them all the way back to Indian Territory by now."

Eli noticed the gentle swelling in Susanna's abdomen, which was beginning to be quite obvious. "How's little Oswald doing?" he asked.

"Oh he's just fine. Or she," Susanna replied. "Starting to move around a little. Still got some months to go, though."

"Where's Thomas?" John asked, looking around the grounds and not seeing any activity.

"He's off to Junction City. He and some of the others got all riled up about a land claim filed by a minor, and they went in to protest. And then to Salina to get supplies. He'll be back tomorrow."

"And left you and the boys and the baby here all alone?"

"I reckon we'll be alright. He made arrangements for us to go over to Michael Healy's place to spend the night. He and his family lit out for Ellsworth when all this Indian scare came up, but said all of us could stay there if trouble started. He's got the biggest home west of Salina, you know. Mrs. Kine and her new baby are going over, too, and Nick Whalen has offered to spend the night. Mr. Whalen will likely look after us OK. The children and I were just getting ready to head over that way when you rode up."

"Well, shucks," Eli said. "I guess that just about lets us out of any chance of getting a bite to eat then."

Susanna laughed. "Well, I reckon I got time to put together a sandwich or two."

Just then her eldest boy, John, came out of the house, and the two men had to explain all over again where they were going and what they were planning.

"Can I come along Uncle Eli? Can I, Ma?" John exclaimed.

The two men laughed. "Well, John, I know you'd be a big help to your uncle and me," Eli said, "but right now your ma needs you to look after her. Not many six year olds have that kind of responsibility, you know."

The older John ruffled the boy's hair, and added "Maybe next time."

Eli and John did not linger at Susanna's. As soon as they finished their sandwiches they were on their way, and by mid afternoon passed the Danish Settlement, where Lorentz and his brother, Peter Christiansen, had their farms. This was as far north and west as the settlements went. Half a mile back they had seen the Lauritzen home where the new Germans were staying.

"Probably ought to get acquainted with them," Eli joked. "Only problem, none of that bunch talks much English, so it's pretty hard to communicate."

About then John noticed a bunch of horsemen in the distance.

"What do you make of that, Eli?" he asked. Eli strained to get a better look. "Looks like cavalry to me," he surmised.

"I don't know," John said. "Could be Indians."

"If they are, we'd best be getting this wagon moving. I keep seeing reflections from their rifles, though, and they look like they're riding in formation. Probably Army."

The two watched the group as they drew nearer. Suddenly Eli exclaimed,"They're Indians alright. Let's get a move on." He snapped the whip over the horses' backs and they turned back towards the creek bed they had just crossed.

The Indians were now in full chase, yelling and whooping as they drew nearer. John and Eli kept looking back to see how fast they were gaining on them.

"Look there," Eli said. "Some of them are peeling off and heading for the Danish Settlement."

"Can't help them none," John answered. "Maybe they'll hear the sound of our shooting, though, and be warned. Over there," he shouted. "Pull the wagon over there on that ridge above the creek bed. We can get down in that gully in the creek and hold them off from there."

As Eli brought the wagon to the ridge, John jumped down and dove for the brush in the river. Eli thought he had time to unhitch the horses and tie them to a tree, but the Indians were upon them before he could even get off the wagon.

"Over here, Eli," John shouted. "Hurry!"

By then bullets were flying all around Eli. He grabbed his rifle and some cartridges and fired at the closest warrior, then made a run for the creek. Just as he reached the embankment he turned back to see an Indian taking aim on him with a rifle. Eli leaped forward, tripped over an exposed tree root, and fell to the ground just as the Indian's rifle exploded. He heard the bullet whistle past his ear as he tumbled down the ledge, then he was beside John who was busy firing at their pursuers.

For some time they waited for the Indians to attack, but the warriors remained on the ledge over the creek bed just out of sight. John and Eli could hear them milling around their abandoned wagon, then the sound of it being driven off.

As they waited for the Indians to attack, they heard the sound of rifle fire off to the south. "They've reached the Danish Settlement," John remarked. When the Indians heard this distant shooting they gave a defiant yell and rode off to join their brothers.

The Danish Settlement, as it was called in 1869, is the present town of Denmark, Kansas. The first of the Danish families to settle there was Erskild Lauritzen, with his wife, Stine, and son, and a single man, Otto Petersen. They erected a log cabin in which they all lived.

In February, 1869, they were joined by the Christensen brothers, Lorentz and Peter, and their families. Peter and his wife had three children. The Christensens built a dugout along the banks of the Spillman, just to the north of the Lauritzens.

In May, George and Maria Weichel and Fred Meigerhoff came to stay with the Lauritzens until they could build a place of their own, and filed a claim on two lots just below Otto Petersen's farm. All of these farms bordered on Spillman Creek.

It was one of those beautiful Kansas days when the sun shone brightly but without the heat that would follow in July and August. A few white clouds drifted in the blue sky, casting shadows which moved quietly across the green hills. Erskild Lauritzen and Stine were enjoying the soft spring-time breeze, as they ambled towards the Christiansen dugout. Their son was playing with the Christiansen children, and Erskild and Stine were off to get him and bring him back home. As they neared the dugout, they surveyed the crops that the Christensens had planted.

"Peter told me that he had planted some corn just over the ridge there, "Erskild said. "Let's go over and see how it is doing."

"But Erskild," Stine replied, "we'd have to cross the creek to get there. I don't want to get my shoes wet."

"Oh, come on. The water's low, and there are stones to step on to get across." Erskild took hold of his wife with one hand as he shifted his rifle to the other, and gently pulled her to the creek and helped her across.

As they came up the bank on the other side of the creek they found themselves facing a dozen Indians. With a wild yell the warriors started towards the two.

"Oh my God!" Stine cried. Erskild raised his rifle and was sighting on the lead warrior when he felt something slam into his chest. He staggered back, tried to raise the rifle again, fell to his knees, then slumped forward flat on the ground.

Stine knelt beside her husband and tried to raise his head, but it rolled lifelessly in her arms. The Indians swarmed around her, and two dismounted. With knives in one hand and rifles in the other they started towards her.

With a sob, Stine grabbed Erskild's rifle and shot wildly at one of the two Indians. Startled, the warrior dropped to his knees, and with a swift motion raised his rifle and fired.

The force of the bullet threw her back across the body of her husband.

In the dugout, Peter and Lorentz Christiansen heard the sound of the gunfire, and hustled the women and children inside the dwelling. They strained to see what was going on through the small slits in the walls of the dugout. The shooting stopped, and the men waited anxiously while the women tried to calm the children. They had three of their own, and the visiting Lauritzen boy.

"What do you suppose the shooting was about?" Peter asked his brother.

Lorentz looked at Peter, then back at the women and children, before answering. "Erskild and Stine were going to come over to pick up their boy. About the right time for them to be out there," he said in a hushed voice. Peter did not answer, but turned once again to peer out into the clearing in front of the dugout. As he watched a number of Indians rode into view. Without hesitation Peter fired at the lead warrior who straightened in his saddle, then fell to the ground. A brief fight followed, with neither side inflicting any damage on the other.

The Indians withdrew for a little, and then appeared again at the edge of the clearing. Lorentz could see they had a torch of some kind.

"Going to try to burn us out," he muttered to Peter, as he fired his rifle towards the group. In the next minute several arrows, with a burning cloth attached to each, were shot towards the dugout.

"Not going to have much luck burning sod, I reckon," Peter observed, as he sent yet another volley towards the Indians, who were keeping a safe distance away.

The Indians made several more desultory attempts to drive the settlers from their dugout, and then with much fan fare, rode off to the south.

"Reckon they're gone for good?" Peter asked.

"I don't know," Lorentz replied. "But I ain't wandering out there right now to see. When it gets dark, if they haven't come back by then, I think we ought to try to get the women and children down to Schermerhorn's Store."

Peter nodded in agreement.

Otto Petersen heard the gunfire up towards the Christensen place. He dropped the hoe he had been working with, and started towards the home he shared with Erskild and Stine Lauritzen. He was unarmed.

He had only gone a few hundred yards when a dozen Indians broke out of the trees ahead of him. Otto sprinted for the cover of the creek bed. His long legs made good time, but not good enough. One of the braves raced past him on his horse, and Otto felt a slight tap on his shoulder. He came to a stop and examined himself, expecting to see blood running down his side. But there was nothing.

The warrior who had punched his shoulder rode on past for another 30 yards and turned his horse around to face Otto. He raised his tomahawk, and gave a loud ear-splitting scream. Otto remembered that Indians liked to count something called coup on their enemies, and sometimes that was enough. They didn't have to actually kill them. Maybe that was all this Indian wanted, and would now leave him alone unharmed. The other Indians had stopped by the edge of the trees, and were watching the two in the field. Every now and then one would yell something to the warrior who was facing Otto, and then laugh derisively.

Emboldened by the thought that they might not harm him, Otto faced the warrior with his head held high. With one last yell, the Indian spurred his horse forward, tomahawk held high in the air. For a moment Otto stood his ground, then his nerve broke and once again he spurted off in a race to the river. He could hear the warrior coming up behind him, and then felt an excruciating pain in his head. He fell to the ground with the tomahawk buried deep in his skull.

The brave dismounted, pulled a knife from his belt, and approached the dead body.

"Oh George! Look! It is snowing! See, Fred. See the snow is falling all about us, and yet it is so warm." Maria laughed as she ran ahead of the two men, trying to catch the cotton tufts blowing in the breeze from the cottonwood trees.

George Weichel smiled. He liked to see Maria so happy. And he had to admit, the cotton was so heavy in the spring air that it almost looked like the blizzards they had known in Switzerland.

Maria ran back to the two men. "Well, Herr Weichel and Herr Meigerhoff! What have you to say to this poor girl that you have brought to this wilderness? This place with huge, hairy beasts and fierce savages lurking behind every bush?"

George gave Maria a loving pat on her rear, and said, "I think maybe we have spoiled this 'poor little girl', Fred, by putting her up in such luxurious accommodations."

They all laughed. They were staying with Erskild and Stine in very crowded conditions. But they had found land to their liking, and had just returned from Junction City, where they filed their claims.

"Yes, such luxury," Maria responded. "Dirt floors, and absolutely no privacy. I don't know why I ever agreed to marry such an oaf." Maria gave George a kiss on the cheek as she said this, and gave a contented laugh once again. "At least I have my two knights in shining armor to protect me. What handsome guardians! And what fierce weapons."

On cue George raised his new Spencer repeating rifle in the air. "That we are, and that we will," he boasted.

The three Germans had just left the Lauritzen household to inspect their new farms.

"Well, Fred," George said, "do you think any of the corn we planted has sprouted yet?"

"Oh you men are such boys," Maria continued. "You have barely put some seed in the ground, and already you have to come see if anything is growing yet."

"Well, not just that," George replied. "We need to be thinking about where we're going to build our house. And I promise you, Maria, it will be the best home on the frontier. Oh, not like we had in Bern, to be sure, but a veritable mansion by homesteader standards."

Their excited conversation was interrupted by the distant sound of gunfire, coming from the direction of the Lauritzen home. There was a moment of silence as they stared at each other, not wanting to express their sudden concern.

"What is that?" Maria finally asked, a slight tremor in her voice. "It is just someone out shooting rabbits, is it not?"

George looked at Fred without comment, then said to Maria, "I'm sure that is just what it is. Rabbit hunting."

As they continued walking to their new farm, Fred said in George's ear, so that Maria could not hear, "I do not think you hunt rabbits with repeating rifles. Nor do so many guns fire all at once."

George quickened their pace and said, "You know what? I am almost out of tobacco. I think we should hike on down to Herr Schermerhorn's store and see what he might have."

"Schermerhorn's Store," Maria repeated. "But that is so far, and it is so late in the day." Then, sensing the looks between the two men, she suddenly realized their concern. "It is the Indians, isn't it? You think the Indians are at our home?"

"To be on the safe side, my dear, I think it is best if we do not return to the Lauritzen home right now. It is probably nothing, and we will feel very foolish tomorrow, but I think we should hasten on to Herr Schermerhorn."

The three walked on in silence, the gaiety of a few moments previous now gone. They did not stop at their new farm but hurried past.

The Dog Soldiers came upon them as they were crossing an open field, just a mile and a quarter west of the present town of Lincoln. With wild yells and shouting they came after them.

"Stay close, Maria," George shouted. He and Fred knelt, and began firing their Spencer repeating rifles at the oncoming warriors. The Indians slowed their advance, and then split into two groups, riding to either side of the trio just out of range of the rifles.

"We should try to get to shelter. Maybe down to the river bed!" Fred shouted.

"Yes —yes," George said. He grabbed Maria's arm and started to pull her with him towards the grove of trees by the river. But the Indians, anticipating their move, cut them off.

George and Fred fired at their attackers, but the moving targets were hard to hit. Just as they fired at an Indian, he would slide over to the far side of his pony and become invisible except for a leg on the pony's side.

"How many rounds do you have left, Fred?" George asked after firing a fusillade of shots at an Indian riding by closer than the others. He was satisfied to see the Indian give a yell, and fall from his horse into the field.

Fred gave a quick check, and turned pale. "I have only the four more shells," he warned.

"I have five more," George replied. "We must be careful with our shots. We need to get to the river."

But every time they started to move, the Indians charged in with guns firing and arrows flying. George and Fred were forced to keep firing, although they now measured their shots carefully.

The Indians sensed that they were about out of ammunition, and kept charging in, then pulling back.

Fred said in a dull voice, "I have no more bullets."

George looked at him and then at Maria. He had just fired his last shot as well.

"Maria, Maria, I am so sorry. Please forgive me. Please …" Then he gave a jerk, twisted half around, and fell to his knees, blood spurting from his chest. Maria shrieked as she saw him fall, and at the same instant Fred fell back with two wounds in his abdomen.

The Indians now were all around them. Maria watched as one brave dismounted, kneeled by George's body and came up with a bloody handful of hair. Then seeing a silver ring on George's finger, he chopped off the finger with his tomahawk, and removed the ring. Another Indian approached Fred. Seeing that he was not yet dead, he fired a shot into his chest at point blank range, then pulled out a knife and peeled back Fred's scalp.

Maria screamed and screamed.

An Indian approached her. "No more scream," he said. Maria did not understand him, nor would it have mattered if she had. She screamed and yelled. Finally the Indian struck her savagely across the mouth, knocking her to the ground, where she lay sobbing.

She was hardly aware of being lifted onto a pony by one of the Indians, and being led away from the field where the bodies of George and Fred lay.

These Indians had come from the north down Spillman Creek, which now joined with the Saline River. Here they met with some of their comrades who had come in from the west, and together the raiding party turned towards the east.

Susanna Alderdice and the children reached the home of Michael Healy where they were going to spend the night.

Nick Whalen, who had an adjoining farm, was already there, along with Bridget Kine and her small child. Tom Noon and his wife, another neighbor, had stopped in for a Sunday afternoon visit. The men had already exhausted their communication skills in discussing in brief sentences the weather and the prospects for a good crop this summer, and had now fallen silent to listen to the women chatter.

"I am looking for some material to make a new dress," Mrs. Kine stated. "But old Ron Schermerhorn doesn't have much of a selection. He did have a white cloth with red polka dots that wasn't too bad." Susanna tried to visualize such a dress, and gave a small shudder. "I guess I'll have to go to Salina. Or even Abilene, "Mrs. Kine continued. "I hear that since the cattle drives from Texas have been coming up to the railroad, a lot of new shops have opened."

"Humph!" Tom Noon snorted. "Most of those new shops are houses of ill repute, is what I've heard."

This silenced the conversation for a moment until Mrs. Noon spoke up. "Does any one know what day this is?"

"Why it's Sunday – May 30, 1869" Mrs. Kine responded.

"No – no," Mrs. Noon said. "I mean what national holiday this is?"

Susanna looked blankly at Mrs. Kine to see if she might have an answer, but it was obvious that she was in the dark as well.

"It's Decoration Day," Mrs. Noon announced. This met with blank stares from the others in the room. "Our Government back in Washington declared last year that every May 30 would be known as Decoration Day," Mrs. Noon continued.

"Decoration Day?" Nick Whalen asked. "And just what are we supposed to decorate - ourselves or our horses?"

"No, silly," Mrs. Noon said. "It is a day to remember those whom we have held dear and who have passed away.

We are supposed to decorate their graves and honor their lives. Kind of a memorial day."

The group was startled by the sound of rifles firing in the distance.

"Indians," Susanna said. "That must be Indians. A bunch attacked a railroad working party a few miles to the west several days ago. They must still be in the vicinity."

Nick Whalen jumped from his chair and headed for the door. "I've got to take the horses at my place into the woods to hide them," he stated. "They are always after horses." With that he disappeared out the front door.

Tom Noon cleared his throat, gave his wife a quick look, and announced "Well, I guess we'll be running along. Our horses are just outside, and I think it best we be on our way."

Susanna looked at them with shock. "You mean you're going off and leaving us?" she blurted.

"We just dropped in to say hello," Tom continued, as he ushered his wife towards the door. "I am unarmed, as you can see, and wouldn't really be of any help even if Indians should come. Which isn't very likely, I'm sure. Come, dear," and he was gone.

Mrs. Noon stood at the door a moment, looked back in the direction of Susanna and Mrs. Kine, but couldn't meet their eyes. Then she too was gone, and Susanna could hear the horses heading out at a gallop.

Mrs. Kine jumped up, ran to the bedroom, and came back with her baby clutched in her arms. As she headed towards the door Susanna cried, "Where are you going?"

"To hide in the river bed," Mrs. Kine replied. "And you'd best do the same." Then she was gone.

Susanna gave a sob as she ran into the bedroom to get Alice, her three month old baby. She came back, grabbed the hand of Frank, her two year old, who had been playing in the corner, and half led and half dragged him towards the door.

Mrs. Kine was halfway to the river. Nick Whalen was no where to be seen. Susanna called to her other two boys, Willis and John, who were playing near the stables. They came at a run, having already realized something was wrong.

"Indians," Susanna yelled when they came close. "We must hide in the creek. Run! Hurry!" And the five of them took off for the creek, the two year old now in tears and having to be dragged along.

Susanna saw Mrs. Kine disappear over the river embankment. "Wait for me!" Susanna cried.

"I can be of no help to you," Mrs. Kine yelled back. "I must look after myself and my child." And then she was gone.

At that same moment Susanna heard the yells of Indians as they rode into the clearing. She looked back, and realized she could not make it to the creek bed. Her legs grew rubbery under her, and she sank to the ground, hugging her baby and Frank close to her. "Run! Run!" she yelled to the older boys. "Run and hide!"

John looked at his mother in desperation, not wanting to leave her, but realized he had no choice. He grabbed Willis by the hand and said, "Come on! Run for it!" They had gone only a few steps before both boys were brought down with arrows in their backs.

Susanna screamed as she saw them go down. Then she was surrounded by a dozen ponies with Indians glaring at her. One dismounted, grabbed Frank, the two-year old, ran a knife into his belly and slit open his chest cavity. Susanna shrieked, "No – No! Please!" but it was over before she could move. Her screams rocked the countryside, and echoed off the walls of the house. Inside the angry war party broke dishes and smashed furniture against the floor.

Clothing was taken from the closets and ripped into shreds. The pantry was emptied of all the goods the Indians could carry.

The Indian that had ripped open Frank's chest said something to Susanna, but she was beyond hearing. With a grunt he pulled Susanna and her baby to a horse, pushed them up on its back, and led them off.

A little over a mile south of the present town of Lincoln, on Bull Foot Creek, John Harrison Strange, age 14, and Arthur Schmutz, also age 14, were digging in the hillside above Mart Hendrickson's house for wild turnips. Mrs. Strange had dropped in at the Hendrickson place for a visit along with her two boys, John and C.C. Her husband, the Reverend John Strange, had gone to Junction City along with Thomas Alderdice, Timothy Kine, Mart Hendrickson and a few others. Another visitor was there also, Mrs. George Green and her two young girls, Lizzie and Bell. It was a beautiful Kansas afternoon, and all of the children were enjoying the fresh air on the hillside, watching John and Arthur digging in the dirt.

"I'm thirsty," Lizzie, age 3, said. "I want some lemonade."

"Me, too," Bell chimed in.

C.C., the same age as John and Arthur, laughed. "OK," he said. "I'll race you down the hill to see who gets to the house first." With a squeal the two girls took off, with C.C. bringing up the rear. John and Arthur watched them go, happy to be rid of the two little pests.

"I hate Sundays," John Strange said. "All you're supposed to do is to be quiet and not play any games or anything. Just rest and do nothing."

Arthur looked at his companion." I guess it must be pretty hard having a dad who is a preacher," he said. "It's bad enough at our house. All I ever hear on Sundays is "Be quiet!

Don't be rowdy! Go read a book or do something quiet! I guess you're not supposed to have fun on Sundays."

"Well, we're going to have fun. Dad's off to Junction City and in a little while we're going after old whiskers, the biggest catfish I ever saw. This time we're going to get him."

"You actually saw him?" Arthur asked.

"Yeah – almost had him, too. Right up to the shore then my line broke and he got away. But not next time, you can bet your cat's pajamas on that."

Three Indians rode into view. The boys stared at them for a few moments, but they appeared to be friendly. They rode up to the boys, speaking in broken English.

"What do they want? What are they saying?" Arthur asked.

"Don't know," John replied. He shifted his shovel to his left hand, then held up his right hand and said "How!" He had heard that is the way you were supposed to greet an Indian.

The oldest of the Indians touched John with his spear, then with a howl rode off. The two boys looked at each other, and gave a nervous smile at the antics of the old man. Then the younger brave, probably the age of John and Arthur, came up to John, and without warning produced a club from his side. In one swift motion he crashed it into John's skull. Arthur watched in stunned horror, then dropped his shovel and took off at a run. He managed only a few short steps before he was felled with an arrow in his back.

Mrs. Green and Mrs. Strange witnessed the slaughter of the two boys from the house. They gathered up the other children and rushed inside. "Oh Lord. Oh Lord," Mrs. Strange kept repeating.

Several of the Indians started for the house, others went to the barn to steal the horses in the corral. Mrs. Green, meanwhile, had been busy. She found two rifles in the drawing room of the house, loaded them, and brought them back to the front room. She handed one to Mrs. Strange, and through the open window began firing at the advancing Indians. Mrs. Strange did the same, shooting at the Indians near the barn. Mrs. Hendrickson tried to keep C.C. and the two girls quiet in the back of the room.

The surprised warriors gave a yell, and withdrew out of range. The women and Indians exchanged shots for a few minutes. At length the raiders decided the shooters inside of the house were too well entrenched, and rode off without the horses.

The women rushed out as soon as they were gone, and carried John and Arthur back to the house. John was dead, but Arthur still lived. His condition, however, was critical. An arrowhead was buried deep in his back.

The various raiding parties of the Dog Soldiers came together and camped that night on Bull Foot Creek. The cool, spring night was filled with the sound of drums and singing of chants, punctuated periodically with wild yells and howls. But rising above it all were the screams of Susanna Alderdice and Maria Weichel as they endured the fate that befell captive women.

Barely a mile away, soldiers camped on Ferdinand Erhardt's farm.

During the night Eli Ziegler and John Alverson left the shelter of the river bed they had been hiding in and made their way down Spillman Creek to Bull Foot Creek. They came upon the Indian camp, which they circumvented, and continued on to Schermerhorn's farm, where they knew the Army was bivouacked. They heard screams coming from the Indian village, not realizing that one of the victims was their sister.

When they reached the Army camp, they related what had happened, and urged the Lieutenant in charge to lead an immediate attack. Eli offered to lead them to the Indian encampment if they would give him a horse. However, the Lieutenant said he had no authority to initiate such an action, and would have to send a courier to Fort Harker to get permission to move against the Indians. Eli and John left in disgust to return to their homes and to warn the other settlers.

Bridget Kine made it to the Erhardt ranch during the early hours before dawn, still clutching her baby. She had hidden in the creek bed under brush growing on the side of the bank, the tops so tall that they arched into the water. The Indians that had come looking for her were so close she could have touched them. But they soon gave up the hunt and moved on. When she finally came out of the creek bed, she saw the bodies of the Alderdice children lying in the dirt in front of the house. Her heart ached for Susanna, but she kept telling herself, "Nothing I could do. Nothing I could do." She stumbled through the night with her baby until reaching the Erhardt's. As soon as they heard her story, they all moved on down to the Schermerhorn store.

The Christian brothers, Lorentz and Peter, and their families, along with the Lauritzen boy who had been playing with their children, left their dug-out, and during the small hours of the night also made their way safely to the Schermerhorn Ranch.

Word of the attack spread quickly through the settlements. The next day a heavily armed group of farmers, including Nick Whalen, made their way back up the Saline, to look for survivors and to bury the dead. Bridget Kine insisted on coming with them.

They found the boy, Arthur Schmutz, still alive at the Hendrickson place, and moved him to the Schermerhorn Ranch.

Moving on up the Saline River, the group came to Michael Healy's home. It was in shambles with windows broken, furniture smashed, and clothes shredded all over the house.

They had been warned by Mrs. Kine what to expect, but still, as they came into Healy's yard, they were totally silent as they surveyed the bodies of John, Willis and Frank, Susanna's three boys, lying quietly in the dirt in front of the house. Several of the group kneeled to examine them further, when one suddenly hollered out, "Hey! This one's still alive. He's still breathing." It was Willis Daily, Susanna's youngest boy by her first husband, alive with an arrow still in his back.

A flurry of activity ensued as they lifted Willis to a wagon, and started him off to the Hendrickson home. Nick Whalen meanwhile slumped onto a chair on the front porch of the house, looking pale and disoriented. He hadn't shaved that morning. His arms hung limply at his side.

"Whalen, you ought to be horse whipped!" someone shouted. "How could you have just ridden off and left two defenseless women and these children to the Indians?"

Whalen looked at the man with eyes that were vacant, and did not reply.

"Yeah, Whalen, you stinking coward," another yelled. "You were supposed to be looking after Mrs. Kine and Mrs. Alderdice and their families while their men were gone. And what did you do? Ran away and left them to the Indians at the first sign of trouble."

The anger swelled among the group as more accusations were hurled at Whalen. Finally, in a weak voice, he managed to say, "I'm sorry. You can't imagine how sorry. I never thought any harm would come to them. Indians usually are just after horses. They don't bother people much. I was just trying to look after my horses. I didn't think the women would be in any danger."

"You know better than that, Whalen," someone shouted. "You know what happened to the Shaw family last year. Killed him and raped his wife and sister-in-law. You were a coward. Scared to death and ran off and left Tom's family and Mrs. Kline to fend for themselves."

"Nothing I could do - nothing I could do," Nick murmured. "Too many Indians."

"Down at the Hendrickson place two women drove them off with no trouble at all," someone shouted. "Seems like you could have done the same."

"We ought to string you up right here and now," another angry voice spoke.

A murmur of agreement spread through the crowd and someone produced a length of rawhide rope. Nick Whalen turned even paler, and staggered back against the front door of the house. The crowd had now changed into a mob, and were yelling and shouting at each other.

Then a woman's voice could be heard above the din. It was Mrs. Kline. "Hold on, men," she said. "There's been enough hurt done here. We don't need to add any more. Mr. Whalen did what he thought was right. We need to let it go at that, and tend to the needs of those that are left."

The shouting abated, and some of the men who had been in a rage minutes before now looked a little sheepish.

"Mrs. Kine's right," someone said. "We came up here to bury our dead and help those that survived, not to add to the trouble we already have. We got a lot of ground to cover yet today. Best be getting on with it."

The group quieted down, picked up their things and moved out.

Nick Whalen staggered back into the empty house. For several hours the sobs of a broken man could be heard emanating through the shattered windows.

The settlers moved on up stream, finding the bodies of George Weichel and Fred Meigerhoff.

"Looks like they put up a good fight before they ran out of ammunition," Peter Christensen said. "Maria, George's wife, must have been with them. Reckon the savages took her prisoner along with Mrs. Alderdice."

After burying the Germans, the group went on to the Danish Settlement, where they found Erskild and Stine Lauritzen. Otto Peterson's body wasn't discovered until sometime later.

Thomas Alderdice learned of his wife's capture and the death of his children while riding home from Salina the next day. Among his companions were the preacher, John Strange, Timothy Kine and Mart Hendrickson.

"Look down the road," Strange said. "Someone's coming like the devil had him by the tail." They could see a lone rider stirring up dust as he pressed his horse forward at a fast pace.

Mart Hendrickson suddenly turned pale and looked like he was about to lose his breakfast. "It's bad, boys, "he said. "Real bad. I hate what I'm seein'. Strange, your boy's been killed. And Tom, all your family's been done in or captured by the Indians."

Thomas looked at Mart in disbelief. "Mart, that's not funny, if that's what you're trying to be."

"Ain't no joke, Tom. I wish it were. I've had this here bad feeling all morning."

The three waited anxiously for the rider to come closer. When he did, he confirmed Mart's visions.

The men all but killed their horses racing back to their homes.

That same day, the Dog Soldiers broke camp, and with their captives, moved northwest at a leisurely pace.

The officer in charge of the troops at Erhardt's farm, to whom Eli and John had reported the raid, received his orders from Fort Harker and sent 2nd Lieutenant T. J. March and about 30 men out that morning to track down the marauding Indians, but they were able to run across only a few small groups who easily evaded them. That night the soldiers gave up the chase and returned to camp.

"Well, Sonny, that's the story of your massacre. The boy Arthur Smultz lingered on for ten days, before dying. They couldn't get the arrow head out of his back. It was in too deep. Willis Daly recovered, and lived to a ripe old age. Mrs. Kine seemed OK at the time, but that day weighed heavy on her mind. In later years, she would have some pretty serious lapses, and ended up in a home for the insane. Forty years later the citizens of the county erected that monument in town you keep talking about in memory of those killed and captured."

Old Joe's voice had grown weaker and more detached as he talked about the events of that day. I think he was exhausted from just thinking about it.

I pulled a piece of paper from my shirt pocket. "It's the list of persons killed and captured that's shown on the monument," I said. "I think you covered them all." I studied the sheet and read out loud.

"Those killed in the raid by the Dog Soldiers were:
Erskild and Stine Lauritzen
Otto Petersen
George Weichel
Fred Meigerhoff
John (Alderdice) Daily
Frank Alderdice
John Strange
Arthur Smultz (who died several days later)
Wounded:
Willis (Alderdice) Daily
Captured:
Susanna Alderdice

Alice Alderdice
Maria Weichel"
I folded the paper and put it back in my pocket.
"I know where we are," I told Old Joe.

"Well, I guess that don't surprise me none since you've been drivin' out here for several days now."

"No, I mean I know whose house this is. Or was. I did some checking at the historical society in town and at the County Recorders Office a couple of days ago when the roads were too muddy to get in here. This is where Michael Healy lived isn't it? You know, the place where Susanna Alderdice and Bridget Kine were when the Indians came."

Old Joe gave me a sly look. "Looks like you done your home work, Sunny," he replied. "Yep, this is the place. Right out there where your car is parked is where Susanna was taken captive and her two boys killed and the other wounded. And down there where the creek curves around is where Mrs. Kine hid under some brushes that hang over the bank. The Cheyenne came into this very house and ransacked it pretty good. And right here where we're sittin' is where old Nick stood when the settlers threatened to hang him. Yessir, a lot of memories stored in this old house."

"I thought so," I said. "Is that why you hang out around here?"

"You got me dead to rights, Sonny. I like to come out here and just absorb some of the atmosphere. Maybe that's where I get all my knowledge of those days."

"I guess I could believe that," I replied, not thinking that I would ever have agreed with any of Old Joe's wild ideas. "Sometimes when we're talking I seem to feel some of those old ghosts hovering around myself."

"But that's not the end of the story," I said. "The Indians took Susanna, her baby and Maria captive. What happened to them?"

Old Joe gave a long sigh, and continued.

CHAPTER 25

"Thomas Alderdice was like a crazed man in the days after the raid," Old Joe said. "He hardly ate or slept. Kept trying to get the Army to put together a company to go after the Indians and rescue his wife and baby. But the Army told him they was just too short handed, and that trying to find an Indian camp in the rolling prairie was harder than finding a needle in a hay stack. General Custer had proved that the year before."

"Finally in desperation Thomas took up the chase all by himself. Half tracking the Indian trail and half just guessing where they might be, he found their camp several days after the raid, about 100 miles from the settlements. He snuck up as close as he could and tried to see if he could spot his wife. Didn't have any luck, but he knew she and the baby had to be there. He high-tailed it back to the settlements to try to get help."

The day was hot. Susanna was soaked through in her dirty dress, which was ripped and tattered from days on the move. Susanna looked at Maria, and wondered how the younger woman could look so cool and reposed in this weather. Off to the west a large thunderhead was beginning to build up, holding the promise of a cooling rain.

After the horrors of their first night of captivity, life had become a little better for Maria and Susanna. They had been

251

taken into the tent of Tall Bull, and were no longer bothered by any of the other warriors. Tall Bull's wives, however, were merciless in their treatment, frequently beating the women with switches if they did not move fast enough, or perform some task to their satisfaction. To them, the two white women were nothing but property, slaves to do their bidding.

Susanna still held out hope of an early rescue. She was sure the Army would be hard on the heels of the Indians. Every day when they were moving she would look back, straining her eyes to see if anyone was following, hoping to see a tell-tale cloud of dust. But there had been nothing.

Susanna's baby was not doing well. Her breast milk had completely dried up over the shock of seeing her children killed, and then being taken captive by the Indians. She begged Tall Bull's wives, and Tall Bull himself, for goat's milk to feed the baby, but was only told, "You feed baby." This was the third day since they had been taken captive. Today, in all the heat, the baby was crying without pause. While Susanna wandered through the camp carrying her child and looking for something she could feed to the baby, Tall Bull walked over, stared at the infant for a moment, then without warning snatched the baby from Susanna's arms.

"Baby cry too much. Not well," he said. Without preamble he wrapped his strong hands around the baby's throat, and with one quick jerk broke her neck. Susanna gave a gasp, then a shriek. "No, no!" she cried.

Tall Bull walked away with the lifeless body.

"Murderer!" Susanna screamed, followed by a shrill cry that could be heard throughout the camp. "You've killed my baby! My poor innocent baby!" she cried again. "The soldiers will find you, and when they do I will see you hang!" Susanna lunged after Tall Bull, but Maria pulled her back, trying to quiet her. Although the two did not speak the same language, the language of sympathy was universal. Susanna fell sobbing to the ground, Maria by her side, holding her closely.

White Buffalo Woman, the oldest of Tall Bull's wives, came to Susanna and Maria lying on the ground. "You never see him hang," she stated. "If white soldiers come, you both die." With that she turned and walked away, singing an ancient Indian chant.

"Old Tom went all the way to Fort Leavenworth looking for help," Old Joe said. "Met with General Schofield, who was the current Military Commander of the District of the Missouri. While he was there he also met with Colonel Custer, and told him his desperate story. Custer was so impressed he even had Tom repeat it to his wife, Libby, but there wasn't much any of them could do. Just weren't enough troopers available.

Schofield told Tom he would alert General Carr, who was in the field in western Nebraska, where the Indians were likely headed, to be on the look-out.

Thomas returned home, and once again rode out to where he had found the Indian camp before. It was abandoned. But there, hanging by the neck from a tree, he found the lifeless body of his baby Alice.

He came home about as dejected as a body can get, his only hope that General Carr might provide a miracle.

General Carr and the troops of the 5th cavalry reported to Fort McPherson in Nebraska, to which they had been reassigned. His orders at the new post were to "drive the Indians out of Republican country." The catch, of course, was in being able to find them. General Custer had shown how difficult that could be in his marches across Kansas the year before. Carr felt he had been lucky in running into the Cheyenne when he was on his way to Fort McPherson. He was not likely to be that fortunate again.

However, he was well equipped with 150 Pawnee Indians as scouts under the command of Major Frank North, and his Chief of Scouts was a person many considered the best tracker in the west, Buffalo Bill Cody. On June 9, General Carr set forth with eight of his companies and the scouts, and wagons loaded with supplies, and headed southeast for the Republican River territory.

Progress was slow in the sandy terrain because of the wagons. Several overturned and were lost. Then one of the officers developed suicidal tendencies, and had to be escorted back to Fort McPherson. Morale of the troops was ebbing fast after only a few days on the move.

Word came to them that Indians had been on a rampage further south along the Solomon and Saline rivers in Kansas where they had taken two women captives. Carr led his troops in a southerly direction, and on June 12 came across a band of about 20 Indians, who quickly crossed the hills and were lost to sight. Carr sent his Pawnee scouts to trail them, but in typical Indian fashion the single trail broke into many trails as the Indians scattered.

Carr spent three more days in a fruitless search for sign of Indians along the Republican. On June 15, after the command stopped for the day to make camp, warriors tried to capture the troops' mules. A contingent of soldiers gave chase, and killed two of the raiders before darkness came.

The next morning the Pawnee Scouts picked up the trail of the attackers, and the 5th Cavalry once again set out in pursuit of the Indians. But again the tracks broke into many paths going in all directions, and the troops had to give up the pursuit.

On June 17, Carr received orders to detach one of his companies and send them to protect settlers on the Little Blue River. The rest of the command continued to hunt for Indians along the Republican, but for the next several weeks saw no sign of them. They moved steadily westward, and had to hunt buffalo for meat as their supplies were running dangerously low. Water was increasingly hard to find, and many of the troopers fell ill.

On July 3, a scouting party ran across an Indian camp that had been evacuated only a day and half previous. While inspecting the abandoned camp, the scouts discovered footprints of a white woman's shoe. This renewed the troopers' determination to catch the renegades.

Three companies of the 5[th,] together with the Pawnee scouts, started off in hot pursuit. But once again the trail dispersed in many directions making it difficult for the soldiers to decide which one to follow. Several days later scouts spotted a dozen warriors in the distance, and the soldiers and Pawnees once again gave chase to the renegades. Three of the Indians were killed, but the rest got away.

Frustrated by their lack of success, Carr turned his troops back to the east, heading back down the Republican. The following day, the troops turned north for a long, 65 mile march towards Frenchman Creek. It was a hot, dry and agonizing march, but on July 10th they came across an old Indian campsite, then another, and finally a third that was only 24 hours old. Once again a white woman's footprint was found in the sand.

Carr felt they were now close to the Indian camp, and selected those troops whose horses still seemed to be fit to take up the chase. At 4:00 the next morning, July 11th, he set forth with 244 men and 50 Pawnee scouts, leaving the wagon trains and the rest of the command behind.

By 2:00 in the afternoon, hope of catching the Indians was fading. It was a hard march, and the horses had been without water since morning. Then the Pawnee scouts sighted animals in the distance, and were sure that this was the Cheyenne camp. The scouts stripped down for battle, and the soldiers made ready for a fight. Buffalo Bill Cody advised Carr to take a wide circular path to the village, coming down from the north where they would be least expected.

Hidden by the rolling terrain, the cavalry rode north and west of where they assumed the Cheyenne village would be. They came within a mile of the camp undetected. Looking over the crest of a hill, they could see the Dog Soldier village just below them. Carr divided the men into three columns, and prepared to attack.

CHAPTER 26

Tall Bull sat against the trunk of a tall cottonwood tree, gazing across the small stream to the reddish, dirt bluffs to the east. His wives and the two white women were busy cleaning up from the noon meal of dried venison and fresh raspberries. The full belly and hot sun made him feel lazy and sleepy.

The village site was good, he thought, nestled in a small valley surrounded and hidden by the rolling hills of the plains. Scouts were posted to the east to look for sign of approaching soldiers, but Tall Bull was not too worried. They had kept well ahead of the riders that had been on their trail, and over a week ago the troops had turned back down the Republican River.

The tribe had come to within a few miles of the Platte before making camp. Several braves were sent to scout the river, several miles to the north and west. They returned with the news that the river was high, and would be difficult to cross. Tall Bull decided to stay where they were for a couple of days, to let the river go down. Besides, the tribe needed time to relax after their grueling march up the Republican.

Some of the Sioux who had ridden with him thought he was being careless, and decided to cross the river right away. They camped a few miles on the other side.

Tall Bull watched the two white women move around the camp. The older one was heavy with her unborn child. She looked tired and worn down, and the younger one not much better. In contrast, his three wives were spry and cheerful, even the eldest. "That is the trouble with white women," he thought, "no strength to endure hardships."

As he watched the busy activity of the camp he thought about the villages that had been destroyed by the white men. The village at Sand Creek, where Black Kettle had put his faith in the white men's words; then the village at Pawnee Fork when the Old Man of the Thunder Hancock had tried to repeat the massacre. But the Cheyenne women and children had eluded him there. Still, they lost their teepees and all their belongings when Hancock burned the village that they had left behind. And then last winter when Yellow Hair Custer had destroyed Black Kettle's village at the Washita. It is time, he thought, that we go to the north to be with our cousins. But it will be hard to leave this place. This place where the Cheyenne have lived, and hunted buffalo, and ridden the vast reaches of the prairie.

Tall Bull lazily swatted at a fly that had landed on his arm, and leaned back and closed his eyes. "The sun is very hot," he thought, as he drifted off to sleep.

Maria moved sluggishly back to Tall Bull's teepee, carrying a bag of water from the creek. Her dress was in tatters, and her arms were sore from being hit with the switch that Tall Bull's oldest wife always carried. Susanna, walking beside her, seemed oblivious to the day.

As the two women entered the teepee, Maria noticed the vacant look in Susanna's eyes. Maria wished she could say things to her to try and comfort her. Since Susanna's baby had been killed, she had lost all of her vitality. She no longer cared what happened, or where they were. The baby she was carrying, now several months into the pregnancy, drained her of all her energy. Maria placed the bag of water on the floor of the teepee and started to sit down when she heard rifle fire outside.

General Carr's attack caught the Cheyenne completely by surprise. Charging down the hill, with the Pawnee scouts in the lead, they scattered the Dog Soldiers in all directions. Everything was a mass of confusion as firing broke out, mingled with the yells of the soldiers and cries of the Cheyenne.

Some of the horses were tied near the teepees, but most were being herded on the hillside by several of the Cheyenne boys One of the boys, realizing what was happening, stampeded the animals into the village hoping that the braves could catch some and be able to escape.

Tall Bull, awakened from his slumber by the sound of gunfire, was quick to size up the situation. He untied his horse, pushed his second wife, Lost Feather, and their daughter onto its back, and gave the horse a whack, sending it on its way.

Susanna and Maria heard the sound of the fighting from inside Tall Bull's teepee. They peered outside and saw the Pawnee scouts shooting at the Dog Soldiers, and thought the Cheyenne were being attacked by another tribe. Then they heard bugles in the distance, and hope surged in their hearts.

They looked out again and saw Tall Bull's wife, White Buffalo Woman, coming towards them with a tomahawk clutched in her hand. Susanna gave a gasp, and pushed Maria out of the teepee ahead of her, yelling "Run! Run!" Maria gave her a questioning look, but sensing the urgency in her voice ran out. She saw several soldiers reining in their horses only a hundred yards away and headed towards them.

Susanna followed, but was not quick enough. White Buffalo Woman struck her with the tomahawk, and she fell to the ground, mortally wounded. Maria, looking back, gave a short cry as she saw Susanna stumble to the ground, but did not slacken her pace. She kept on running towards the soldiers. But even as she lunged forward she felt a hard jolt to her shoulder which knocked her off her feet. Raising herself on her knees, she saw blood streaming down her chest, and realized she had been shot. She looked back, and saw Tall Bull's youngest wife staring at her, slowly lowering the pistol in her hand. Then the ground seemed to swirl around her, and the brightness of the day dimmed into darkness.

Two of the soldiers dismounted and rushed to Maria's side, trying to stop the bleeding and revive her. As she opened her eyes, her first thought was of Susanna. She tried to tell the soldiers to help her, but they didn't understand. With their help she rose to her feet, and led them to Susanna.

The soldiers looked at the deep gash in Susanna's head, and turned away. Maria fell beside her, and although her shoulder was in great pain was able to roll her friend over. Susanna had a smile on her face, and looked more at peace than Maria had ever seen her. Maria felt Susanna's body stiffen for a moment, and then it relaxed as death made its claim on her. Still her lips remained in a slight smile.

"She is happy," Maria thought. "She is with her children."

Tall Bull, after sending Lost Feather and her child off on his horse, cried out to his warriors, "All of you who have no horses, follow me to the bluffs." A dozen warriors and women, including Tall Bull's other two wives, raced for the protection of the bluffs, the Pawnee scouts and soldiers in hot pursuit.

At the mouth of the ravine, Wolf with Plenty of Hair staked himself to the ground with a dog rope, indicating that he would fight to the death, unless his comrades could rally around him and pull the stake from the ground. The fighting was so fierce that none did, and Wolf with Plenty of Hair was killed where he stood.

A fierce battle ensued, with the Cheyenne suffering devastating losses. Tall Bull's youngest wife, Moon Flower, was one of the first to die with a bullet in her heart.

Tall Bull hacked steps in the wall of the bluffs with his tomahawk to get to a higher elevation. From there he could better fire on the Pawnee and soldiers below. As he peered over the ridge looking for a target, a bullet struck him in the forehead, and he fell back into the ravine.

For a moment, everything seemed out of focus to Tall Bull, but abruptly his eyes cleared. Looking up, he saw three of his brothers mounted on horseback at the top of the bluffs, holding the reins of a fourth pony. The horse was magnificent - a black and white stallion with a star outlined on its forehead.

Tall Bull looked at the warriors more closely, and recognized Roman Nose, Black Kettle and Lean Bear. They motioned for him to join them. Tall Bull thought it was strange that Black Kettle would be there, but found that he held no animosity towards him. He was, after all, a Cheyenne brother.

Tall Bull ascended to the top of the bluff, and mounted the black and white horse. Everything moved in slow motion. The sound of the fighting had faded until it was just a dim noise in the background.

Lean Bear said, "Come," and turned his horse towards the west. There before them was a trail blazed in gold, rising from the ground gradually up to the sky. It was the Hanging Road, the trail to the land of Hemmawihio, the Wise-One Above.

The four warriors began their ascent to the other world.

The rout of the Dog Soldiers was complete. Fifty-two Indians, including some women, were killed, and seventeen women and children captured. Among these was White Buffalo Woman, Tall Bull's oldest wife, the only person to survive from the bluffs.

The horses of the 5th Cavalry were so exhausted from their long march and then the fight that they were unable to give chase to those that escaped.

That night a fierce thunderstorm moved onto the troops from the west, drenching the soldiers and washing the spilled blood deep into the ground. The next morning was damp and mist lay heavy on the hills. Stillness descended on the land, and men moved through the camp like ghosts floating in the dim light.

As the soldiers prepared to move out, Susanna Alderdice, wrapped in buffalo hides, was buried in a grave on the hillside. The soldiers still didn't know her last name. General Carr stood by the burial site, and said a few words in her memory.

"Dear Lord, we are happy that you saw fit for us to rescue these two women from the clutches of the savages. But we regret that this one, whom we now turn over to your mercy, was killed. She saw much hardship in this life; may she now revel in the glory of your kingdom. Amen."

A corporal stepped forward and said he would like to read from the scriptures. The General nodded, and the young man produced a weathered pocket-sized Bible from his shirt. He said he would like to read of God's promise for a better world, when wars and strife and killing would all be behind us. He opened the Bible to the 2nd chapter of the Song of Solomon, cleared his throat, glanced around, and began to read:

"For lo, the winter is past, the rain is over and gone. The flowers appear on the earth; the time of the singing of birds is come, and the voice of the turtle can be heard in our land.

The fig tree putteth forth her green figs, and the vines with the tender grapes give a good smell. Arise, my love, my fair one, and come away."

When he finished, the soldier closed his bible, looked around, and then continued.

"I guess that's one of my favorite passages in the Bible – especially the part about the voice of the turtle being heard in our land. I guess I didn't even know the turtle had a voice – at least I've never heard it. Too much noise in our world, I reckon. Horses neighing to each other, guns barking, Indian war drums beating, people shouting to each other. So we don't even know when the turtle's tired and worn out, or when he's happy, or when he's hungry or hurting. And I guess because we never hear his voice, we don't much care."

"But the Bible says that someday the voice of the turtle will be heard in the land. That must mean that someday we will all be quiet, and we will be listening. And we will listen because we care about what the turtle has to say. And if we care about that, it must mean that we will be listening to each other, too, and that we care what each of us thinks and feels - whites and Indians alike. And maybe we will be kinder to each other, and not have to fight and kill each other. That ought to be a better world than this, don't you think?"

The men around the grave glanced at each other, and shifted uncomfortably on their feet. The question went unanswered. The bugler played Taps, and the sound echoed across the hills.

The camp was uncommonly quiet as the troops moved out. Only the occasional sound of someone slapping leather, the snorting of a horse, and the sounds of hoofs pressing against the soft earth. As the company of soldiers and scouts disappeared over the ridge, voices could be heard singing an old campfire ballad. Then that too faded away, and only the sound of the wind, rustling through the tall prairie grass, remained.

Old Joe was quiet for a long stretch after telling about Susanna's burial. I almost felt that he was mourning her death. There didn't seem to be anything left to say, so I gathered up my notes. When I was ready to go I looked at Old Joe, wanting to thank him once again for his insight on those turbulent years. His eyes were sunken further into his wrinkled face, and his heavy eyebrows looked like they might come crashing down over them at any time.

I felt awkward, and mumbled my thanks. He didn't respond, just looked straight ahead, and rocked slowly back and forth in his chair, seemingly oblivious to my presence.

Finally I went back to the car, started it up, and drove to the edge of the yard. I stopped, looked back at the house, and waved goodbye, but Old Joe didn't wave back. I put the car in gear and headed back to town.

EPILOGUE

Several months before my book was published I returned to Lincoln to hunt up Old Joe. I had a couple of questions I wanted to clear up about the massacre. I went out to the old house where we had always met, only to find the west side of the structure blown down and the roof partially collapsed. The only thing still standing was the east wall and the fireplace in the middle of what used to be the living room. There was no sign of Old Joe.

I rummaged through the debris, and on the fireplace mantle I found an old corn cob pipe. It looked just like the one Old Joe smoked, although this one didn't look like it had been lit for a long, long time.

I visited the neighbors on either side of the old homestead, but nobody had ever heard of nor seen an old man hanging around the place. In town I tried to find the attendant at the gas station that had originally directed me to Old Joe, but he couldn't be found either. The owner assured me nobody by his description had ever worked there.

I guess I'll never know what happened to Old Joe. Sometimes I wonder if he even existed. I get this crazy idea that maybe all the discussions I'd had on that rickety old porch were with an empty, tortured house. A house whose walls had been impregnated with terror on that day in May by six people – one who later lost her mind, three who were killed, and two others who would die in the weeks ahead. A house that felt the anger of Cheyenne Indians who had raced in the yard and ransacked the home. A house that had absorbed the grief of Tom Alderdice when he came to view the spot where Susanna and his children were set upon by the Cheyenne. A house that felt the deep shame and anguish of a man who had deserted his guests in the face of danger. A house inhabited by spirits of the past.

A house, as Old Joe had said, that had a story to tell.

NOTES

Near as I can tell, Old Joe's story is pretty much the way it happened. I tried to check on some of his statements, and they seemed to be pretty factual, as indicated in the following references.

CHAPTER 1

The Cheyenne have several stories on the origins of the tribe. Old Joe's account was not an origin story, however, but a description of how they came to America. It is also told by Maria Sanchez, on page 168 of her book *Love Song to the Plains* written in 1961. Most anthropologists believe the Indians didn't have to sail across the Bering Strait, however, but crossed on dry land which connected Asia and America at that time.

The mythical Sweet Medicine, and his predictions about the coming of the horse and white men, has been described in several books, including *by Cheyenne Campfires*, written by George Bird Grinnell and first published by Yale University in 1926.

It has been estimated that over 1 million buffalo wandered across the plains when the white man first came on the scene. Almost immediately their numbers started to decrease. Geoffrey C. Ward, in the book *The West*, published by Little, Brown and Company in1996, states that although the near extinction of the herds is attributed to white hunters who wantonly killed them, the decline had actually started before due to draught, diseases introduced with cattle, competition with horses for fodder in the green valleys, and the increasing number of Indians depending on them.

CHAPTER 2

A comprehensive look at the life of Black Kettle has only recently been documented in a book by Thom Hatch, *Black Kettle, the Cheyenne Chief Who Sought Peace but Found War*, written in 2002 and published by John Wiley and Sons. Old Joe's accounts pretty much agree with this book.

CHAPTER 3 & 4

The Battle of Chickamauga, Georgia, was one of the bloodiest to be fought in the Civil War up to that time. The fighting raged for two days. The Union forces finally fell back to Chattanooga, leaving the field to the Southerners. It was declared a Southern victory, but the South failed in their determination to take Chattanooga. When it was over the Union forces had lost 16,336 men, while the Confederate casualties ranged anywhere from 18,000 to 20,000.

Dr. Jeff Broome, a professor of history and philosophy at Arapahoe College in Littleton, Colorado, has done extensive research into the lives of Thomas and Susanna Alderdice, including Tom's role in the Battle of Chickamauga and the background of Susanna's first husband, James Daily. His book, *Dog Soldier Justice: the Ordeal of Susanna Alderdice in the Kansas Indian Wars*, published by the Lincoln County Historical Society in 2003 is one of the most comprehensive descriptions of the Lincoln County massacre that has been written.

Fort Leavenworth, where James Daily served for most of his 100 day enlistment, was the first fort to be located in Kansas. It served as the launching point for many Indian campaigns and is the oldest U. S. Army fort to be in continuous existence west of the Mississippi. Currently it supports the U.S. Command and General Staff College. It is on the eastern edge of Kansas, just to the north and west of Kansas City.

CHAPTER 5

Charles and William Bent, and their business partner St. Vrain, an ex-trapper, established Bent's Fort in 1833 on the north bank of the Arkansas River to conduct trade with the Indians and with Mexico. It is estimated that100 men worked at the fort at its peak. George Bent, the son of William Bent and Owl Woman, describes the fort in George Hyde's book *Life of George Bent* published by the University of Oklahoma Press in 1968 as follows: "There were Indian women of a dozen different tribes living at the fort, and a large number of children. Something was always going on....In fall and winter there was always a large camp of Indians just outside of the fort.... The trade room was full of Indian men and women all day long; others came just to visit and talk, and there was often a circle of chiefs sitting with my father or his partners, smoking and talking."

After the Mexican War in 1852 and with increasing tensions between whites and Indians, the fur business fell off and it was no longer profitable to maintain such a large trading post. The Government offered to buy the fort from Bent, but he felt the price was not right. As a result he blew up part of the fort and moved 38 miles downstream to establish a newer and smaller fort. The old fort, which has come to be known as Bent's Old Fort, was not completely destroyed, and for a while was used as a stage station. Today Bent's Old Fort has been carefully reconstructed and is a

National Historic Site. Located just a few miles outside of La Junta, Colorado, it is well worth the drive to visit.

Bent's New Fort was sold to the Government in 1859, and was named Fort Fauntleroy. It was later changed to Fort Wise, after Governor Wise of Virginia, but when the Civil War broke out was renamed once again to become Fort Lyon, where Major Wynkoop was stationed and where Black Kettle was told to take his people before the Sand Creek Massacre. It is located on Highway 50 just 8 miles west of Lamar, Colorado.

CHAPTER 6

Major Wynkoop played a major role in the settling of the west. He migrated to Kansas from Philadelphia in the 1850's, and then joined the rush into Colorado when gold was discovered in the Pikes Peak region in 1858. He worked as a bartender in Denver, then was elected sheriff for Arapahoe County and later for Jefferson County. In 1861 he received a commission as second lieutenant in the First Colorado Volunteers, and rose to the rank of Major. He served under Colonel Chivington in the battle with the Southerners at Glorietta Pass in New Mexico. Before being assigned to Fort Lyon he was the commander at Camp Weld near Denver. When he resigned from the Army he became the Indian Agent for the Cheyenne from 1864 to 1868. Little is known of him after he returned to the East.

CHAPTER 7

The Sand Creek Massacre is still remembered as one of the worst atrocities in the history of the west. Congress initiated several investigations into the matter and all were unanimous in the view that the slaughter of the Indian camp was unconsciable. The House of Representatives Committee on the Conduct of the War reported: "As to

Colonel Chivington, your committee can hardly find fitting terms to describe his conduct. Wearing the uniform of the United States, which should be the emblem of justice and humanity, holding the important position of commander of a military district, and therefore having the honor of the government to that extent in his keeping, he deliberately planned and executed a foul and dastardly massacre which would have disgraced the veriest savage among those who were the victims of his cruelty."

In 2000 Congress authorized the creation of the Sand Creek Massacre National Historic Site, but as yet the National Park Service has been unable to acquire sufficient land at the location to establish the memorial.

Medicine Woman Later, Black Kettle's wife, who was wounded at Sand Creek, was reputed to have been shot nine times, and showed these wounds to the peace commissioners in 1865, when they met at the Little Arkansas.

CHAPTER 8

After the raids at Julesburg, the Southern Cheyenne moved to the north to join with the Sioux and the Northern Cheyenne. The Cheyenne had split into the two groups around 1826. George Bent, in the book *Life of George Bent*, tells how surprised he was at the appearance of their northern cousins. Whereas most of the Southern Cheyenne wore cloth leggings and clothes, the Northern Cheyenne still dressed mostly in buffalo skins and animal hides. Also there were considerable differences in their language. Nevertheless the southerners were welcomed as brothers.

CHAPTER 9

The magical war bonnet that Roman Nose wore has been mentioned in a number of books about the Cheyenne and the west. In the Time-Life book, *The Indians*, published in 1973, it is described as follows: "It was painted with black pigment made from a tree that had been set on fire by lightning. A single buffalo horn was placed at the front. The skin of a kingfisher was tied to the top (its magical effect would be to close up bullet wounds instantly, just as water instantly closes up when a kingfisher dives in a pool). A bat was tied to the right side (the bat flies through the dark and cannot be caught; hence the wearer of the bonnet could fight safely at night)."

CHAPTER 10

Old Joe's story of how Thomas Alderdice might have met Susanna - through an old Army buddy, Houstan Anglin - follows the explanation given by Dr. Jeff Broome, mentioned earlier, in his book, *Dog Soldier Justice, the Ordeal of Susanna Alderdice in the Kansas Indian Wars.*

CHAPTER 11

I could find absolutely nothing to back up Old Joe's description of George Weichel's involvement in the Seven Weeks War in Austria. Indeed very little is known for sure about the lives of George and Maria, and Fred Meigerhoff, except that she was very young and pretty, and they seemed to be pretty wealthy. There are conflicting versions of whether they were from Bern or Hanover, although Old Joe's description would satisfy both explanations. His thoughts on the matter would certainly fit in with the times and place.

CHAPTER 12

In 1867, General Hancock was stationed at Fort Riley, which was situated on the Republican River roughly 150 miles west of Fort Leavenworth. It was built to protect travelers on the Santa Fe Trail. Currently it is the home of the Army's First Infantry Division, First Armored Division.

Hancock met with the Cheyenne chiefs at Fort Larned, which was established in 1859 in Central Kansas. In the 1860's it served as an agency of the Indian Bureau. Today it is one of the best surviving examples of a frontier Army post and a National Historic Site.

George Armstrong Custer, who accompanied Hancock to the Cheyenne village at Pawnee Fork, graduated from West point in 1861, at the bottom of his class. However, his daring and bravery during the Civil War won the admiration and respect of his superiors, and he rapidly advanced to the rank of Brigadier General. He was present at the surrender of the Confederacy at Appomattox. At the conclusion of the war he was reduced to the rank of Lt. Colonel and joined the regiment at Fort Riley in November 1866.

Henry Stanley, the reporter who was with the Hancock expedition, is best known for his explorations in Africa, where he was sent to find David Livingston, who had disappeared into the dark regions of the interior. His famous words, when he found the explorer on Lake Tanganyika, were "Dr. Livingston, I presume?"

CHAPTER 13

Several western forts were mentioned by Old Joe in relating the travels of Custer in trying to find the Cheyenne, and then his subsequent desertion to visit his wife. These included Fort Hays in Western Kansas, which was established in 1865 to protect military wagons along the Smoky Hill Trail. Several structures still stand, and have been designated as a State Historical site.

Fort Wallace was near the Kansas-Colorado border, north and west of Dodge City. All that remains of the fort today is the old post cemetery.

Fort Harker, originally named Fort Ellsworth, was located near Ellsworth, Kansas. It was established in 1866 and served as a supply depot and a distribution point for all of the forts in Colorado, New Mexico, Arizona and northern Texas. Today most of where the fort was located is on private property.

The Cheyenne were delayed for the council meeting at Medicine Lodge because they were in the middle of their ceremony to renew the Medicine Arrows. A good description of these arrows and the renewal ceremony is contained in George Bird Grinnell's book, *By Cheyenne Campfires*, published by the University of Nebraska Press and the Yale Press in 1926. The Medicine Arrows, four in number, were considered sacred and protected the tribe from sickness and gave them strength and health. They were given to the tribe by one of their legendary medicine men, Sweet Medicine. From time to time, the Cheyenne would hold a ceremony to renew their power, taking them from their bundles, and perhaps making new shafts and rebinding them. There were many reasons for a renewal ceremony – to atone for a wrong done, to ward off evil, or to give victory in battle. The ceremony usually lasted four days.

CHAPTER 14

George Bent and his wife left the Cheyenne tribe in 1868 to live the rest of his life with the white men in Denver. His brother, Charlie, however, remained with the tribe and became a leader of the Dog Soldiers. He was wounded in a raid in 1868, came down with malaria, and died shortly thereafter.

The Kansas Historical Marker east of town that described the three women being left "half dead on the prairie" has been replaced by a new one that tries to present a more balanced view of the troubles of that time. In doing so all of the specificity of the incidents has been lost. There is no mention of the ordeal of the women in the new marker, only saying that in 1868 Cheyennes attacked settlements along the Saline and Solomon rivers. Likewise the 1869 massacre and capture of two women that the original marker described has been toned down to being a "conflict" in 1869 between the Cheyennes and settlers, with no mention of the women. Sometimes the realities of history are softened in the telling to the point that the significance and drama are entirely lost.

Old Joe was apparently not exaggerating when he talked about Mart Hendrickson's ability to receive visions. These were well documented in Adolph Roenigk's book, *Pioneer History of Kansas*, published in 1933.

CHAPTER 15 - 19

Going south on Yuma County Road KK, about 40 miles north of Burlington, Colorado, the landscape is marked by gently rolling hills and depressions, much like the swell and dips of the ocean, only on a grander scale. As you come to the crest of a hill, you can see for miles, for there are no trees to block the view, only prairie grass blowing in the breeze. However, this can be deceiving, for across these miles are numerous vales and depressions which could conceal entire villages, hidden until you come to the hills surrounding them.

Approaching one of these crests on County Road KK, the land suddenly dips into a green valley, unexpectedly lined with cottonwood trees and willows. A small stream flows eastward at the bottom of the valley – the Arickaree River. Normally only a trickle of water runs through it but in flood season it can become a roaring river.

This is the site of the Battle of Beecher's Island. Today it is a quiet and serene place, isolated from the rest of the world, but if one listens closely to the soft blowing wind, you can still hear the sound of the shouts and gunfire that occurred those many years ago. Alongside the creek bed there is an 18 foot granite monument dedicated to the men who fought here, erected by the states of Colorado and Kansas in 1905. The original monument was placed on the island itself, but was damaged in a flood in 1935. The monument was then moved to its current location. However, part of the inscription on the base was never recovered, which contained the names of the scouts who were killed and wounded. Still remaining is the part which lists the names of those who escaped without any wounds. The first name on the list is Thomas Alderdice, and the last is Eli Ziegler.

The question of how many were killed in the battle would never be fully answered. The Indians some years later claimed that only 9 braves were lost. Some of the volunteers swore it was at least 200. The monument puts the number at 75, including Roman Nose, the most feared and notorious of the Cheyenne warriors. Forsythe's Scouts lost six killed, and 15 wounded. The shape of the island as it was in 1868 has become somewhat vague and ill-defined. A flood in 1935 changed the path of the meandering river, and water no longer runs on the south side.

CHAPTER 20

The massacre of the Pawnee Indians at Mulberry creek is also described by Miss Elizabeth Barr in the *Pioneer History of Kansas*, Adolph Roenigk, 1933. The incident was never officially investigated, however, and no record exists of the fight. When asked about the lack of an investigation years later, according to Miss Barr, Thomas Alderdice replied, "The Government did hold an investigation at that time, but no witnesses were found that knew anything about the matter."

CHAPTER 21-24

Old Joe's story of the massacre pretty much agrees with accounts given in Adolph Roenigk's book, *Pioneer History of Kansas* and Dr. Broome's book, *Dog Soldier Justice, the Ordeal of Susanna Alderdice in the Kansas Indian War.* The arrow head removed from Willis Daily can be seen today in a glass exhibit at the Lincoln Historical Society in Lincoln, Kansas.

The ordeal of Mrs. Kine haunted her for the rest of her life, and in 1896 she was admitted for treatment at the Kansas Insane Asylum.

CHAPTER 25-26

Old Joe never said who killed Tall Bull. William F. (Buffalo Bill) Cody maintained that he fired the fatal shot, but others made a similar claim, including Major Frank North and Lt. George Mason. But it was Buffalo Bill who held the smoking gun in his Wild West Show, where the Battle of Summit Springs was reenacted over and over in the cities of the East and the capitols of Europe.

Likewise it is not clear who killed Susanna Alderdice and wounded Maria Weichel. Old Joe maintained that it was Tall Bull's wives, but in other accounts of the raid some have said it was Tall Bull himself.

Maria Weichel recovered from her injuries, and later remarried. It is said that her new husband was the hospital corpsman who tended her wounds, but it is not known for certain. In going through the belongings left by the Indians, almost $1,500 was found by the Pawnees and troopers. $845 of this was turned over to Maria Weichel in the form of currency and gold pieces by the soldiers, out of sympathy for her ordeal at the hands of the Indians. It is not clear what happened to the rest.

Thomas Alderdice later remarried and had eight children with his second wife.

Eli Ziegler and John Alverson moved to Salem, Oregon with their families sometime after this raid.

The death of Tall Bull broke the spirit of the Cheyenne Dog Soldiers. Never again would they freely roam the vast reaches of the Kansas and Colorado plains. Some that escaped at Summit Springs returned south to join with Little Robe's tribe, others went on to Montana and lived with the Northern Cheyenne and Sioux.

The battle site at Summit Springs remains today much as it was 140 years ago, unchanged by the passage of time. The main difference is that a few cattle dot the grassy hillside instead of buffalo. The location is in an isolated and somewhat lonely section of eastern Colorado, about 13 miles south and east of Sterling. A dirt road going east from State Highway 63 terminates at the location.

In 1933 a memorial was erected at the site by the Logan County Lions Club to commemorate the battle. The original placard on the monument is now broken and many of the rocks imbedded in the cement have been lost. A new bronze sign was placed on the north side of the memorial in 1966.

A dozen yards away another monument has been erected in honor of the Cheyenne shepherd boy who stampeded the horses into the Indian camp, which allowed many of the tribe to escape, and for Tall Bull and the other Cheyenne chiefs who died there. When viewed by the author, pieces of animal bone and rocks had been placed at the foot of the monument, and a broken Indian necklace and woven dream catcher were tied to the top and on a bush behind the monument. It was dedicated by the grandson of Tall Bull in 1969, with the prayer that the tribes and all white men might live together in harmony. The top of the monument contains the words:

"Our lands are where our dead are buried"

If this be the case, the plains of Kansas and Colorado truly belong to both the Indians and the settlers who together lived and struggled and died there.

The site on the hillside where Susanna Alderdice was buried remained unknown and unmarked until the summer of 2004, when a project to find the grave was initiated by Dr. Jeff Broome, whose book "*Dog Soldier Justice; the Ordeal of Susanna Alderdice in the Kansas Indian War*" has been referenced several times in this book. Dr. Broome was also instrumental in leading an initiative to erect a memorial in honor of Susanna, which was dedicated on July 11, 2004, and which stands beside the other two memorials mentioned above.

The words etched on the Pioneer Monument in the courtyard at Lincoln, Kansas, which inspired this story, still resonate in our minds:

"Remember the days of old"

It is to this thought that this book is dedicated.

Made in the USA
Middletown, DE
30 October 2015